Aliens and Linguists

South Atlantic
Modern Language Association
Award Study

Aliens and Linguists

Language Study and Science Fiction

Walter E. Meyers

•

The University of Georgia Press
Athens

Copyright © 1980 by the University of Georgia Press
Athens 30602

All rights reserved

Set in 10 on 13 point Optima type
Printed in the United States of America

Library of Congress Cataloging in Publication Data

Meyers, Walter Earl, 1939–
   Aliens and linguists.
   (South Atlantic Modern Language Association award
study)
   Bibliography.
   Includes index.
   1. Science fiction—History and criticism.   2. Linguis-
tics in literature   3. Communication in literature.   I. Title.
II. Series: South Atlantic Modern Language Association.
Award study.

PN3448.S45M46   809.3'0876   79–23574
                ISBN 0–8203–0487–5

for R. B. White

Contents

Acknowledgments

It is always a pleasure to be able to thank people who have been helpful, and to confirm a long-standing belief that an interest in science fiction is almost always the sign of a generous nature. Those who have aided me include both close friends and strangers, and here I have the opportunity to express my gratitude. Among those who suggested or furnished works that have made this study more comprehensive than it would otherwise have been are Ben White, Wes Ives, John Chalmers, and Isaac Asimov. Those who helped by reading parts of the manuscript (often correcting mistakes I had not noticed) included R. D. Mullen, Douglas D. Short, and R. V. Young. Institutional aid is less easy to attach to individuals, but none the less welcome: my thanks go to the School of Humanities and Social Sciences at North Carolina State University and to the Department of English at that school for support that enabled me to research the field and to complete the manuscript; to the staff of the Interlibrary Loan Department at the D. H. Hill Library, who have been thoroughly courteous and efficient; to the journal *Science-Fiction Studies*, in which an earlier version of Chapter 2 appeared; and to *Analog* and its former editor, Ben Bova, for permission to reprint the letter found on pages 115–16. Finally, I would like to thank Rollin Lasseter, in whose class it all began, and the students in English 376 ever since, who remind me why I do these things.

Aliens and Linguists

1

"The Godlike Science"
and Science Fiction

Soon after his creation, Victor Frankenstein's monster, abandoned by his maker, hides in a shed behind a shepherd's cottage. He lurks there for several days, observing the members of the little family living inside, studying them with the greatest pleasure:

> By degrees I made a discovery of still greater moment. I found that these people possessed a method of communicating their experience and feelings to one another by articulate sounds. I perceived that the words they spoke sometimes produced pleasure or pain, smiles or sadness, in the minds and countenances of the hearers. This was indeed a godlike science, and I ardently desired to become acquainted with it.[1]

Even in Mary Shelley's embryonic science fiction, we see a concern with problems of communication; communication, with language as its chief discipline, is centrally important to an enormous portion of science fiction, and crucial to its understanding. Why this should be so is the subject of this book.

My procedure in this work has been to survey the uses, whether sound or unsound, to which writers in the field put linguistics. And the first thing to be noted is the striking contrast between the wealth of language problems in science fiction and the relative poverty of linguistic explanation. Recent years have seen a number of introductory critical works bent on discussing the "science" of science fiction, to show how the field achieves that alchemical mix of art and science that is its distinguishing characteristic. A writer might, for example, be invited to contribute an essay to one of these works showing how a particular problem in physics or genetics underlies one of his stories. But we notice a gap in works of this kind: they neglect linguistics. This omission is doubly curious; first, there has been no shortage of criticism pointing to (if not demonstrating) the importance of language to the genre. Robert Plank twenty years ago noted the great increase in literary stature of science fiction, and commented that the burgeoning of the field "must, obviously, be a symptom of whatever it is that is peculiar about the present state of our civilization. But what is that? One expects science fiction to be particularly concerned with science, in the usual sense of the word. It is surprising to find that this is not so. These systems of fantasy are, rather, preoccupied with communication." [2]

The neglect of linguistics is strange for another reason: writers of science fiction frequently congratulate themselves for keeping up to date on research in the various fields they explore in their art. Many indeed argue that the writer of science fiction lays himself under a special obligation to be competent in, or at least conversant with, advances in knowledge. As Harry Harrison phrases it, "Sf cannot be good without respect for good science. This may be a tautology, but it is so often ignored that it must be clearly stated. This does not include time machines, space warps, and the fifth dimension; they will continue to exist in the hazy borderland between sf and fantasy. But it *does* include everything else in these stories once the warp has been jumped or the centuries spanned." [3] In fact, Harrison rates a knowledge of "the basic facts of the science he is writing about" as the science-fiction writer's primary duty (p. 57).

But I suspect that when Harrison and similar commentators use the word *science*, they unconsciously but regularly restrict its meaning to the natural sciences. Thus, in Arthur C. Clarke's collection of articles *Time Probe: The Sciences in Science Fiction* (Dell, 1967), we find no essay on linguistics. It might be argued that the humanities receive the least attention given to traditionally defined fields of study in science fiction, but the social sciences get not a great deal more. And even when critics turn to the role of the social sciences, language and its study are almost always omitted. When Willis E. McNelly edited an introductory chapbook for the College English Association, *Science Fiction: The Academic Awakening* (1974), he included an essay by Leon E. Stover on "Social Science Fiction," an essay that cited outstanding examples of science fiction stories by discipline. There we find coverage of political science, anthropology, economics, psychology, and history, but again, nothing on linguistics. The whole state of affairs is explained in this way by a lecturer (who looks much like an electric eel) at the Galactic University: "It is typical of the sexual races [among which are humans] that the flair for physical engineering is rather stronger than the instinct for communication" (Judith Merril, "The Lonely" [1963; rpt. *Best of Judith Merril*, p. 238]).

Several studies have made a start toward correcting this imbalance, most notably M. J. E. Barnes's *Linguistics and Languages in Science Fiction-Fantasy* (Arno, 1974). The present work is aimed at extending and to some extent correcting these early efforts, at introducing to each other linguistics and science fiction, two fields with such marked similarities. It is commonplace for linguists (at least) to regard their discipline as the most scientific of the humanities (or as the most humanistic of the social sciences, depending on which direction the linguist is facing). And, as we have seen, writers of science fiction often feel themselves to be operating as artists under constraints of scientific accuracy unique to their field and irrelevant to the rest of literature.

Finally, linguistics can help us understand and evaluate the phenomenon of science fiction. Beverly Friend, the science-fiction editor of the Chicago *Daily News*, notes that "an added benefit from studying SF, and one that is often overlooked by the teacher of English, is its natural tie-in with linguistics and language study." Friend's aptly named essay "Strange Bedfellows: Science Fiction, Linguistics, and Education,"[4] points out the close connection between linguistics and two frequent themes in science fiction, contact with aliens and the use of language for thought-control. As we will see, the value of linguistics as a critical tool is not limited to these two, common as they are, but can be useful over a much broader and deeper array of science-fiction themes.

The material surveyed here is chiefly American, with a large helping of British fiction, a blend typical of the genre as a whole. For the most part it is recent—the past thirty years have been the focus of this study, although from time to time an older work is brought forward for comparison, or as a specially notable example.

At this point in introducing my subject, I would now turn to a definition of science fiction if I were continuing in the time-honored way. I would specify as precisely as I could just what it is that I have surveyed. But I have resolved not to yield to this temptation; the definition of science fiction is a bog of opinion into which the academic criticism of the field too often sinks; each party to the argument draws its limits and cites its examples to no one's real satisfaction. Certainly, science fiction has some relation, either linear or hierarchical, to fantasy and utopias. And it has some relation to myth and fable, probably one of purpose. And it has some relation, though perhaps an illegitimate one, to weather forecasting and city planning. It diverges from reality no more than economic theory, and is more useful. It is more concerned with human happiness than urban renewal is, and is more aesthetically pleasing. If much of science fiction is wretched art, it is precisely in step with modern painting and music and architecture, though it has not equalled the excesses of either elitism or mindlessness notable in all these fields. But to avoid arguments on these topics and many more like them, I will assume we all agree on what science fiction is. If certain examples I cite seem misplaced, there will be others sufficient to make the point. Let us forget limits for the moment, and range freely from Frankenstein's monster to Michael Valentine Smith and from Gandalf at the gates of Mordor to John Carter on the sands of Mars.

II Although I offer no formal definition of science fiction here, I would note that there are several distinguishing characteristics of the genre, characteristics that come near to gaining general acceptance by critics. One of these is the strong didacticism that marks the field. If the teaching function of science fiction is examined closely, it turns out to be of two kinds. The first is a didacticism of purpose; science fiction can act as a vehicle for the arguing of the author's point in just the same way that a medieval morality play or one of Donne's sermons does. More particularized is the second kind of didacticism, one of method rather than purpose, and it is this second kind that especially marks the genre. Here is what I mean by didacticism of method: let us suppose that when Larry Niven and Jerry Pournelle wrote *The Mote in God's Eye* (1974), they did so not to advance *laissez-faire* capitalism, nor to argue the rightness of vegetarianism, nor to strike a blow for compulsory education, but rather to write an entertaining story. They nevertheless have some teaching to do, since the story concerns the human reception of an alien spacecraft; because of necessities of the plot, Niven and Pournelle have that spacecraft powered by an engine that would certainly be unfamiliar in its operation to many of their readers. Therefore, in chapter 6, "The Light Sail," they work into the dialogue a short lecture on its principles:

> The Sailing Master looked at him quizzically. "You knew we were dealing with a light-sail propulsion system, sir?"
> "Naturally."
> "Then look here." Renner's nimble fingers made a green curve on the view

screen, a parabola rising sharply at the right. "Sunlight per square centimeter falling on a light sail decreases as the square of the distance from the star. Acceleration varies directly as the sunlight reflected from the sail." (P. 54)

And so on for several pages. Although we are assured later "It's high school physics!" the authors do not count on perfect recall on the part of their readers; on the contrary, they explain as they go, using a didactic method, even though their purpose may be pure entertainment.

When we apply this notion of didacticism of method to those stories concerning language and its problems, we see that the author faces an even larger difficulty. Given the American system of education and the kind of reader who enjoys science fiction, I would think that there is a fairly good chance that the writer can presume that his reader will know something about the laws of thermodynamics, or at least the laws of motion in Newton's system. It seems probable that the reader would be acquainted with at least the idea of cloning in biology, if not the process. In fact, if the story deals with a question of astronomy, there is probably a very good chance that the reader does not have to be told the sort of things that the television networks so painstakingly explain when they cover a manned mission to the moon.

But the situation is much different with language. Can the writer presume that his reader knows how the laws of analogy operate in the development of natural languages? Will the reader know what the phonemic principle is, or what a recursive rule is? Almost surely not. Even if the writer works hard to make himself as competent in matters of language as he is in physics or chemistry, that competence will somehow or other have to be transferred to the reader while the story is proceeding. For this reason it is best, I think, not to be too demanding in our examination of linguistics in science fiction. When Jack Vance, in *City of the Chasch* (1968) has a human on another planet hear the aliens "speaking in harsh consonants and broad vowels" (pp. 17–18), he is using terms that, while they have no precise linguistic significance, are still suggestive and in common use. In short, he is getting as technical as his audience will allow without his stopping to instruct the reader in phonology. And in the description of alien languages, just as in the techniques of learning a language, the principle *omne ignotum pro magnifico* rules: if the author wishes to dispense with "harsh" and "broad" as descriptive terms and simply make up some exotic labels of his own, how many readers will know the difference?

Thus Frank Herbert in *Dune Messiah* (1969) has a group of characters sitting around using "a *mirabhasa* language, [with] honed phalange consonants and jointed vowels. It was an instrument for conveying fine emotional subtleties" (p. 12). "Honed phalange consonants and jointed vowels"—unless they are talking with their hands, this description doesn't make much sense.

It would be equally a mistake, though, to say that because this sort of thing happens from time to time, an investigation of the linguistics in science fiction is a fruitless undertaking. It is a commonplace that a great deal of learning and research gets stuffed away in odd corners of science fiction, and some of those corners, if just by chance, turn out to be linguistic ones. Consider the sentences quoted above from Herbert; along with the phonological foolishness occurs the word *mirabhasa*. This I took to be a deliberate coinage, and, with that assumption as the starting point, the word unfolds, rich with significance, in the context in which it appears. The *-bh-* suggested a construction from Indo-European or Sanskrit roots; consulting Sir Monier Monier-Williams's Sanskrit-English Dictionary, I found that *bhasha* means "speech, language," and that *mrī*, a root meaning "death" (compare Latin *mors*), has an alternate form *mir*. And while these characters are using their "death-language," they are plotting the assassination of the central figure of the novel. An investigator put off by the meaningless description of sound would have missed the subtle and creative use of a new word.

Herbert's strange juxtaposition illustrates the problems a writer faces in dealing with questions of language. If we make a rough division of language into phonology, syntax, and semantics (including the lexicon), only two of these categories are likely to suggest themselves as matters of interest to the author. Under the influence of the misinformed who, since Dr. Johnson's day, have been saying that English has no grammar, the writer will scarcely think the field of syntax worthy of much plowing (there are, of course, the great exceptions to this statement, some of which we will see later). If the writer's notions of "grammar" are limited to subject-verb agreement, and the use of the comparative adjective with two and the superlative with three or more, he really has no models to go by. The great majority of the writers examined in this study speak English as their mother tongue. Couple the limited perception of grammar given to them by the schools with the serene transparency of a language for its native speakers, and it is small wonder that syntax attracts little interest; the wonder is that it attracts any at all.

The other two areas, phonology and semantics, are patently much more interesting to the layman, and hence more likely to serve as the central concern of a story. Surely the two most frequent kinds of arguments about language concern the pronunciations of words and the meanings of words. But we have already seen an illustration of the difficulty of discussing sound in language, and we will encounter more copious examples later. If a writer goes to the trouble of making himself knowledgeable about phonology, he will have no vocabulary at hand in which to share his inventions with the reader. And in the short story, a predominant form of the genre, there is little room for explanatory digressions. Thus a writer most often says that a language sounded harsh or broad, musical or rasping, this or that, and lets it go.

On the other hand, no great number of specialized terms is needed to discuss meaning. The writer is therefore free to be as playful and inventive as he wishes. And since meaning on the word level is more accessible and familiar to the layman than any other kind of meaning, it is with that kind of meaning that we begin our study.

III Starting with meaning at the word level is a process that in some senses repeats the history of investigations of language in Western thought, because some of the earliest of the Greek speculations about language deal with defining the meaning of words. From that early time to the present, writers have taken a sensitivity to the meaning of words to be absolutely basic to their craft, and we find as good examples of that sensitivity in science fiction as in any other genre.

At the most elementary level is the introduction of an alien word together with a denial of the exact translatability of that word in an effort to emphasize the "otherness" of the society which produced it. Poul Anderson in "Lodestar" (1973; H. Harrison, ed., *Astounding: John W. Campbell Memorial Anthology*) has a character complain about the difficulty of recruiting a crew for a spaceship, saying that he was not able to enlist the whole crew from his own *choth*. The word *choth*, we are told, "designated a basic social unit, more than a tribe, less than a nation, with cultural and religious dimensions corresponding to nothing human" (p. 17). While Anderson might have conveyed the same meaning by using the familiar words *clan* or *totem*, the use of the new coinage stresses the alienness of the situation, and its difference from the situations that might be suggested by *clan* or *totem*. Thus Anderson bestows precisely the denotation he wants on the word, while avoiding unwanted connotations of words already in currency.

Some writers have brought to a higher level the use of words purely as vehicles for connotation. When a coined term is given without definition, it brings to the context in which it appears only the associations suggested by its form; if the wordmaker perceives those associations keenly, they can help establish the tone of the story by connotation alone. We know we are reading comedy from the first words of Theodore Sturgeon's "The Hurkle Is a Happy Beast" (1949; rpt. R. Silverberg, ed., *The Science Fiction Bestiary*): "So on Lirht, while the decisions on the fate of the miserable Hvov were being formulated, gwik still fardled, funted, and fupped" (p. 12). Although we later learn that the gwik are the dominant species of the planet Lirht, none of the other words are ever explained, nor do they need to be. To speakers of English, the verbs *to fardle, to funt,* and *to fup* sound as if they describe ridiculous acts, and that is all they need to do. Quite different is the opening of Robert Sheckley's "Game: First Schematic" (*Can You Feel Anything When I Do This?* [1971]): "He looked down at himself: he was wearing a collarless blue shirt and red shorts— A leather mitaxl was strapped to his left hand. In his right hand he held the daenum, its four-foot length heavy and reassuring" (p. 46). Some sort of sporting event, possibly on a future Earth, is going on, but exactly what mitaxls and daenums are we never find out, no more than we would expect to find out, in a contemporary sports story, the exact nature and construction of a first-baseman's glove. In Sheckley's story, as in Sturgeon's, the words are there for the associations of their sounds: whatever a mitaxl is, it is a serious thing, just as a gwik is a comic thing. The connotations, not the denotations, justify the terms.

The use of words in this way serves a more important purpose than just the establishment of tone, for what is science fiction if it is not exotic? New societies, new forms of life, are key elements in the appeal of the genre. If through the use of language the author adds an extra imaginative dimension and at the same time provides the reader with a new perspective from which to view his own society, something special indeed has been accomplished. In *The Left Hand of Darkness* (1969) Ursula Le Guin has her narrator reflect on a term of utmost importance in the alien society of the planet Gethen: "No doubt this was all a matter of *shifgrethor*—prestige, face, place, the pride-relationship, the untranslatable and all-important principle of social authority in Karhide and all civilizations of Gethen" (p. 10). When we find that etymologically the word *shifgrethor* means "shadow," we are given a new perspective on the often insubstantial basis of human power relationships.

The best writers of science fiction take special pains to provide us with these new perspectives. It is only in bad science fiction that the alien being acts like a costumed human, differing from the familiar only in appearance. In the hands of the masters of the genre we are constantly reminded through the use of new terms, new metaphors, and the very turns of phrase that our accustomed ways of thinking are not the only ones. C. M. Kornbluth pictures aliens in his "The Slave" (1957; rpt. *A Mile Beyond the Moon*) who are blind; they have some discrimination from a heat-sensitive organ; they can read minds, to a degree; but their tactile sense is highly developed and is the mainstay of their perceptions. Hence many of their metaphors are based on touch rather than on sight. Their writing system is much like Braille, and a human (the slave of the title) has learned to read it. His alien master, doubting his ability, comments, "'If it amuses the fellow to pretend that he can read, I see no obstacle [he says to a subordinate]. And if it contributes to the efficiency of your department, we all shine that much brighter.' (More literally, with fuller etymological values, his words could be rendered: 'If it amuses the fellow to pretend that he fingers wisdom, my hands are not grated. And if it smoothes your quarry wall, we all hew more easily')" (p. 117).

And finally, the use of words in this way provides an extremely efficient method of characterization. We are never told directly what the Martians in Robert Sheckley's *Mindswap* (1966) look like, but we form impressions immediately when we hear one say "This son-in-law I have always distrusted, since he is a fancy dresser and owns twenty pairs of chestprops, although his wife my daughter hasn't even got a matched set of scratchers. But it can't be helped, she dug her burrow, now she has to crawl in it" (p. 25).

Among current writers, Jack Vance's work is especially notable for this playful use of "untranslatable" terms. He is always careful when writing of alien languages that the reader be aware that Vance (or the narrator) is ostensibly translating the speech of the characters. Vance will typically footnote one of the early speeches of the characters to reinforce this point. In his award-winning story "The Last Castle" (1966; rpt. B. Aldiss and H. Harrison, eds., *Nebula Award Stories: Two*), an aristocrat comments on a revolt among the servant classes: "The dogs have stolen our power-wagons, otherwise I'd be tempted to ride out and chivvy the rascals home with a whip" (p. 87). The cool, somewhat distant voice of the slightly pedantic narrator footnotes the speech with this explanation:

> This is only an approximate translation and fails to capture the pungency of the language. Several words have no contemporary equivalents [these are humans of the far future speaking]. "Skirkling," as in "to send skirkling," denotes a frantic pell-mell flight in all directions accompanied by a vibration or twinkling or a jerking motion. To "volith" is to toy idly with a matter, the implication being that the person involved is of such Jovian potency that all difficulties dwindle to contemptible triviality. "Raudelbogs" are the semi-intelligent beings of Etamin Four, who were brought to Earth, trained first as gardeners, then construction laborers, then sent home in disgrace because of certain repulsive habits they refused to forgo.
>
> The statement of O. Z. Garr, therefore, becomes something like this: "Were power-wagons at hand, I'd volith forth with a whip to send the raudelbogs skirkling home." (P. 87)

IV The samples above only glimmer with the kind of light a linguistic investigation can shed on science fiction. In the chapters to follow, I hope to show that the field abounds with plots in which language problems are necessarily present, and with situations which linguistic methodology can help us understand and evaluate. Every single story in which a character travels in time and every single story spanning a long period involve questions of historical change of natural languages, a subject surveyed in chapter 2. Chapter 3 considers the question of the alien being and the "differentness" of an alien communication system, and points out, together with chapter 4, that the first aliens we need to deal with, indeed that we are already trying to speak to, are located not in a distant star system but right here on earth. Chapter 5 moves to the kind of alien that comes first to mind when science fiction is mentioned, the intelligent creature from another planet. In that section the linguistic search for the universals of human language is applied to the variety of means of communication with which authors have endowed their extraterrestrial aliens. Chapter 6 continues this theme, showing how intimately linguistic questions are involved in first-contact stories. All the chapters to that point discuss plots implying that someone has to learn a new language, and chapter 7 examines the various means writers have used to smooth that task, showing how closely science fiction follows topics of current interest in the popular science press. The next two chapters discuss time-honored ways of avoiding language problems: chapter 8, in which I skirt the morass of defining science fiction, looks at the automatic translator, while chapter 9 explores some language-related questions of telepathy. Chapters 10 and 11 deal with those works that might be thought classics of language and science fiction, tracing the development of linguistics through major works in the genre. Finally, chapter 12 attempts a wider usefulness, examining some of the things that linguistics and science fiction together can tell us about society.

This book argues that, Beverly Friend's title to the contrary notwithstanding, linguistics and science fiction are not strange bedfellows; their meeting on common ground should be expected, and the exploration of their intermeshing may be not merely interesting but highly useful, perhaps even crucial to our understanding of ourselves. I cannot phrase this argument better than Ian Watson has done:

> It seems indisputable that we are witnessing nowadays a necessary convergence of what used to be regarded as the most diverse areas of knowledge: Physics, Cosmology, Biology, Mathematics, Logic, Linguistics. Each is needed now to throw light on the fundamental problems of the others. And this convergence—which demands some highly speculative "leaps into the Beyond"—is something which the Science Fiction imagination can and should explore. The problems of this world here and now are urgent—the social, economic, ecological problems; and science fiction should deal with these. At the same time, I think it must find a way of dealing with these epistemological problems. For science fiction is a literature of the Beyond, as well as a literature of the impact of change on Man. It deals with the Beyond in a historical sense: the Future, that is rapidly becoming the Present. It must also deal with the Beyond of knowledge—without losing touch with a sense of the social base of Man, whose knowledge this is. For, just as we are here making our world and our society, so in another sense we are engaged in the making of the universe through that which is at the root of our social being: our language.[5]

2

The Future History and Development
of the English Language

After reading an earlier version of this chapter, Thomas Pyles, the author of
The Origins and Development of the English Language, remarked that he
had not realized what a rich field of linguistic problems science fiction
provides. Indeed, very few people, even those well acquainted with the
genre, realize the large part language plays; John R. Krueger observed that
"in perhaps one-third or thereabouts of s-f stories, problems of language
and communication raise their head, though not always playing a major
role."[1] On reflection, this high percentage becomes understandable: for
example, only science fiction requires its practitioners to put down on
paper their estimates of the language of the next decade, the next century,
or the next millennium, since only science fiction offers stories of travel
into the future. Similarly, stories of travel into the past require that science-
fiction writers share with writers of historical novels a concern for older
forms of language. Science fiction as a genre, then, has a special relationship within the field of language studies to historical linguistics.

Historical linguistics is that branch of the discipline that examines the
very noticeable habit languages have of changing through time. Every college sophomore who takes the survey of English literature confronts evidence of that change, from an incomprehensible sample of Old English,
through a more-or-less difficult helping of Chaucerian Middle English, to
the Early Modern English of Shakespeare, still patently different from our
own. Although such evidence should be obvious[2] to everyone who reads
widely, one's attitude toward change is probably more important than the
evidence itself in terms of how it is perceived, and that attitude warrants
close investigation.

The present state of American English is decried by such a large part of
the public (by newspaper columnists, television commentators, and

others in a position to know) that we might think they would be doing their best to promote as much change as possible, on the grounds that things could hardly get worse. But that is clearly not the case, since one of the tenets of the naive observer is that change is always bad. In 1934, Murray Leinster published "Sidewise in Time" (rpt. I. Asimov, ed., *Before the Golden Age*), a short story that illustrates that tenet. The premise of the story is that many universes exist simultaneously, each one resulting from a different outcome of a key historical event. For example, when it's 1934 in one world, it's 1934 in all, but in some the Civil War was won by the Confederacy. The tale begins with an "upheaval of nature" that shuffles parts of the different universes together unpredictably. A professor of mathematics leads a group of his students into a universe where the Roman Empire never fell; there the Romans discovered and settled the New World, but otherwise they have not changed much: they still have centurions, chariots, slaves, and the like. One might have expected their language to have changed over the centuries, as indeed it has: Leinster's professor overhears a villa owner speaking "a curiously corrupt Latin" (p. 570).

Words used to describe historical change often carry a heavy freight of opprobrium—"debased" frequently appears, as in Poul Anderson's "The Sharing of Flesh": "It was a debased form of Lokonese, which in turn was remotely descended from Anglic" (1968; rpt. I. Asimov, ed., *The Hugo Winners*, 2 : 771), or in John Morressy's *Stardrift* (1973), where we read of the "unruly gibberish that served as *lingua franca* in space, the debased end product of the long decay that had begun in the last centuries of Old Earth" (p. 105).

More than three decades after "Sidewise in Time" the same attitude toward linguistic change still persists, but of course professors of mathematics no longer speak Latin, so it has become necessary to have the change noticed, as in the next example, by an expert. The English-speaking crew of a spaceship from our own time (give or take a few generations) lands in the North America of the future in Philip José Farmer's *Flesh* (1960). The ship's anthropologist identifies the language of the natives: "It's English. But farther from our brand than ours was from Anglo-Saxon. . . . It's degenerated, in the linguistical sense, far faster than was predicted." He has a reason for the degeneration, too: "Probably because of the isolation of small groups after the Desolation. And also because the mass of the people are illiterate" (p. 25). Perhaps degeneration in the linguistical sense is not as derogatory as degeneration in the ordinary sense, and we see here a small gain for education, but it would be interesting to know whom the author had in mind when he spoke of someone's making predictions of the rate of language change. It is a useful assumption (one which we will examine later) that the rate of at least some linguistic change is constant.

But it seems that anthropology has degenerated since our time, too. American structural linguistics began with the work of men who were as much anthropologists as linguists, men like Franz Boas, Edward Sapir, and Leonard Bloomfield. Bloomfield's first great work was a grammar of the language of the Menomini Indians, and Sapir's celebrated pupil, Benjamin Lee Whorf, did most of his work "in the field." It is hard to image scholars like these (or any anthropologist since) regarding linguistic change as "de-generation." Nor do anthropologists or linguists predict either particular changes or the rates of change. Yet the writer of science fiction need not have attended a university course to avoid mistakes like these: had he looked, he would have found advice within the genre on handling the different states of a language.

In 1953, L. Sprague de Camp, a well-known writer himself, published a book of excellent counsel for the would-be author. One section specifi-cally discusses language: "What if your characters are 'really' speaking a past or future variety of English? If they are using past English, have them speak as the past speakers would have spoken unless the form is so archaic that it makes hard reading. You can use the English of the time of Milton or Shakespeare (if you know how) as it stands."[3] But good advice is still just advice: as de Camp notes, "you can never be so careful as to avoid all mistakes," referring to his own *Lest Darkness Fall* (1939), that, as he says, "threw my modern hero back into sixth-century Rome. I caused my characters to make a few remarks in Gothic to lend authenticity to the scene. After the book appeared I got a letter from a professor saying that while he liked the story, did I realize that I had caused a couple of these Gothic-speakers to use the nominative case when they should have used the vocative?" (p. 179).

Verb and pronoun forms of the second person singular are particularly troublesome to some science fiction writers. R. D. Mullen points out a bril-liant exception to this generality in Theodore Sturgeon's "To Here and the Easel," where pronominal usage reinforces the theme of the story.[4]

As Charles F. Hockett has noted,[5] the knowledge of linguistics shown in science fiction, a genre whose authors claim a special interest in accuracy, is low in general; we may add that it is abysmally low when it comes to historical linguistics. Hockett no doubt had in mind stories like Nat Schachner's "Past, Present, and Future" (I. Asimov, ed., *Before the Golden Age*), which strings linguistic improbabilities through ten millennia and mocks grammarians at the same time. In that story, printed in 1937, a lieutenant of Alexander the Great is preserved in a chamber hewn from the rock of a live volcano; he wakes far in the future in the company of Sam Ward, an American soldier of fortune of our own time. Though but a mere adventurer, Sam is a college man:

> Kleon's face lighted with gladness and a certain astonishment. "You speak Greek, Sam Ward, yet you speak it as a barbarian would. The accents are false and the quantities wrong." Sam grimaced wryly at that. His professors at college had been most careful in inculcating those accents and quantities. They represented the true Attic Greek in all its purity, they had averred. (P. 932)

A comment about the history of English in particular is still likely to be ludicrously wrong in science fiction. A brief documentation of that charge would list, for instance, the story stating that speakers of the Northumbrian and Sussex dialects of Old English could not understand each other (Frederik Pohl and C. M. Kornbluth, "Mute Inglorious Tam," *Fantasy and Science Fiction* [October 1974], p. 112), the story that labels Chaucer's Parson's Tale "Old English" (Richard Wilson, "A Man Spekith," in Wollheim and Carr, eds., *World's Best Science Fiction 1970*, p. 1),[6] and the story in which the omniscient narrator says that a character struck "the final vowels of [his] words with a grunting emphasis in the curious brogue of Middle English" (Ed Jesby, "Ogre," in E. L. Ferman, ed., *Best from Fantasy and Science Fiction*, 18th Series [1972], p. 69). This ineptitude appears in general, nonfiction works as well. Pointing to the adoption of Gaelic in Eire and Hebrew in Israel as national languages, Willy Ley claims that the number of languages has increased in modern times ("One Planet, One Language," *Galaxy* [February 1960], p. 104), showing that he is unaware of the disappearance in the eighteenth century of Cornish and much more recently of Dalmatian and a large number of American Indian languages.

One of the authors cited earlier, Philip José Farmer, deserves a special exemption from the charge of historical inaccuracy. In novels such as *The Fabulous Riverboat* (1971) and other works in his "Riverworld" series, characters who speak the English of different historical periods frequently encounter one another (for example, Mark Twain meets King John), and Farmer's comments on their language are consistently accurate, implying much research and a general familiarity with the facts of language change.

The last bit of evidence on the history of English deserves quoting at length. Professor Hikhoff, a character in Harvey Jacobs's "The Egg of the Glak" (E. L. Ferman, *Best from F&SF*, 18th Series), teaches the history of English at a university. He has apparently informed the narrator that the Great Vowel Shift was caused by the Norman Conquest, a piece of misinformation that casts doubt on the competence of the committee that tenured Hikhoff:

> If it were not for Hikhoff, I would know nothing of the vowel shift, though it altered my life and fiber. For it was this rotten shift that changed our English from growl to purr.
>
> Look it up. Read how spit flew through the teeth of Angles, Saxons, and Jutes in the good old days. Get facts on how the French came, conquered, shoved our vowels to the left of the language, coated our tongues with velvet fur.
>
> For Hikhoff, the shift of the vowels made history's center. *Before* was a time for the hairy man, the man who ate from the bone. *After* came silk pants, phallic apology. (P. 242)

Although the humor allows us to forgive Jacobs much, his story remains a textbook example of what Thomas Pyles described as the mistaken notion that William the Conqueror was rather like Paul Valéry.

Surely, some of these errors arise from ignorance of the facts, but others arise from a misunderstanding of the mechanisms of linguistic change. In Larry Niven's "The Fourth Profession" (1971; rpt. D. A. Wollheim, ed., *1972 Annual World's Best SF*), an alien has pills for sale that will bring their purchasers mastery of assorted fields of knowledge. An earthman comments to a friend,

> "The pills must be very old."
> He pounced. "How do you know that?"
> "The name for the pill has only one syllable, like fork." (P. 9)

The point here is that the author thinks that the short words are the oldest words. As he says in a recent nonfiction article, "*Tasp* is short and easy to say. Such words give away the fact that they are in common currency throughout a culture, like *lamp* and *pan* and *pen*." [7] The correctness of this observation would vary from language to language, and even English furnishes abundant counterexamples of short words that are neither old, e.g., *jet, gene,* and *erg,* nor widespread throughout the culture, e.g., *tosh, quaich, kip,* and *scutch.* Unlike rocks, words do other things than wear away.

Thankfully, some few writers handle linguistic change accurately and to good effect in their fiction. Since science fiction writers customarily work on a grand scale in time as well as in space, these skillful few can plot over centuries, making the change of a language not just part of the atmosphere but a device to forward the action. Alexei Panshin does just this in his novel *Rite of Passage* (1968). The work deals with the growing up of a young girl, the narrator, who lives in a colossal spaceship. The colony of thousands on the ship is almost self-sustaining, visiting planets only to trade or to place on their surfaces the adolescents of the ship, who must survive a trial period on an often hostile world before being accepted as adults by the ship's society. The heroine and her classmates are to be set on a planet last visited 150 years before. Although the thought that the language may have changed in that time apparently occurs to no one, the speech of the children betrays their origin to the planet-dwellers almost at once. The girl survives several dangers before finding a friendly native who will teach her to speak in a way that will not draw attention to her. In the education that follows, both sound change and differences in morphology are illustrated:

> We worked on my speech for a couple of hours that day. Some of the changes were fairly regular—like shifted vowel sounds and a sort of "b" sound for "p," and saying "be" for "is"—but some of the sounds seemed without pattern or sense, though a linguist might disagree with me. . . .
> I couldn't tell you off hand what all the changes were—I think rhythm was a large part of it—but I did have a good ear. I suppose that there was a pattern after all, but it was one I only absorbed subconsciously. (Pp. 205–6).

With only a little knowledge and care, a writer can use language change like any other detail of his imaginary world, developing it as a plot device, or as a mirror of custom, or, as in the next two examples, as a vehicle for humor. Michael Moorcock's novel *An Alien Heat* (1972) is set in the far future when today's languages are mistakenly thought to have been merely dialects of a single tongue. When a woman from nineteenth-century

England is brought to that time, she is addressed by a character with more confidence than accuracy in his reconstruction of her speech: "Good evening, fräulein. I parle the yazhik. Năy m̀-śai pă."[8]

Poul Anderson's characters in "Supernova" (*Analog* [January 1967]) are more accurate, just unlucky. Their adventure takes place when interstellar travel is possible; voyaging to a particular planet, though, is infrequent because of the large number of inhabited worlds. A merchant ship travels to Eriau, a planet not visited in two centuries, and although the crew studies the local language during their passage, they discover on landing that "two hundred years back, Eriau had been in a state of linguistic overturn." The merchants find themselves in a position like that of a man who learns the English of 1400 only to land in 1600. When they reach Eriau, primed with their hard-won language facility, they find they aren't "even pronouncing the vowels right." In a clever touch, Anderson uses different stages of English to show the embarrassment of the traders. They speak like this: "I pray forgiveness, Hand, if perchance in mine ignorance I misuse thy—uh— your tongue. Naught was intended save friendliness. Hither bring I news of peril impending, for the which ye must busk yourselves betimes lest ye lose everything ye possess." And they find themselves answered thus: "Frankly, I am dubious. You claim Valenderay is about to become a supernova—" (p. 14).

But unfortunately treatments like these are the exceptions. In general the treatment of linguistic change in science fiction is like the sky on a hazy night: a few bright spots seen through an obfuscating fog. When we look more specifically at the treatment of the future development of English, the fog does not lift.

II De Camp in 1953 had also outlined the principal concerns of a writer who turns his attention to language-to-come, whose characters speak a "future variety of English." He stated reasonably that "we may presume that English will go on changing (perhaps more slowly than hitherto because of the spread of literacy and world-wide intercommunication) so that in a thousand years it would be unintelligible."[9] And writers have had an illustrious example since long before de Camp wrote. H. G. Wells's *The Time Machine* (1895) is usually thought of as the beginning of the theme of time travel in science fiction, and in that novel the central character goes to the future and hears "a strange and very sweet and liquid tongue," of which he understands not a word.[10] He has to learn the language in the usual way, and never does get very good at it. Like the Time Traveler, many a willing or unwilling subject has, since 1895, visited or viewed the future as his author conceived of it, and it is just this large body of evidence that allows us to compile our survey of post-modern English.

Surprisingly few stories that describe the future of English hypothesize any sort of influence from other languages. When one does, however, that other language is almost certain to be Russian. Sterling Lanier's "Such Stuff as Dreams" (Analog [January 1968]), hints at an amalgamation when a character uses "Slavang, the language of Terra," (p. 91), where Slavang is perhaps a blend of Slavic and English. Sometimes the most casual of comments implies profound social, as well as linguistic, changes: in James Blish's "This Earth of Hours" (in Galactic Cluster [1959]), a spaceship from Earth is named the Novoe Washingtongrad.

The most offhand sort of comment may even affect our understanding of the story's meaning. Ursula Le Guin's story "The New Atlantis" (in R. Silverberg, ed., The New Atlantis [1975]), pictures a future United States under a thoroughly despotic federal government. The critic Darko Suvin labels her society "a well-identified American variant of admass Fascism" and "a fairly standard American radical nightmare," [11] appearing to miss Le Guin's indications of the contemporary model she is using. The society is much more the sort of nightmare that Barry Goldwater might have than one of George McGovern's. Although Suvin notices the "Solzhenitsyn-like Rehabilitation Camps" of the story, he does not mention one linguistic clue in a comment the central character makes about her husband: "He's never been able to publish any of his papers, in print; he's not a federal employee and doesn't have a government clearance. But it did get circulated in what the scientists and poets call Sammy's-dot, that is, just handwritten or hectographed" (p. 75). Sammy's-dot is a folk etymology of Russian samizdat, the term in current use in the Soviet Union to describe precisely the kind of underground publishing Le Guin writes of.

Usually when Russian has some influence on the future of English, it is limited, as in Le Guin's story, to the borrowing of words. The most often discussed example of such influence is Anthony Burgess's A Clockwork Orange.[12] There, in the not-too-distant future, British teenagers speak a slang called Nadsat; in this slang, words like ptitsa, deng, moloko, and *droog* are straightforward English transliterations of the Russian words for 'bird,' 'money,' 'milk,' and 'friend'; *veck* shows a clipped form of *chelovek* 'man'; and even folk etymologies are represented by terms like *gulliver* (from *golova*, 'head') and *horrorshow* (from *horosho*, 'good'). The resemblance of these last two items is even closer if we remember that the characters of the novel speak a dialect that loses *r*'s except before vowels. Richard C. Meredith uses the same method as Burgess, interspersing some Russian words in his English, and adds a different use of contraction and perhaps a suggestion of change in pronunciation in the speech of a character from the twenty-fifth century: 'Wha'tam wrong *tyepyer* ['now']? . . . I wan' to know where I'm—*Gdye* ['where']?" ("Choice of Weapons," *Worlds of Tomorrow* [March 1966], p. 136). In general, though, speakers of English can look forward to a rosy future, one in which they can travel where they wish with firm confidence that the shop signs will proclaim "English Spoken Here."

The more chauvinistic among us may think that when all the world speaks English, the world is getting the better of the deal. In Arthur C. Clarke's novel *Childhood's End* (1953), the millennium arrives, and Clarke enumerates its benefits: "There was no one on earth who could not speak English, who could not read, who was not within range of a television set, who could not visit the other side of the planet within twenty-four hours" (p. 72). Presumably they all have tea at four, too. Although Clarke is an Englishman, he seems to dread the task which the average American fears more than any other: that he will have to learn a foreign language. And naturally the easiest solution is to have everyone else learn English: "Schwartz had spoken with them several times. They understood English well enough—all galactic races did; Schwartz imagined it would become the interstellar lingua franca as it had on Earth" (Robert Silverberg, "Schwartz Between the Galaxies," *Stellar 1*, ed. J.-L. del Rey [1974], p. 115).

A similar solution to the language barrier is supposed by Isaac Asimov in his novel *The Caves of Steel* (1953; rpt. *The Rest of the Robots*); the central character reflects that "English might not be the 'English' of Shakespeare or Churchill, but it was the final potpourri that was current over all the continents and, with some modification, on the Outer Worlds as well" (p. 266). David Samuelson quotes this passage in his *Visions of Tomorrow*, suggesting two reasons for the supposition of a universal English at the same time that he points out its improbability: "Even allowing for the tendency of communications technology to standardize language and retard change, such a situation after 3,000 years in a civilization of fifty-odd planets not in constant contact with one another is at least improbable, from a linguistic point of view." He notes further that the preference for English as the universal language is conventional, "even in the science fiction of other countries." My own experience confirms this statement, with the exception of Russian science fiction. Samuelson also notes that the writers' desire for a common language for their characters exists throughout literature, and is not limited to science fiction. But he does suggest a reason more specific to the genre: "The wishful thinking which lies behind the science fictional assertion of one common tongue in the future is, I suspect, related to the scientist's desire to communicate across international or interlingual borders as freely with words as with mathematical and technical symbols." [13]

Whatever the reasons may be for any given author, we do find an occasional story in which neither English nor Russian becomes the new world tongue: Poul Anderson's novel *Tau Zero* (1970) has Swedish fulfilling that high function in the twenty-second century, but speakers of English are entitled to hope that merely an alternate universe is depicted there.

If science-fiction writers lean toward the universal spread of spoken English, many are pessimistic about the future of written English. Sometimes full-scale nuclear war reduces most of the population to illiteracy, as in Walter Miller, Jr.'s critically praised *A Canticle for Leibowitz* (1960). Or it may be an invasion from outer space, causing a hard-pressed society to undergo great deprivations from military necessity, as in Algis Budrys's "For Love" (1962; rpt. F. Pohl, ed., *Seventh Galaxy Reader*). In that story, a young man is described as "educated—or mis-educated; show him something not printed in Military Alphabet and you showed him the Mayan Codex" (p. 3). But most often future illiteracy simply reflects the linguistic pessimism so often expressed in the pages of *Time* or *Newsweek*, a pessimism which sees the use of *media* as a singular noun as the harbinger of the collapse of civilization. Thus we find scenes like the one in Samuel R. Delany's story "Time Considered as a Helix of Semi-Precious Stones" (*Driftglass* [1968]). In the Times Square of New York a hundred years from now, "the ribbon of news lights looping the triangular structure of Communication, Inc.," spells out its headlines in Basic English (p. 224). A similarly gloomy outcome appears in Robert Sheckley's *Mindswap* (1966). The

thirty-two-year-old hero of this story, in no way out of the ordinary, learned
to read at age twelve; after twenty-eight years of formal education (including four years of post-graduate work), he is employed in a toy factory,
fluoroscoping the products for defects. When he wants information on a
subject, he adjusts the comprehension rate of his encyclopedia to "simple," and settles down to a chummy lecture from a magnetic tape. In their
skepticism about education (public education only—rarely is fun poked at
advanced scientific research), science-fiction writers share the media-
approved attitude of the larger society around them.

III Science-fiction writers face problems that *Time* and *Newsweek*
avoid, though, when they imagine the language of the future. Often
their solution to those problems is simply to ignore them. For example,
consider a work of extraordinary scope, *The Quincunx of Time* (1973),
whose author, James Blish, displays knowledge that he fails to use. The
story concerns a machine called the Dirac, which transmits messages faster
than light, but which has the unforeseen capability of picking up every
message sent on a Dirac transmitter at any time in the future. We find that
Blish knows about language change: when its possessors first listen to the
Dirac, someone remarks, hearing an apparently meaningless message, "I
suppose it's whatever has happened to the English language—or some
other language—thousands of years from now" (p. 104). Despite this
promising hint (the character is mistaken in this particular case), there is
no change whatsoever in the English of any message quoted in the book
though the characters intercept, and we read, communications dating
from 2091, 2973, 3480, 6500, and even 8873.

In *The Quincunx of Time*, Blish provided a more recent example of the
kind of story a colleague had complained of in 1953. Fletcher Pratt, a
versatile writer not limited to the field of science fiction, contended that
"most science fiction writers have another irritating habit that does nothing
to win friends for the art: the habit of being extremely slipshod about language. . . . The time travelers hop three thousand years into the future and
find people still speaking idiomatic New York English. (How many people
today speak any language that was used in 1000 B.C.?) I do not mean this
happens every time, but it takes place often enough to constitute a rather

general criticism, and it is one of the reasons why non-science-fiction readers tend to regard the art as the property of a cult."[14]

It is not hard to find stories in which language-change ceases utterly as a result of the author's inadvertence or ignorance. Back in 1933, Laurence Manning's "The Man Who Awoke" (I. Asimov, ed., *Before the Golden Age*) showed this flaw. The hero awakes after a full five thousand years, a rather extended period, yet one that nevertheless fails to hamper the ease of his communication with the people of that time:

> The surprising thing, when he came to think about it, was that the man's speech was plain English, for which he was thankful. There were new words, of course, and the accent was strange to his ears—a tang of European broad *A*s and positively continental *R*s. He was wondering if radio and recorded speech had been the causes of this persistence of the old tongue. (P. 352)

The only new words in the story appear very early: a character asks the hero, "Wassum, stranger! Where is your orig?" meaning "Welcome, stranger. Where is your village?" On reflection, the fact that a language has undergone some phonological shifts and added some new words in five thousand years would seem far less remarkable than the fact it had changed so little, yet even as limp and unlikely an account of language change as Manning's came as a surprise to one adolescent reader. In a preface to the story, Isaac Asimov recalls that as a youth, he had noticed that "Manning's view of the future involved not merely new inventions, but new societies, new ways of thought, new modifications of language."[15]

Note that Manning at least makes an attempt to cover his stunning implausibility by pointing to recording devices. Even this minimal amount of face-saving is absent from Clifford Simak's 1931 story, "The World of the Red Sun" (I. Asimov, ed., *Before the Golden Age*). In this, the time travelers leave 1935, but something goes amiss:

> They stared at one another in the half-light.
> "Then this isn't the year 7561," stammered Bill.
> "No, more likely the year 750,000, perhaps even more than that."
> "The time dial was wrong then."
> "It was wrong." (P. 200)

Shortly after their arrival, a mob of barbarians overpowers them and takes them captive: "'March,' said one of them, a large fellow with a protruding front tooth. The single word was English, with the pronunciation slightly different than it would have been in the twentieth century, but good, pure English." Later the travelers overhear more conversation among the savages, "but, although the tongue was English, it was so intermixed with unfamiliar words and spoken with such an accent that the two could understand very little of it" (p. 203).

To prove the near-impossibility of even this limited understanding, we can explore a linguistic method called glottochronology. If a language community splits into two groups, each having little or no contact with the other, their once common language will change over a period of time until the groups speak mutually unintelligible tongues. Part of this divergence will result from sound-changes in the speech of the two communities, but part will consist of the replacement of words. With glottochronology, a sample of one or two hundred words is carefully chosen, called the "core vocabulary." These are words for the lower numbers, body parts, simple physical phenomena, and the like, presumed to be resistant to technological obsolescence. The theory assumes that the rate of replacement in the core is constant, and just as the decay of a radioactive carbon isotope can be used to date archaeological specimens, so can the decay of the core vocabulary be used to date the time of separation of the two language groups. For example, English and German were once one language. Compare English *heart* and German *Herz*; both have changed in sound from their ancestral Germanic form, but they still demonstrate their common origin, and are therefore called "cognate," meaning "born together." On the other hand, German *Kopf* has the same meaning as English *head*, but these two are not cognate, and show the replacement (in German) of one of the core terms.

According to glottochronology, after one thousand years about 81 percent of the core vocabulary will remain in the two languages. But the curve falls off rapidly; after five thousand years, the time-span of "The Man Who Awoke," only 18 percent remains. By ten thousand years, only 2 percent of the core vocabulary is preserved. The precision of glottochronology is controversial, but in "The World of the Red Sun," we are talking about 750,000 years; that the two men could understand even a single word would be breathtakingly surprising, yet the phenomenon receives no further mention.

Glottochronology was known to a more recent writer; in Larry Niven's

Ringworld (1970), humans contact first one, then another, isolated community, which they have reason to believe were once part of a greater civilization. Since they possess the ubiquitous automatic translator, they hear the speech of these two groups in their own language. One character regrets the device, since he realizes that "knowing how far the two languages had diverged since the breakdown of communication, he might have been able to date the fall of civilization" (p. 228).

But when we return to the 1930s, the decade of Manning's and Simak's tales, we find story after story showing the severe retardation or complete stoppage of language change (even though the fact of language change was then well known and described in detail). Perhaps the swift receding of the imaginative horizon in those days brought about a kind of dizziness, clouding the writers' perception of mundane considerations. Or was it that writers in that first flush of dealing with years in the hundreds of thousands simply lost their perspective, and spoke of eons as if they were centuries? The "Seeker of Tomorrow" in Eric Frank Russell and Leslie T. Johnson's 1937 story of that name invents a time machine and travels 300 years into the future—and finds no change in the language. He goes further, to 34,656 A.D.—still no change. Finally, after journeying through 150,000 years, "he needed a period of convalescence, during which [says a dweller in that far time] he has learned how to speak our language. You will find that he can speak with fair fluency, the reason for this being that his own language proved to be the root of ours" (rpt. D. Knight, ed., *Science Fiction of the Thirties*, p. 372). There is a curious foreshortening here, as if all those passed-by years had had no greater duration than the seconds it took to traverse them. But whatever its cause, this petrification of language seems to begin with science-fiction pulps.

Lest it be thought that this unsophisticated attitude has disappeared in more recent years, consider Ray Bradbury's "Forever and the Earth" (1950; rpt. G. Conklin, ed., *Big Book of Science Fiction*), which followed Manning's and Simak's stories by almost two decades. In Bradbury's story, the writer Thomas Wolfe is resurrected in 2257 A.D., yet apparently the language has changed not at all in three hundred years. Bradbury freezes English in this story for sheer convenience to his plot: as great a writer as John Dryden was, we would hardly bring him back to write a modern British novel. Yet if "Forever and the Earth" is to be a proper homage to Thomas Wolfe, Bradbury must ignore the knowledge he had shown two years earlier in 1948, in "Pillar of Fire" (rpt. A. Boucher, ed., *A Treasury of Great Science Fiction*, vol. 1); his central character in that story is awakened after a sleep of like duration and fears that "his use of archaic terms" might lead those around him to guess he is not one of them (p. 149).

As the Bradbury example suggests, the forties were no freer of the flaw than the thirties. In "Dear Charles" (1946; rpt. *Twists in Time*), Murray Leinster has a character write a letter to a descendant of his in 3400; eventually he travels there, meeting his posterity in person. The people of that future time seem to have no trouble at all reading the lengthy letter or understanding his speech when he arrives, nor does he find any difficulty with their speech. Even in the fifties, some of the best-known writers of the genre showed this flaw, not through the few centuries of "Forever and the Earth," but through several millennia, as evidenced in Theodore Sturgeon's "The Stars Are the Styx" (1950; rpt. H. L. Gold, ed., *Galaxy Reader of Science Fiction*), in which Earth sends out a fleet of ships to set up a network of matter-transmitters around the galaxy. The job will take six thousand years to complete, but the crews of the ships will be thrust "into space-time and the automatics [will hold] them there until all—or enough—are positioned." The returning crews won't have aged at all, and will be heroes to boot: "Their relatives, their Earthbound friends will be long dead, and all their children, and theirs; so let the Outbounders come home at least to the same Earth, the same language, the same traditions" (p. 191). Just how everything, including language, is to be held changeless for six thousand years is not explained.

A. E. van Vogt seems never to have let linguistic plausibility constrain him. In *The Weapon Shops of Isher* (1951; rpt. A. Boucher, ed., *A Treasury of Great Science Fiction*, vol. 1), a man moves forward in time, quite unexpectedly, seven thousand years. Apparently, English is still spoken. In fact, the first person from the future that he meets, a girl in a shop, does not remark at his speech at all. They converse freely before she realizes (and not from his language) that he is not a contemporary of hers. It takes a still longer period before the man himself is convinced that he has left 1951.

The result is the same whether the time traveler goes forward or backward; in Leigh Brackett's *The Sword of Rhiannon* (1949) a man goes back a million years into the past of Mars, but has no problem communicating with the natives in his modern Martian language. He does have something of an accent, however. But even a million years is not the limit. The prize for arrested development must go to Arthur C. Clarke's *The City and the Stars* (1956). There are actually two cities figuring in the book, Diaspar and Lys, which have been without contact for a full billion years. Alvin, the hero, makes a trip from one city to the other, the first human to do so throughout this geologic time span. We are told that he "had no difficulty in understanding the others, and it never occurred to him that there was anything surprising about this. Diaspar and Lys shared the same linguistic heritage, and the ancient invention of sound recording had long ago frozen speech in an unbreakable mold" (pp. 69–70).[16] Although Clarke's unchanging language puts an intolerable strain on the willing suspension of disbelief, the oddest thing about this linguistic will-o'-the-wisp is its complete needlessness. Granted that the plot may require immediate communication to take place, still, the people of Lys are endowed with another of science fiction's more bewhiskered conventions, telepathy. If he had chosen, Clarke could have had them read the traveler's mind instead of boggling ours, and the continued mutual intelligibility of the languages of the two cities could have been dispensed with. Next to this, Manning's use of a new word or two seems like philological scholarship.

Clarke, like Manning before him, points to sound-recordings not just as a retarder of change, but as an absolute barrier to it. Some more recent writers are not so sure: Joe Haldeman's *The Forever War* (1974) assumes that by A.D. 2450 English will have undergone drastic changes that make it almost unintelligible to someone of our time. Yet other novels, published that same year, still offer us languages that remain unchanged over millennia and light-years for reasons less convincing than tapes and records. One naive explanation occurs in Doris Piserchia's *Star Rider* (1974). The novel depicts a time, thousands of years from now, when humans hop all over the galaxy quickly and easily. The heroine is held captive on a planet she has never seen. One of her kidnappers (whom she has never seen before, either) asks, "Why do you suppose we speak the same language?" She answers, "Your people probably copied it from mine, then when yours came to Gibraltar [the kidnapper's planet] they decided not to change it" (p. 97). It might be argued that the heroine is an extremely untutored fourteen-year-old who knows next to nothing about anything. But whatever the state of her knowledge, there is no sign throughout the book that anybody speaks a language in any way different from anyone else's.

The Mote in God's Eye (1974), by Larry Niven and Jerry Pournelle, notes in one section that universal languages invariably fragment (p. 233), and mutual consent seems like a feeble way to forestall that outcome. But other methods with more teeth in them have been recounted, such as one found in Zach Hughes's *The Legend of Miaree* (1974):

> We stem, of course, from a common source, all of us, from the rim worlds to the outposts toward the center. But as the centuries passed, as worlds became more isolated and independent from the parent civilization around Terra II, we began to develop variations in language. . . . Accents changed. Although it never reached the point where one man could not understand another, there was a different ring in the ear when one conversed, for example, with a rimmer and with a center worlder. . . . We are, in spite of our far-flung travels, one people. And the lengths to which we have gone to keep it that way, among them the enforcement of the standard language regulations, are for the good. (P. 71)

And the regulations are stringent: earlier in this novel, a university professor warns a student about his regional dialect, and notes it as a mark of provincialism. "Provincialism leads to nationalism. On the isolated planet of Zede II it was allowed to grow. Until, as one would cut out a cancerous growth, we eliminated it" (p. 36). The method of elimination—destruction of the planet—is surely the literary high-water mark of vigorous prescriptivism.

IV These horrors, linguistic and otherwise, are not universal in science fiction. There are works that deal knowledgeably and artistically with the future of English, and in examining some of those, we begin with the language of a time close to our own. In Alfred Bester's "Of Time and Third Avenue" (1951; rpt. D. Knight, ed., *A Century of Science Fiction*), a man named Knight buys a 1990 almanac; the purchase would not be noteworthy, except that the time is 1950. Although Knight is unaware of his good fortune, the people of 1990 are not, and they send an official back to 1950 to retrieve the almanac, thereby preventing any unwanted repercussions arising from Knight's knowledge of the future. In the history of a language, forty years is only a moment—barring cataclysmic occurrences, we would not expect a great deal of change—and there are no great differences in the language of Boyne, the man from 1990. His speech sounds a little odd (a bartender thinks he might be a foreigner),[17] and he uses a few words coined after 1950. At the climax of the story, he has just about convinced Knight that any gain he might make from reading the almanac would be, in a sense, cheated from history rather than won through his own efforts. At the peroration of his speech, Boyne proclaims, "You will regret. You will totally recall the pronouncement of our great poet-philosopher Trynbyll, who summed it up in one lightning, skazon line. 'The Future is Tekon,' said Trynbyll" (p. 61). The story uses language change convincingly, in a way that is both clever and understated, and contains no linguistic gaffes to distract the reader's attention and diminish his enjoyment.

Not all visitors from the future are as trustworthy as Boyne. C. M. Kornbluth illustrates the dangers of gullibility in his short story, "Time Bum" (*A Mile Beyond the Moon* [1953]). A real estate agent and his wife, a science-fiction buff, suspect an odd stranger of being from the future (this is not as fantastic as it may seem; he gives them good cause). A clandestine search of his house turns up a newspaper page bearing the date July 18, 2403. It reads:

TAIM KOP NABD:
PROSKYOOTR ASKS DETH

Patrolm'n Oskr Garth 'v thi Taim Polis w'z arest'd toodei at hiz hom, 4365 9863th Strit, and bookd at 9768th Prisint on tchardg'z 'v Polis-Ekspozh'r. Thi aledjd Ekspozh'r okur'd hwaile Garth w'z on dooti in thi Twenti-Furst Sentch'ri. It konsist'd 'v hiz admish'n too a sit'zen 'v thi Twenti-Furst Sentch'ri that thi Taim Polis ekzisted and woz op'rated fr'm thi Twenti-Fifth Sentch'ri. Thi Proskyoot'rz Ofis sed thi deth pen'lti will be askt in vyoo 'v thi heinus neitch'r 'v thi ofens, hwitch thret'nz thi hwol fabrik 'v Twenti-Fifth Sentch'ri ekzistens. (P. 77)

The story is too good to spoil by quoting any more. It suffices to note that this English of the "Twenti-Fifth Sentch'ri" differs from our own only in its orthography. Both Bester's and Kornbluth's stories limit linguistic change to such comparatively superficial matters.

Respellings are not frequently used, on the whole, as a device to illustrate the English of the future. One or both of two simple methods are probably the most often seen: the noting of some difference in pronunciation, and the insertion of a few words. Bruce McAllister uses the first of these in his story "Benji's Pencil" (E. L. Ferman, ed., *Best from F&SF*, 19th Series [1969]). It concerns the short career of another of those characters satirized so effectively in Woody Allen's *Sleeper*, the frozen hero. (Since his name is Maxwell, a more appropriate name might be "freeze-dried.") He is revived after two hundred years, and is told that although the written language had not changed much, "inflections and the sectional dialects often make it hard for a 'new' person to understand" (p. 302). The speaker, the Introducer, has made a special study of the pronunciation of "past spoken languages" in order to speak to the reawakened. The first time Maxwell hears the new form of the language, it sounds to him like "nasalized English, chopped but softer than German" (p. 303). The impressionistic description of the sounds comes as a surprise, since Maxwell had been an English teacher, and one might have expected him to possess a more effective vocabulary to describe the changes.

In "Benji's Pencil," we are simply told about the new pronunciations, but an author may occasionally choose to demonstrate them, at least for a short stretch. This method differs from respelling—note that in the quotation from "Time Bum," we are dealing with written English, and have no direct information about pronunciation. Damon Knight's "Extempore" (1956 as "The Beach Where Time Began"; rpt. *Best of Damon Knight*) is a time-travel story, and the central character asks, at one point, "'What year is this?' . . . 'Thairty-five twainty-seex, Mista Rossi!'" (p. 149), where the use of what is sometimes called "literary dialect" is intended to show the effect of time on the language.

The second method mentioned above is the introduction of new words. All the usual ways of forming words are represented in the coinages found in science fiction. They include new formations such as *skazon* in Bester's "Of Time and Third Avenue" above, or *goffin* in James Blish's "A Work of Art" (1956; rpt. *Best Science Fiction Stories of James Blish*); they include old words used in new senses, such as *golden* in Samuel R. Delany's "The Star Pit" (*Driftglass* [1967]), in which the adjective is the term used to name the border-line psychotics who alone can withstand the mental stresses involved in piloting inter-galactic ships; and they include old words put together in compounds with new senses, such as *diradah* in Philip José Farmer's *Flesh*. As a character explains, the word means "the aristocrats. I think the word originally was deer-riders. Only the privileged are allowed to ride deer. *Diradah*. Analogous to the Spanish *caballero* or French *cavalier*. Both originally meant *horseman*" (pp. 25–26).

The very pinnacle of success for the literary word-coiner is to have his new term embraced by the users of the language at large. This has happened several times through the intermediary of science fiction, and the same writer was responsible in two of the more interesting cases. In 1942 Robert A. Heinlein's story "Waldo" was printed (rpt. A. Boucher, ed., *Treasury of Great Science Fiction*, vol. 1). The title character of the story has myasthenia gravis, and he invents a device to allow him to strengthen and steady his manipulation of objects. He inserts his hands and arms into the machine, and the movements of his limbs are transmitted to and replicated by mechanical arms, the size and strength of which can be adjusted to suit the particular task. In the story, although the inventor titles the machine "Waldo F. Jones's Synchronous Reduplicating Pantograph," the patented invention finds wide use, and "the ubiquitous and grotesquely humanoid gadgets [become] known universally as 'waldoes'" (p. 182), much to his chagrin. As Anthony Boucher comments, such machines now "exist (for the handling of radioactive matter) and are known, properly and gratefully, as *waldoes*" (p. 6).

Heinlein's addition of *waldo* to the English vocabulary was much more direct and purposeful than his second brush with lexicographers, which came about either by sheer coincidence or cosmic irony, depending on your point of view. In 1963, a conference was held at Brown University to plan the compilation of a large-scale sample of edited American English. The sample was to be coded on magnetic tape in a computer-accessible format, making it available as a standard data base for uses of various sorts. One of its subsequent uses was in the compilation of the word-list for the *American Heritage Dictionary*. It was decided that the corpus to be encoded would consist of about a million words, all published in the United States in 1961, divided into five hundred samples of about two thousand words each. As W. Nelson Francis, one of the compilers, says, "The actual selection of the specific samples in each category was done at random. In most cases the holdings of the Brown University Library and the Providence Athenaeum were treated as the universe from which the random selections were made." [18] The categories of the samples range widely, covering a predetermined range of all varieties of edited American English, from press reportage to Westerns to learned articles. Category II.M. consists of six samples of science fiction, and as luck would have it, one of those samples is a passage from Robert A. Heinlein's *Stranger in a Strange Land*. As a result, among the words of modern American English listed in a work compiled from the tape—Henry Kučera and W. Nelson Francis's *Computational Analysis of Present-Day American English* (Brown University Press, 1967)—are the words *grok, grokked,* and *grokking.*[19]

Inventive as the preceding examples are, they are not the best that science fiction has to offer in comments on the future of English. Individual words and pronunciations come and go, and their appearance and disappearance shows no special creativity. In fact, Thomas M. Disch has complained specifically about this point as part of a more general criticism of the field: "For some reason, most fiction, in proportion as it advances toward the farther reaches of space and time, grows lackluster and olive drab. Perhaps it's only that against backgrounds so exotic the pulpy tissue that constitutes 80 percent of most sf becomes, more noticeably, lifeless. It does not grate nearly so much when Perry Mason sits down to a steak dinner for a chapter as when the same dinner is served on Aldebaran V in the year 2500. Even at a meal of hydroponic glop the table settings don't change; some few new words are introduced, but the syntax is immutable."[20]

An author needs rather more imagination to conceive of a change in the language that goes beyond word-formation, and the conception is doubly imaginative if the author can, at the same time, suggest a plausible reason for the change. An example of this more satisfying treatment of future English is found in David Karp's *One* (1963). Karp's excellent dystopian novel is set near the end of the twentieth century. The dictatorial government of England of that time uses two major weapons to enforce conformity among the masses: its hidden one is a network of informers who regularly report any forbidden word or action; the other weapon, just as secret in its purposes but open in its operation, is a growing religion, the Church of State. Church of State members are notable by their speech—they speak of themselves in the third person "as if they did not exist by themselves but only as part of a third group. *Me, my, I, mine* did not exist in the language of the Church of State families" (p. 18). In sketching a change in pronoun usage, Karp has gone the inventors of new words one better, and in selecting religion as the reason for the change, he has picked a force powerful enough to make the change possible. He even has historical precedent on his side—witness the continued Quaker use of *thee* after the word had become obsolete for most speakers.

George Orwell picked the same period for his much better known and much brassier *Nineteen Eighty-Four.* The adaptation of English in that novel, Newspeak, deserves its own study, but Newspeak, with the whole Ministry of Truth behind it, seems not as effective, nor nearly as feasible, a means of thought control as the simple change of pronouns Karp depicts.

The changes we have seen so far occur in what might be called Standard Future English. Statements about dialect are infrequent in science fiction, and the use of several different social or geographical variants of the same language is rare indeed. It is tempting to attribute this omission to a general ignorance about dialect; science fiction's occasional comment about present dialects is sometimes astonishingly misinformed: a character in one novel claims that Great Britain in 1950 had fifty-seven mutually incomprehensible dialects.[21] It is therefore a pleasant surprise to find a story that not only shows an awareness of dialect, but illustrates it in a refreshingly irreverent way.

In "The People Trap" (1968; rpt. E. Ferman, ed., *Best from F&SF*, 18th Series), Robert Sheckley puts his hero through a Land Race, a contest in the teeming streets of an anarchical future Manhattan. The winner of the race receives an acre of stripped land, and the contest provides diversion and hope for the jammed-in masses. During the race, the hero seeks a ride from the piratical captain of a Hoboken contraband runner: "'Ye seek passage of *uns?*' he declared in the broad Hobokenese patois. 'Thin ee we be the Christopher Street ferry, hai?'" The captain mistakenly gets the idea that the hero has a wife and children:

> "Woife and tuckins?" the captain enquired. "Why didn't yer mention! Had that lot myself aforetime ago, until waunders did do marvain to the lot. . . ."
> "Aye." The captain's iron visage softened. "I do remember how, in oftens colaim, the lettle blainsprites did leap giner on the saern; yes, and it was roses all til diggerdog."
> "You must have been very happy," Steve said. He was following the man's statements with difficulty. (P. 35)

Steve puts his finger on the chief problem the writer faces: if there is little change in the language the characters are using, the reader has no trouble understanding it; if there is a great difference in the language, then the writer simply states that his characters are speaking in Old High Martian or the twenty-fifth-century development of a present tongue, and writes his dialogue in the English we know. But midway between these two extremes lies difficult ground. Samuel R. Delany solves the problem nicely in *Nova* (1968): some of his characters speak as natives a dialect of English that differs syntactically from that of the rest. The foreignness of their syntax keeps the reader linguistically aware of the exotic setting, while the familiar spelling and vocabulary allow him to understand what they say with a minimum of difficulty. Delany can therefore present whole pages of conversation in the dialect, which essentially consists of a verb-final sentence pattern:

> Perhaps your cards of Prince and me will speak?
> In this race, the universe the prize is.

Auxiliary *do* has disappeared from questions in the dialect:

> What the cards about this swing into the night say?
> Where Prince and myself among the cards fall?
> Captain Von Ray, you well the Tarot know?[22]

One sentence, however, if not a misprint, comes close to the border of unintelligibility; a woman reading the Tarot cards remarks that one's fate is etched in the lines of the face, and Von Ray, pointing to his scarred face, asks: "From the crack across mine, you where those lines my fate can tell will touch?" But this sentence is not representative of the generally easy flow of the dialect.

A second, perhaps even more successful, example of an ambitious attempt to represent language change occurs in Robin S. Scott's story, "Who Needs Insurance?" (1966; rpt. B. Aldiss and H. Harrison, eds., *Nebula Awards Stories: Two*). In order to withstand a threat from outer space in 2106, Earth needs to increase her numbers of people with extrasensory perception. One such, the twentieth-century hero of the story, was killed in a raid on Ploesti in 1943, thus effectively preventing him from reproducing. A time-traveler comes to our present from 2106 and changes the personal history of the hero-narrator, keeping him safe through World War II, Korea, and helicopter duty in Viet Nam, thereby saving his precious genes for the future. In the story, the time-traveler answers in the English of his day when the hero encounters him for the first time:

"You the guy who saved my bacon at Ploesti and in the chopper last year?"
"Yo. I be the guy." He pronounced "guy" almost like "gooey." I couldn't
place the accent. (P. 57)

The narrator, linguistically naive, describes the sound of the language im-
pressionistically, and misunderstands its verbal system: "He spoke with
broad vowels and clipped consonants, somewhat like a Yorkshireman I
had served with in Korea. And he had trouble with verbs. 'Thought' was
'thinked,' 'ran' was 'runned,' and so forth" (p. 58). The traveler has, of
course, no trouble at all with his verbs. In the English of 2106, a process has
continued that has been going on for a thousand years, the regularization
of strong verbs. Scott extends the process to all verbs, even modal aux-
iliaries, giving them weak past tense and past participial forms. The only
exceptions are *have*, which remains *had* in the past rather than the expected *haved*, *set*, which remains *set* rather than *setted*, and *make*, which
remains *made* rather than *maked*:

> So you see, Colonel Albers, I goed back through time to 1943, set up shop in
> London, and when I had made the power source I goed on to Libya and in-
> stalled it in your aircraft. Then I comed back to 1950, getted this building as a
> base, and comed on up to 1980. . . . Each time then, I comed up to the next
> five-year check to see if a letter from you will'd indicate that the steps I had
> tooked had beed effective. (P. 60)

Although there is ample evidence of the leveling of *am* / *are* / *is* to *be*, there
are no instances in the time-traveller's speech of a verb in the third singular
present, so it is impossible to say if that inflection has also been lost. The
one occurrence of *is* probably shows a slip of the pen, but the two of *might*
and the one of *tooked* (rather than *taked*) may show the continuation of
relic forms.

Even these few petrified forms, however, are missing from the variety of
future English found in Philip José Farmer's "Prometheus" (1961; rpt. *Down
in the Black Gang*), a story which shows the variety of English inflections
deliberately simplified. In "Prometheus," a race of intelligent birdlike beings are given the gift of language by a human. In the English he teaches
them, not only are verbs and nouns regularized, and the form *is* eliminated,
but even pronouns are made unvarying, with the present-day objective
form used in all cases. In his farewell speech to his pupils, the human says:

"Each day at noon, when the sun highest, a male or female choosed by you must do this before you and for you."

He took a piece of bread and dipped it in the water and ate the piece, and then he said, "And the Choose[d] One must say so all able to hear,

"'With this water, from which life first comed, me thank me Creator for life. And with this bread, me thank me Creator for the blessings of this world and give me self strength against the evils of life.'" (P. 175)

The intensity and beauty of the whole passage from which this sample is taken belies the apologetic attitude of the character in his justification of the dialect he has created. When berated by a human associate for teaching the creatures a pidgin, he defends his ouster of *is* on the grounds that "there's a recent tendency in English to drop it in conversational speech, and I'm just anticipating what may become a general development" (p. 146). And he reveals his estimation of the relative worths of "standard" and "nonstandard" English: "As for teaching them lower-class English, I'm doing that because I think that the language of the illiterates will triumph. You know how hard the teachers in our schools have to struggle to overcome the tendency of their highclass students to use button-pusher's jargon" (p. 146). It is sad that the character cannot learn from his own actions; he makes the unwarranted assumptions (and very popular ones they are) that the uneducated are the sole source of innovation in language, that change is necessarily bad, and that bad language pushes out good, through some strange linguistic application of Gresham's Law. Just give the birds a couple of centuries to perform their ritual, and an attempt to change its language will be met with as fanatical a resistance as meets those who wish to revise the Book of Common Prayer.

Surprisingly, some of the changes that Scott and Farmer envision had already been suggested in *Astounding Science Fiction*. In 1938, L. Sprague de Camp published an article entitled "Language for Time-Travelers,"[23] discussing and illustrating historical change. Although de Camp's brief essay is badly dated in many areas (that of dialects, for example) by more modern work, his article is still generally sound and more tolerant of change than many more recent stories. Had his advice been heeded, fewer errors would be discussed in the early pages of this chapter.

We can now generalize a bit about historical linguistics in science fiction. First, science fiction is a window not into the future but into the present: in its stories we see what the writers know about language in general and historical linguistics in particular. Sadly, that knowledge is seldom more than that of the man in the street. In fact, exactly the same ignorance, anxieties, and misconceptions show up in the majority of science fiction. It is not surprising, though, that science-fiction authors should be so much more inventive with photons than with phonemes, and so much more knowledgeable about the future of galaxies than about the past of their own language. The schoolteachers of many of these writers no doubt wasted their students' time and tried their patience with interminable myths about *shall* and *will*, *continual* and *continuous*, and other pedantries, hardly leaving time for real instruction about language, had they been competent to provide it. Science-fiction writers show us what is common knowledge about language change, and it's a paltry amount indeed.

On the whole, though, the genre is optimistic—perhaps the competent treatments we have seen point to a time when the First Sound Shift will be as familiar to authors as the First Law of Thermodynamics. And although we know that some are wrong—those authors who expect no change at all in our language through thousands of years—some could be right. Perhaps some of the changes cited here will occur. In fact, one of the characters in a novel by Isaac Asimov makes a comment about our language that will certainly be spoken someday: "'This is the English the linguists are always talking about, isn't it?' he asked, tapping a page" (*End of Eternity* [1955], p. 160).

3

Resident Aliens: Mummies and Machines

Of all the branches of literature, science fiction is one of the most interesting, in part because so much of it deals with basic yet unsolved problems. The study of language presents many such problems, in definitions as well as in details: what sort of communication systems are we willing to count as language? Bee dances? Gibbon calls? Religious glossolalia? Similar questions arise whenever a science-fiction story presents (as frequently it does) an intelligent alien.

If we take *alien* in a broad sense to mean simply "the other," then we need not leave Earth to speak with aliens. For the alien may be different in time or in type. Under the heading of a difference in time fall those stories that deal with the everyday work of an archaeologist attempting to decipher the language of a people vanished from history. Those stories will make up the first category examined here. Under the heading of a difference in type we find stories of the second and third categories. In these two, we can stay at home and speak to aliens if we, like Dr. Frankenstein, talk to our own creations, or, like Dr. Dolittle, talk to the animals. Both machines and animals are resident aliens, so to speak, and if we assume a fictional intelligence for them, then in speaking to them we are communicating with aliens. In surveying the science-fictional uses made of these themes through this and the next chapter, we find that linguistics has a centrally important place in evaluating as fiction the stories that embody such communication.

I With a few exceptions, the stories that deal with the deciphering of a dead language are rather well informed. If we can judge from the reactions of science-fiction writers, possibly the two linguistic events most impressive to laymen were the discovery of the Rosetta Stone and Michael Ventris's deciphering of Cretan Linear B. Reference to these two successes turns up in many stories. And the two events illustrate one of the most intractable features of natural languages, a feature that demonstrates how

Herculean a job decipherment is. Languages are closed systems; that is, the relationship between any bit of language and any bit of reality is a symbolic and therefore arbitrary one. There is nothing doggy about the word *dog*, and any other group of sounds, say, those represented by *cat*, would serve equally well to denote canines. Even so-called onomatopoeic words are primarily a matter of convention, as words for sounds and noises show: although English dogs say *bow-wow*, French ones go *gnaf-gnaf*, German ones go *wau-wau*, and Japanese, *wung-wung*. According to John Algeo, when a door slams, it does so only in English; a Dutch door goes *plof*, and a Russian door goes *bats*.[1] If words like these have so little contact with reality, we can more readily appreciate the arbitrary character of language in general.

Therefore, to decipher a dead language, one must have some way of getting into the circle, of finding a connection between something inside the system and something outside it. Just such an entry was provided for Egyptian hieroglyphics when Napoleon's troops discovered the Rosetta Stone in 1799. The stone is incised with three languages, Greek, demotic Egyptian, and Egyptian hieroglyphics. The assumption (later confirmed) that the same message was thrice repeated in these languages provided the connection from Greek, which was known, to hieroglyphics, which were unknown. This connection enabled Thomas Young and François Champollion to break the closed circle.

Anthony Boucher knew about the Rosetta Stone, and used the knowledge for a detail in his "Expedition" (1945; rpt. G. Conklin, ed., *The Best of Science Fiction*). One of his Martians says that they "could never have deciphered the ancient writings of the Khrugs without the discovery of the Budarno Stone which gave the same inscription in their language and in an antique form of our own" (p. 745).

Ira Levin shows his familiarity with the Rosetta-Stone procedure of decipherment in *This Perfect Day* (Random House, 1970). In this novel he depicts a future society that has unified the whole world under a grinding tyranny. Only one language (perhaps English, although it is never identified) is in use. A secret nonconformist has acquired some foreign-language books and examines them clandestinely, trying to find some truth about the past. He recognizes that several different languages are represented in the texts he has, and sets to work first on Italian, but makes little progress beyond the obvious cognates. He has no way into the circle. But one night he finds a book in French containing an essay by a founder of the world-state, an essay already available to him in the world-language. Now he has a parallel text which serves as his Rosetta Stone: "The value of what he had found, as he began to perceive it, held him motionless. Here in this small brown book, its cover clinging by threads, were twelve or fifteen pre-U-language pages of which he had an exact translation waiting in his night-table drawer. Thousands of words, of verbs in their bafflingly changing forms; instead of guessing and groping as he had done for his near-useless fragments of Italiano, he could gain a solid footing in this second language in a matter of hours!" (p. 111)

As both reality and fiction demonstrate, the deciphering of a dead language requires immense good fortune. Perhaps from awareness of this fact, science-fiction writers are often skeptical of the possibility of decoding dead languages on other worlds. M. John Harrison's *Pastel City* (1971) and James Blish's "No Jokes on Mars" (*Anywhen*, 1970) picture alien landscapes littered with inscribed stones that are absolutely indecipherable because, as Blish tells us, they have "no connection to Earthly languages" (p. 149), and hence their would-be interpreters have no way inside the circle. William Rotsler expresses well the human frustration caused by this situation: "We stopped momentarily at the Royal Bar; the back wall was a single massive slab of petrified fiber, carved with a convoluted design that could have been purely decorative, the Martians' Eleven Commandments, a political ad, or a shopping list. It was beautiful, but unreadable" (*Patron of the Arts* [1973], p. 103).

But not all authors feel this way; if some show an unqualified pessimism, others show an invincible optimism that defeats both the problem and common sense. In A. E. van Vogt's "Resurrection" (1948; rpt. D. Knight, ed., *Toward Infinity*), aliens land on a long-dead Earth. They find a museum containing a mummy, and since they have a device to revive anyone, no matter how long expired, they use it. The chief biologist explains: "Our speech experts have been analyzing the recorded voice mechanism which is a part of each exhibit, and though many languages are involved— evidence that the ancient language spoken at the time the body was alive has been reproduced—they found no difficulty in translating the meanings. They have now adapted our universal speech machine, so that anyone who wishes to need only speak into his communicator, and so will have his words translated into the language of the revived person. The reverse, naturally, is also true" (p. 300). Now, many a reader must have visited a museum or gallery with recorded lectures in English discussing the exhibits. And it is not impossible to envision an exhibition with recorded lectures in several languages for the convenience of foreign visitors. But this must certainly be the only instance of an Egyptian display where the lecture is *in* ancient Egyptian. Let us suppose that present disagreements about the vowels of ancient Egyptian are solved by some unimaginable discovery; it still seems that the museum in the story has gone to considerable trouble for a very, very limited clientele.

Almost as mystifying is James Blish's "Surface Tension" (1952; rpt. *Best Science Fiction Stories of James Blish*). In this story, a colonizing human spaceship crashes on a planet nearly covered with water. Unable to escape yet unwilling to die without issue, the survivors use cellular material from their own bodies to manufacture tiny people (less than one-hundredth of an inch long) to inhabit freshwater ponds on the planet's one swampy continent. They would like to leave a message for their descendants, and therefore look at the problem of deciphering from the other end: "They won't get the record translated at any time in their early history. They'll have to develop a written language of their own, and it will be impossible for us to leave them any sort of Rosetta Stone or other key. By the time they can decipher the truth, they should be ready for it" (p. 19). The second part of the story takes place long afterward, when the micro-Lilliputians have succeeded in understanding some of the message; but without any kind of key, it is impossible to say how they achieved even this partial success. Their ancestors may have used pictures, as did the doomed race in Arthur C. Clarke's "The Star" (1955; rpt. I. Asimov, ed., *The Hugo Winners*): "They left thousands of visual records and the machines for projecting them, together with elaborate pictorial instructions from which it will not be difficult to learn their written language" (p. 126).

The aliens of "The Star" arrange for their language to be deciphered. Clarke's story is very short, and consequently gives no details of how they hoped to facilitate that result. But even if Clarke had dealt with their plans at length, he could not have presented a more thoughtful account than that which we find in a 1927 story, Cecil B. White's "The Retreat to Mars" (rpt. G. Conklin, ed., *The Best of Science Fiction*). White tells of the failure of a

Martian attempt to colonize Earth eons ago. When it becomes clear to them that they will not succeed, the Martians decide "to build a monument to their endeavors, so that as time went on and intelligence returned to this planet [Earth], a record of their attempt, and data of the most useful kind, would be available to those who found it" (p. 664).

To this end they bury three huge cylinders on Earth, one of which is found ages later by an explorer in Africa. The explorer, who narrates the story, has his entrance to the cylinder barred by a massive lock which can be opened only if the would-be entrant understands that the keys to the lock must be operated in a manner determined by instructions written in a duodecimal number system. The explorer operates the keys in the needed sequence and enters the chamber, where he sees doors leading from galleries on several levels. He opens one at random and finds the room behind it stacked from floor to ceiling with numbered boxes, which, on inspection, prove to contain picture books. The pictures, by the way, bear a remarkably prescient similarity to holographs.

Deciding to be systematic about it, the explorer goes to room number one and opens box number one. "It contained what I may liken to a child's primer, profusely illustrated. . . . The second volume contained composite pictures—simple actions of human-like creatures and so on. I saw at once that it would be quite easy for a man of average intelligence to learn this unknown language with the aid of this wonderful primer" (pp. 660–61). White describes in some detail how the lessons, starting from the simplest of word definitions, become progressively more complicated. After a few weeks, his hero comes to the end of the language course, and translates its final sentence: "First read volume one, case three. A complete catalogue of the contents of the library will also be found in this case" (p. 664). It contains as well a dictionary and instructions in the use of the library.

The Martians in White's carefully conceived story knew they would not be back, and with forethought arranged their materials to aid decipherment. But the Martians of H. Beam Piper's "Omnilingual" (*Astounding* [February 1957]) make no provision for their extinction. Consequently the story concerns the efforts of a team of human archaeologists on Mars involved in one of the most detailed accounts of a decipherment in science fiction. The author knows about linguistic archaeology: names like Ventris, Grotefend, and Friedrich are dropped in conversation, and the characters knowledgeably mention the successful efforts with Hittite, Egyptian hieroglyphics, and the Mycenaean Greek of Linear B. But the story has a point to make: as James Blish, writing under the pseudonym of William Atheling, Jr., puts it, Piper's thesis "is that translating a tongue which belonged to a scientific culture is a problem inherently different from, and in the long run easier than, translating a pre-scientific language—because the basic clues are not philological, but physical."[2] The archaeologists of the expedition are hoping to find something to get them into the closed circle of the Martian language. One of them comes close to despair: "There is no Rosetta Stone, not anywhere on Mars," but is answered, "We'll find one. There must be something, somewhere, that will give us the meaning of a few words, and we'll use them to pry meaning out of more words, and so on. We may not live to learn this language, but we'll make a start, and some day somebody will" (p. 11). Pictures don't seem to help much: "They had found hundreds of pictures with captions; they had never been able to establish a positive relationship between any pictured object and any printed word" (pp. 11–12). But the "something" does turn up eventually. The heroine of the story finds the names of the elements and the Martian number system by means of a labelled periodic table; "And there would be other tables—astronomical tables, tables in physics and mechanics, for instance—in which words and numbers were equivalent. . . . And pick out the chemistry textbooks in the Library; new words would take on meanings from contexts in which the names of the elements appeared" (p. 44). The summation of Piper's argument is delivered by the head of the expedition: "Physical science expresses universal facts; necessarily it is a universal language. Heretofore archaeologists have dealt only with pre-scientific cultures" (p. 46). Unfortunately, these words end the story with a classic anticlimax, but the fact remains that Piper has thought his problem through, and imagined a real method for deciphering the language of a technological culture. Blish (as Atheling) perhaps justifiably thinks Piper's "assumptions about the continuity of symbols" from culture to culture are doubtful, but Blish himself in "Surface Tension" offered far less to the reader, and can hardly speak as an expert.

In stories that deal with vanished human civilizations, authors have the immense advantage of dealing with their aliens from the inside, as it were. The humans dead and gone were nonetheless humans. Even when the story deals with a dead alien culture, the author can make sure (as H. Beam Piper does in "Omnilingual") that his aliens were much like humans. That option is not open to writers working in the second category, that of stories dealing with machines.

II When we turn from aliens to machines, we enter a field where science fiction is hard pressed to keep ahead of reality. The fact is, people have been talking to machines for years in specialized computer languages through the intermediary of electric signals. What is not so well known is that the machines, for almost a decade, have been answering in natural languages, especially English, often without people being aware of it. I am not talking about something like a recorded message for an answering service—the message there is unvarying—but a message that will change unpredictably in response to a changing context.

Current machine speech is of two kinds: the more ambitious is called synthesized speech, and the sound is produced entirely by the machine. Robert A. Heinlein, in *The Moon Is a Harsh Mistress* (1965), equips a computer with this capability. A character explains the method: "Voder-vocoder is very old device. Human voice is buzzes and hisses mixed various ways; true even of a coloratura soprano. A vocoder analyzes buzzes and hisses into patterns, one a computer (or trained eye) can read. A voder is a little box which can buzz and hiss and has controls to vary these elements to match those patterns. A human can 'play' a voder, producing artificial speech; a properly programmed computer can do it as fast, as easily, as clearly as you can speak" (p. 99). The machine, by the way, speaks much better than Manuel O'Kelly, the human quoted. In 1967, a speech synthesizer at the IBM Development Laboratory at Research Triangle Park in North Carolina employed seven different control signals to produce the buzzes and hisses (and other sounds) mentioned above. One produced a monotone vowel, three added resonances of the vocal tract, one added nasals, one added fricatives (sounds like s, z, and so on), and the final control varied the intonation of the phrases. The production of such speech must be directed, and that task, as Heinlein indicates, can be performed by a human or a computer. The final product attains a level of naturalness that makes it difficult for a naive listener to distinguish it from a human voice.

The second kind of machine speech, called machine-generated, assembles prerecorded segments of human speech in whatever order is needed. It is this type that is already widespread in commercial use. In this method, as two of its developers write, "The computer extracts the required information from its storage file and codes a message which directs the audio response unit to transmit a sequence of spoken words answering the inquiry with the most recent data on hand. These words are drawn from a prerecorded vocabulary stored in spoken form in the unit. Each vocabulary is created for the particular customer's application."[3] Thus, if one dials an obsolete telephone number, a computer notes the number that has been called, and assembles an answer something like this: "I'm sorry. The number you have dialed, 123-4567, has been changed. The new number is 765-4321." Eventually, we may expect to get a bank balance, find prices of groceries or common stocks, in short, receive almost any kind of information from machine-generated speech at the other end of the line.

A robot uses machine-generated speech in Philip K. Dick's story "Autofac" (1955; rpt. R. Silverberg, ed., *Beyond Control*). Although the robot begins with a recorded preamble, it switches to machine-generated speech very soon: "The optimistic voice clicked out and a second voice came on. It resembled the first, but now there were no intonations or personal mannerisms. The machine was utilizing the dead man's phonetic speech-pattern for its own communication" (p. 57).

With what reality already offers, communication with machines in science fiction will hardly reach unattainable levels. The linguistic abilities of fictional machines sometimes surpass those in existence, but only in degree (such as miniaturization or mobility), not in kind. Instead, what we have in recent science fiction is an insight into the attitudes of writers, rather than imaginative extrapolations.

As might be expected, many writers use the machine as a symbol of human depersonalization, and the machines sound simply mechanical. William F. Nolan characterizes his "computerized ship's voice" as "metallic, emotionless," in a stage direction to his "Promises to Keep: A Science Fiction Drama" (*Alien Horizons*, 1974), continuing a tradition at least as old as John W. Campbell's "Last Evolution" (1932; rpt. L. del Rey, ed., *The Best of John W. Campbell*). In this early tale, we often hear "the vibrationally correct, emotionless tones of all the race of machines" (p. 13). In Isaac Asimov's "It's Such a Beautiful Day" (1954; rpt. *Nightfall and*

Other Stories), so mechanized has the world become that students listen to a "vocalizer's mechanical voice" as a model for their pronunciation of English (p. 256). Firmly within this tradition is one of the most famous robots in science fiction, the "robass" or mechanical mule, in Anthony Boucher's "Quest for St. Aquin" (1951; rpt. M. Mohs, ed., *Other Worlds, Other Gods*). In this frequently anthologized story, a persecuted church has gone underground in a world devastated by nuclear war. For a journey through that world, a priest is mounted on the robass: "'I am a new model. Designed-to-provide-conversation-to-entertain-the-wayworn-traveler,' the robass said slurring the words together as though that phrase of promotional copy was released all at once by one of his simplest binary synapses" (p. 178). The emotionless voice had been described earlier, when the robass asked something of the priest with "no querying inflection to the question. No inflection at all—each syllable was at the same dead level" (p. 178). Obviously, some information is lost when intonations are lost, and even the robass is aware of the deficit. At one point, it is forced to paraphrase to make clear its comment on something the priest has said: "'No,' said the robass, 'I do not mean no period. I mean no question mark with an ironical inflection'" (p. 183). The vocal flaw annoys the robass, and it muses that the defect must not have been present in a perfect robot it has heard legends of. Only twenty-five years after Boucher wrote, his story is technically obsolete. In fact, the problems of adding pitch, stress, and juncture (the transitions between words and phrases) to machine-produced speech were mastered well before William F. Nolan wrote the passage quoted at the beginning of this section. Writers who now speak of emotionless mechanical voices do so either through ignorance or, more probably, because they value the symbolism involved more highly than scientific accuracy.

Jack Williamson confirms that readers of the genre are used to connecting mechanical voices with depersonalization in his "Jamboree" (1969; rpt. R. S. Wilson, ed., *Those Who Can: A Science Fiction Reader*). Manipulating the attitude that sees the voice of the machine as symbolic of the loss of human identity, Williamson pictures a group of children in a regimented future society in which their conformity is ensured by a warden-robot named Old Pop. Old Pop's voice is pliable; it is variously described: "Its smooth, sad voice dripped over him like warm oil"; "the . . . loud words swelled out like big soap-bubbles bursting in the sun"; "Pop's voice turned downy soft, the slow words like tears of sadness now"; and "Pop laughed like a heavy chain clanking." In an afterword, Jack Williamson explains that he sought irony "in the contradiction between Old Pop's speech and its mechanical reality" (p. 17). Just as Shakespeare's satiric "My Mistress' Eyes Are Nothing Like the Sun" is a sure confirmation of the currency of the Petrarchan conventions (otherwise its satire would go un-recognized), so does the irony of Williamson's "Jamboree" prove the widespread recognition of an emotionless, mechanical voice as a symbol of the loss of human identity.

Depersonalization directly caused by machines is shown most keenly when writers outline the effect of machines on their creators by having the humans become themselves like the machines. Cecil Snyder has a charac-ter in his *Hawks of Arcturus* (1974) address a machine in "the flat modulated voice reserved for computers" (p. 77), following the example of Walt Sheldon's machine in "I, the Unspeakable" (1951; rpt. H. L. Gold, ed., *Galaxy Reader of Science Fiction*), which instructs the humans who con-sult it to "use approved voice and standard phraseology" (p. 250).

The theme of depersonalization can be intensified by making the human being a physical part of the machine. Anne McCaffrey incorporates a hu-man into the control system of a spaceship in "The Ship Who Sang" (1961; rpt. with revisions in D. Allen and L. Allen, eds., *Looking Ahead*). The story also contains a large amount of nonsense, such as the achievement by the bottled heroine of a vocal range in song from bass through soprano through "diaphragmatic control." She does strange things to her vocal tract: "By relaxing the throat muscles and expanding the oral cavity well into the frontal sinuses, she could direct the vowel sounds into the most felicitous position" (pp. 243–44). If we take the words literally her palate must be made of rubber instead of bone; if the words are meant to indicate that the heroine lowers the soft palate and allows sound to resonate in the nasal cavities, then the achievement is universal—anyone can do it.[4.]

Larry Niven economizes in "Becalmed in Hell" (1965; rpt. E. Ferman and R. Mills, eds., *Twenty Years of the Magazine of Fantasy and Science Fiction*); in this story the spaceship controls accommodate only the brain and nervous system of a human being. Though stemming from signals from a human brain, the voice of the ship is necessarily mechanically produced, and under stress loses something. As another character notices, "his voice was a mechanical, inhuman monotone; he wasn't making the extra effort to get human expression out of his prosthetic vocal apparatus" (p. 48).

Surely the ultimate depersonalization, almost a loss of identity, is shown in Frederik Pohl and Jack Williamson's *Starchild* (1965). In their novel, set in the far future, a gigantic computer rules the world, and bends humans to its purposes. It has solved the problem of machine-human communication by inventing a new language, dubbed Mechanese. But learning the language requires humans to dedicate themselves completely to the task; they become the acolytes of the Machine. "The Machine, counting time in nanoseconds, could not wait for laggard human speech. Accurate in every either-or response, it had no need for redundancy" (p. 86). Redundancy in human speech consists of the transmission of lexical or syntactic information more than once; for example, in a sentence like "The machines are in control," the plurality of the subject is shown twice, by the *s* on *machines*, and by the plural form *are*; similarly, the fact that *machines* is a noun is twice indicated, first by being preceded by *the*, and second by the *s* of the plural. Redundancy is thought to be a desirable part of communication systems, since it allows the message to be interpreted even if part of the signal is lost due to unavoidable noise in the system. But if the system is so perfect that there is no noise, then redundancy becomes undesirable because it slows down the transmission of information. This is the case with Mechanese.

To understand the design of Mechanese, we must be aware that a phoneme is the minimally distinguished unit of sound in a given language. In English, for instance, the words *pat* and *bat* differ only by their first sounds; *p* and *b* are classified as separate phonemes in English because native speakers agree that *pat* and *bat* are different words. Analyses of this kind establish about forty or forty-five phonemes in English (the exact number depends largely on theoretical and procedural considerations that have no applicability here). We must also be aware that a morpheme is the minimum meaningful unit in a language. A word like *hatracks* is composed of three morphemes, *hat, rack,* and *s,* meaning "plural." The number of morphemes in English is certainly less than the number of words, because a word like *deoxyribonucleic*, unique as it seems, is made from the morphemes *de, oxy, ribo, nucle,* and *ic,* which have wide use in many, many words. A conservative guess would place the number of morphemes in English somewhere between 50,000 and 100,000. With this information, we can evaluate what Pohl and Williamson say about Mechanese.

Mechanese, they tell us, "is built upon a principle of economy already familiar: . . . one syllable for one sentence. Obviously, that requires a large number of syllables" (p. 123). To achieve the requisite number, Mechanese uses tones as phonemes; its speakers must absolutely distinguish fifty separate musical pitches. Now, some human languages use pitch as part of their system: in Mandarin Chinese, for instance, a sequence of phonemes like *bee* has three different meanings depending on the pitch at which it is spoken. The pitch discrimination of Mechanese acolytes must be perfect (they are helped somewhat by strings of "tonal beads" which they carry and use like pitch pipes). In English, the sound *mmm* has no particular meaning nor, in the abstract, would it in Mechanese. But when that particular nasal phoneme is spoken at a certain pitch in Mechanese, it has an associated meaning—it is a morpheme. The morphemes can then be strung together to make a very economical utterance: what would be a single syllable in English is, in Mechanese, a sequence of morphemes making a whole clause, if we add their ordering as part of a syntactic system. Suppose, for example, that the topic of an utterance comes first, followed by any modifiers, followed by any comment on that topic. Suppose, too, that we have the following morphemes (the numbers represent the distance in pitch from a low tone chosen as the base—say, the lower end of the range of a trained singing voice): o^{19} a modifier meaning plural; g^{19} "transistor"; r^{19} "my"; and b^{15} "tired." Then *gorb*, sung like a much condensed version of the opening of Beethoven's *Fifth Symphony*, is the clause, "My transistors are tired."

The learners of Mechanese, to control this complexity, must sacrifice every human concern; as the Machine's translators, they are rewarded for their services by having a socket implanted in their foreheads, allowing electricity from the Machine to directly stimulate the pleasure centers of the brain. They have become appendages of their mechanical master.

Not all machines in science fiction either exemplify or insist on emotionless speech. Some, in fact, have a fluency and naturalness to their conversation that a human might envy. Here again, John W. Campbell was one of the pioneers; a mechanical voice in "The Machine" (1935; rpt. L. del Rey, ed., *Best of John W. Campbell*) is described as "peculiarly commanding, a superhuman voice of perfect clarity and perfect resonance. It was commanding, attracting, yet pleasant" (p. 47). John Brunner creates a versatile robot in "You'll Take the High Road" (*Three Trips in Time and Space* [1973]). His robot is programmed with "a whole vocabulary of objurgation" (p. 73), and like more than one syndicated columnist, appreciates the chance to use a learned construction. As he says, speaking of another robot, "I'll swear that autonome is older than I am, but here it is, still functioning as though it were fresh off the assembly line. Say, did you notice? I just used a subjunctive! Hearing that beautiful English reminded me I haven't fully exploited my diction circuits lately" (p. 87).

Slightly different is the talent of Willis, a robot in Philip K. Dick's *Galactic Pot-Healer* (1969). Willis not only speaks, but switches dialects at will, and has a sense of humor to boot. He shows all these accomplishments when addressed by a human character, Joe Fernwright:

> "Willis," he said.
> "Yassuh."
> Questioningly, Joe said, "'Yassuh'? Why not 'Yessir'?"
> The robot said, "I jes' done bin readin' Earth history, Massuh Fernwright, suh."
> "Are there bone beds here on Plowman's Planet?"
> "Well, Massuh Fernwright, Ah don' rightly know. Ah gues' dat you'all kin as' de central computator iffen—"
> "I order you to talk correctly," Joe said.
> "You'all gotta say 'Willis' fust. Iffen you'all wan' me tuh—"
> "Willis, talk correctly."
> "Yes, Mr. Fernwright." (P. 77)

As the excerpt shows, Fernwright is not only humorless, but supremely confident that he knows what's right and wrong in language.

The most fluent robots in science fiction are the work of Ira Levin in his novel *The Stepford Wives* (1972). Since they are designed to look exactly like human beings, the proper word for the creatures is *androids*, a word coined by Jack Williamson, but listed without etymology in the dictionaries.[5] Whatever name we use, they result from the assembling of an impressive array of specialized skills: "Mr. Ferretti is an engineer in the systems development laboratory of the CompuTech Corporation. . . . Mr. Sumner, who holds many patents in dyes and plastics, recently joined the AmeriChem-Willis [builder of *the* Willis?] Corporation, where he is doing research in vinyl polymers," and on and on through men skilled in microcircuitry and optical sensors to "'audioanimatronics' at Disneyland, . . . the moving and talking presidential figures featured in the August number of *National Geographic*" (pp. 116–17). The androids must be perfect replicas of the men's wives, because they are intended to replace the women after they have been murdered by their husbands.

The voices of the Stepford substitutes are machine-generated: in one scene, a wife is being measured, so to speak, for her replacement. She is approached for a recording of her voice, and is given a plausible reason for her unwitting cooperation in the construction of her surrogate:

> "I've got this project I've been working on in my spare time," he said. . . . "Maybe you've heard about it. I've been getting people to tape-record lists of words and syllables for me. . . ."
>
> "They tell me where they were born, . . . and every place they've lived and for how long. . . . I'm going to feed everything into a computer eventually, each tape with its geographical data. With enough samples I'll be able to feed in a tape *without* data, . . . maybe even a very *short* tape, a few words or a sentence—and the computer'll be able to give a geographical rundown on the person, where he was born and where he's lived. Sort of an electronic Henry Higgins. Not just a stunt though; I see it as being useful in police work." (P. 73)

The heroine remarks, "My gosh, there's a lot," when she sees the list of words she is asked to record. Indeed, there would have to be a lot; from the tapes will come the vocabulary of the androids, who are nonetheless restricted in the subjects they will discuss and the answers they will give to questions. The single drawback to the success of a similar scheme in the real world would seem to be money; anyone who doubts that the hardware is available is advised to visit Disneyland.

One final word about the voices of machines. Since such a voice is produced to specifications, it can be made to sound any way the designer wants. The heroine of Dean Koontz's *Demon Seed* (1973) takes advantage of this potential to become Electra through electricity when she designs her computerized house as a combination father and lover:

> The hidden speaker broadcast a voice which was gently masculine. She envisioned a strong man, graying at the temples, perhaps, steady along the jaw, eyes clear and blue. More than six feet tall. Broad shoulders. Large hands. Smiling, all the time smiling. She had undergone seven hours of psychological testing in order to obtain the proper voice tapes from the house's main com-

puter. This was the voice that was supposed to key all the desirable reactions in her psyche: security, happiness, reliance. (P. 2)

More often, writers are less explicit, and more often, too, the voice of the machine, especially if it is a spaceship, is made to sound like a woman, almost certainly because of a preponderance of male central characters. E. C. Tubb, in his "Evane" (1973; rpt. D. A. Wollheim, ed., *1974 Annual World's Best SF*), creates a machine which "had been vocalized on the basis of psychological necessity. . . . The voice . . . was soft, mellifluous, the voice of an actual woman or something designed on computer-optimums. . . . It was mellow, devoid of the stridency of youth" (p. 136). Not just the voice of a woman, but the voice of an older woman. In Damon Knight's "Stranger Station" (1956; rpt. D. Allen and L. Allen, eds., *Looking Ahead*), a character in an orbiting space station calls his station's voice "Aunt Jane"; it says, "I'm here to protect and serve you in every way" (pp. 219–20). A spaceship with a woman's voice is transparent symbolism; it does not require any great psychological insight to understand why the tube that in actuality connects an astronaut with the ship is called an umbilical.

4

Resident Aliens:
Monkeys and Marine Mammals

We have long felt the desire, even the need, to speak to the creatures around us, a need which parrots and the like do little to satisfy. But perhaps we have lost the knack. In 1711, a "Widow Gentlewoman" advertised a school to teach "Birds of the loquacious Kind, as Parrots, Starlings, Magpies, and others . . . not only . . . to pronounce Words distinctly, and in a proper Tone and Accent, but to speak the Language with great Purity and Volubility of Tongue." Opera lessons were available for birds with good voices, as was instruction in Italian or French for a slightly higher fee. Finally, the widow promised that "if they are Birds of any Parts of Capacity, she will undertake to render them so accomplish'd in the Compass of a Twelve-month, that they shall be fit Conversation for such Ladies as love to chuse their Friends and Companions out of this Species." [1]

In the twentieth century we still are fascinated with teaching English to animals—Frank Herbert has called the talking animal one of the "classic myth ingredients" of science fiction [2]—no matter what that animal may be. Much recent writing in the speculative field has insured that dolphins will have their day, to such an extent that one of Katherine MacLean's exploring submarines has as its crew "a mechanic, a field naturalist, a specialist in dolphin language, and a xenobiologist and universal linguist" ("Small War," 1973; R. Elwood and V. Kidd, eds., *Saving Worlds*, p. 61). But talking dolphins, which we shall discuss in more detail later, are relative newcomers to the field. Most older science fiction and much recent writing concentrates on more accessible animals. Dogs, certainly the species closest at hand, seem to play a surprisingly small part. In Clifford D. Simak's "Census" (1944; rpt. *City*), dogs are surgically altered to make them capable of speech, [3] and in his "Desertion" (1944; rpt. *City*), a newly acquired telepathic skill on the part of humans reveals that dogs have been capable of communication all along, but lacked the means to express themselves.

"Blood" is a similarly endowed dog in Harlan Ellison's "A Boy and His

Dog" (1969; rpt. D. A. Wollheim and T. Carr, eds., *World's Best Science Fiction 1970*). The time of the story is 2024, after one or more major wars. Civilized society endures in small underground enclaves, abandoning the ruined surface to packs of teen-aged gangs and assorted non-joiner delinquents, one of whom is Blood's master, Vic. Or maybe Blood is the master; at least he seems the smarter of the pair. In the dialogue below, Blood is trying to annoy Vic by calling him "Albert." Vic speaks first:

> "Find! I ain't kidding!"
> "For shame, Albert. After all I've taught you. Not: 'I *ain't* kidding.' 'I'm *not* kidding.'" (P. 195)

Purists or not, dogs play little part in stories concerning animal communication. And even two of the three cited above use telepathy as their method. Because telepathy presents linguistic problems of its own, we will postpone its consideration to a later chapter, and consider only observable systems here.

Talking animals have had a history in literature that is long and, with the exception of the serpent in the Garden of Eden, honorable. Balaam's ass speaks plainly, after her mouth is opened (Numbers 22 : 22–30), and Greek and Roman literature is full of bestial conversation.[4] So pervasive is the theme that many commentators have suspected it fills some human need. J. R. R. Tolkien saw "the desire to converse with other living things" as the expression of a profound wish to escape from one of our greatest limitations:

> On this desire, as ancient as the Fall, is largely founded the talking of beasts and creatures in fairy-tales, and especially the magical understanding of their proper speech. This is the root, and not the "confusion" attributed to the minds of men of the unrecorded past, an alleged "absence of the sense of separation of ourselves from beasts." A vivid sense of that separation is very ancient; but also a sense that it was a severance: a strange fate and a guilt lies on us. Other creatures are like other realms with which Man has broken off relations, and sees now only from the outside at a distance, being at war with them, on the terms of an uneasy armistice.[5]

Yet the desire often shows itself in the form of humor, at least in English, where we must turn to Chaucer for the first example. The voluble eagle of *The House of Fame* begins the long tradition, seen in its modern form in "A Boy and His Dog," of animals that not only talk, but are noticeably smarter than the humans in the story.[6]

Jonathan Swift, therefore, had plenty of illustrious predecessors when he invented the Houyhnhnms. Cheerfully ignoring bestial anatomy, Swift has Gulliver describe the Houyhnhnm language as "pronounce[d] through the nose and throat." Gulliver, it will be recalled, describes the Houyhnhnm speech as "graceful and significant" (L. Landa, ed., *Gulliver's Travels and Other Writings*, p. 189), and modern science fiction maintains the tradition of equine elocution in Alan Dean Foster's "Dream Done Green" (1974; T. Carr, ed., *Fellowship of the Stars*). In his story, set in the far future, Foster tells us that "the human Micah Schell found the hormone that broke the lock on rudimentary animal intelligence and enabled the higher mammals to attain at least the mental abilities of a human ten-year-old" (p. 2). One horse in the story far outpaces ten-year-olds; he is a genius in fact, speaking eighteen languages in "a mellow tenor that tended to rise on concluding syllables, only to break and drop like a whitecap on the sea before the next word" (p. 4).

Given the right hormone and a good education, Foster's horse does well indeed, but most writers who deal with this theme postulate some kind of physical change that gives the lower animal the capacity for speech. Sweeting, a character in James R. Schmitz's *The Demon Breed* (1968) is a seven-and-a-half-foot otter, "the product of a geneticist's miscalculation." The king-sized animal's forebears "were a development of a preserved Terran otter strain, tailored for an oceanic existence. The coastal rancher who'd bought the consignment was startled some months later when the growing cubs began to address him in a slurrily chopped-up version" of his language (p. 50). The rancher's surprise is understandable; speech is rarely heard from an otter, even in science fiction. Primates more often serve as raw material, perhaps because the changes necessary to endow them with speech are not so drastic.

Genetic mutation, as in Sweeting's case, has been the mechanism for these changes for a long time, as the genre goes. In 1939, L. Sprague de Camp published "The Blue Giraffe" (rpt. R. Silverberg, ed., *The Science Fiction Bestiary*), in which an eccentric scientist exposes baboons, among other animals, to radiation from "an electronic tube of some sort, built to throw short waves of the length to affect animal genes" (p. 77). The offspring of the mutated baboons (who inhabit a wildlife preserve) increase in size and wit, and a ranger teaches them to speak Xhosa, a Bantu language. De Camp describes the heads of the baboons as altered only in size, and in this he took what ultimately proved to be a false step. It is well established that no nonhuman primate has the anatomy to produce the range of sounds of a human language.[7] Computer simulation of primate vocal range was unknown when de Camp wrote, of course, but there had been indications, even in science fiction itself, that without changes in bone structure and musculature, the baboons could not have mastered the phonology of Xhosa or any other human language.

Whether an ape can master a language that does not have sounds, such as a sign language, is another question, one not directly germane to the discussion at this point, but one positive answer (among others) appeared in Charlton Laird's "A Nonhuman Being Can Learn Language."[8] Laird discusses the education of just one of the several chimpanzees now being taught a system of communication by a variety of methods. This chimp, Washoe, was instructed in a project at the University of Oklahoma. Though only time will settle the matter, the confident assertion of Laird's title would be challenged by some linguists, or, for that matter, by some science-fiction writers, who are frequently well-read in areas that concern their stories. In 1938, Manly Wade Wellman implied some of the problems involved in an ape's use of a vocal language in "Pithecanthropus Rejectus" (rpt. D. Knight, ed., *Science Fiction of the Thirties*). The narrator of the story, an ape, tells of early memories of pain, saying, "As I learned to speak and to comprehend, I found out the cause of those pains. I was told by the tall, smiling blond woman who taught me to call her 'Mother.' She explained that I had been born with no opening in the top of my skull—so needed for bone and brain expansion—and that the man of the house—'Doctor'— had made such an opening, governing the growth of my cranium and later stopping the hole with a silver plate. My jaw, too, had been altered with silver, for when I was born it had been too shallow and narrow to give my tongue play. The building of a chin for me and the remodeling of several tongue-muscles had made it possible for me to speak" (p. 423).

Since Wellman's day, other ways of dealing with the problem of anatomy have been imagined, although the same result is aimed at; Frederik Pohl and Jack Williamson, the authors of "Doomship" (1973; rpt. D. A. Wollheim, ed., *1974 Annual World's Best SF*), use a topical method to account for their newly speaking species: genetic engineering instead of surgery or chance mutation through radiation. In the process of describing the method, they give a more direct statement of the difficulties involved:

A chimpanzee is simply not human. His physiology is one count against him. He cannot develop the brain of a human being because his skull is the wrong shape—and because the chemistry of his blood does not carry enough nourishment to meet the demands of abstract thought. He cannot fully master speech because he lacks the physical equipment to form the wide variety of phonemes in human language. The molecular-biology people knew how to deal with that. They could do things like widening the angle of the cranium called the kyphosis, thus allowing the brain to round out full frontal lobes, or restructuring tongue and palate, even adding new serum components to the blood like the alpha$_2$ globulins that bind human hemoglobin. (P. 58)

Their altered chimps have foreheads, speak fluently, and in general comport themselves creditably.

Old ideas in science fiction never die; they don't fade away, either. In 1960, J. G. Ballard returned to de Camp's method for a detail of his story "The Voices of Time" (rpt. *Chronopolis and Other Stories*). The central character has a chimp whose ancestors' genes have been altered by radiation. We are told that the animal is "about as intelligent as a five-year-old child" (p. 9), but he has only a two-hundred-word vocabulary, which would be extremely unimpressive in a five-year-old, so much so that brain damage or retardation would be suspected. A better handling is that of a writer new to science fiction, although celebrated elsewhere: Paddy Chayefsky's first novel, *Altered States* (1978) is as hard a science fiction tale as one could wish. In it, a man has his body regress through eons of evolutionary development, and the proto-human form it assumes is not equal to the demands of speech. X-rays reveal that his "hyoid bone seemed to be elevated, the base of the tongue broadened and the pharyngeal space shorter than is normally found" (p. 87), all characteristics that prevent him from speaking, as they prevent the higher primates from speaking a human language. Chayefsky's thorough groundwork is obvious (he knows about the experiments of the Gardners, for example), and his novel is the better for it.

Talking to the animals, of course, should be a two-way street: instead of teaching the dolphin or chimpanzee to speak English, the linguist could concentrate on learning the animal's language. Stories of this sort, as might be expected, are rarer; a notable one is Ursula K. Le Guin's *jeu d'esprit*, "The Author of the Acacia Seeds and Other Extracts from the *Journal of the Association of Therolinguistics*" (1974; T. Carr, ed., *Fellowship of the Stars*). Her brief satire, almost shorter than its title, presupposes a whole new field of linguistics: as the title of her mythical journal suggests (from Greek Θήρ–, "wild animal"), its subject is the languages of animals, and its discovery procedures are efficient enough to make commonplace the deciphering of the languages of mammals, birds, even insects: "No known dialect of Ant employs any verbal person except the third person singular and plural, and the first person plural. In this text [the acacia seeds of the title], only the root forms of the verbs are used; so there is no way to decide whether the passage was intended to be an autobiography or a manifesto" (p. 171). Insects do have various kinds of communication systems, many of which have been deciphered, if that word can be used for systems that are hardly languages.

Ants, for example, communicate by leaving trails of chemicals called pheromones when returning to the nest from a food source. Alfred Bester explains the process while using it in a story, providing an excellent example of the mixing of science with fiction that, when done well, defines the genre for many of its readers. In Bester's "The Four-Hour Fugue" (1974; rpt. D. A. Wollheim and A. Saha, eds., *1975 Annual World's Best SF*), a man with an extremely keen sense of smell, an important employee in a perfume company, nightly somnambulates about the city. His disappearances coincide with a series of unsolved murders, and an investigator thinks she has the answer to the mystery; she believes that the sleepwalker goes into amnesiac trances, or fugues, stimulated by pheromone trails. As she explains,

> "Pheromones are external secretions which excite other creatures into action. It's a mute chemical language.
> "The best example of the pheromone language is the ant. Put a lump of sugar somewhere outside an ant hill. A forager will come across it, feed and return to the nest. Within an hour the entire community will be single-filing to and from the sugar, following the pheromone trail first laid down quite undeliberately by the first discoverer. It's an unconscious but compelling stimulant."
> "Fascinating. And Dr. Skiaki?"
> "He follows human pheromone trails. They compel him; he goes into fugue and follows them."
> ". . . But what trails is he compelled to follow?"
> "The death-wish." (P. 176)

Although it is a fiction that would-be human suicides leave pheromone trails, it is true that ants do, which explains why they always manage to join a picnic en masse. Obviously though, communication by pheromones is strictly limited; it is involuntary on the initiator's part, and concerns only a single subject—the route to a food source, in the case of the ant.

The location of food is also the sole subject of a better-known insect communication system, one that is iconic in nature rather than chemical: the nectar dance of honeybees. When a worker returns from a nectar source, she performs a figure-eight-shaped dance on the wall of the hive, in which the size, frequency, and orientation of the figures show the direction and distance to the source. The great German biologist Karl von Frisch was the first to understand the system.[9] His findings appeared in the early years of this century, and were almost immediately incorporated into science fiction. In W. K. Sonnemann's "The Council of Drones" (1936; rpt. D. Knight, ed., *Science Fiction of the Thirties*), a man has his mind transferred to the body of a queen bee as the result of an experiment. While carrying out his reginal duties, he says, "I paused once in my labors to observe the pollen dance of a worker bee, and again to observe the nectar dance of another, those peculiar dances they perform to announce the finding of a new supply in the field" (p. 332). Knowledge of earthly bees' communication system leads a more recent hero to try (unsuccessfully) to make himself understood to giant alien bees who have captured him in Barrington J. Bayley's "The Bees of Knowledge" (1975; rpt. D. A. Wollheim and A. Saha, eds., *1976 Annual World's Best SF*). But while bees and ants find their methods useful, pheromone trails and bee dances lack the quality of open-endedness possessed by all human languages, the quality that allows the users of the language to discuss any subject they wish.

In the eighteenth-century school for starlings, the widowed gentlewoman purported to teach birds grand opera. The same pretense continues in Le Guin's fiction; in a contributor's note to the future *Journal of Therolinguistics*, we find that at least some birds have an opera of sorts of their own: "Indeed it seemed strange that a script written almost entirely in wings, neck, and air should prove the key to the poetry of short-necked, flipper-winged water writers. But we should not have found it so strange if we had kept in mind that penguins are, despite all evidence to the contrary, birds. Because their script resembles Dolphin in *form*, we should never have assumed that it must resemble Dolphin in *content*" (p. 173). Meaningful motion—*kinesics* is its name in linguistics—is a theme to which Le Guin has returned several times. She has used it in alien societies in a work discussed in the next chapter, and with earthly animals in "The Author of the Acacia Seeds" and "Mazes" (1975; R. Elwood and R. Silverberg, eds., *Epoch*). "Mazes" is told from the point of view of a rat in a Skinnerian experiment. At first the rat welcomes being placed in the maze, because it gives him the opportunity to communicate in what we learn is the normal way for rats—a sort of dance, a language of movement. The experimenter and the rat mutually frustrate each other; as the rat says,

> I noticed early that from time to time it [the human] would move its curious horizontal mouth in a series of fairly delicate, repetitive gestures, a little like someone eating. At first I thought it was jeering at me; then I wondered if it was trying to urge me to eat the indigestible fodder; and then I wondered if it could be communicating *labially*. (P. 81)

The rat has never considered a vocal language; indeed, the very thought seems strange to him: "It seemed a limited and unhandy kind of language for one so well provided with hands, feet, limbs, flexible spine, and all; but that would be like the creature's perversity, I thought" (p. 81). The tone of the story is depressing; the kinetic language of the rat is just as unsuspected by the experimenter at the end as it was at the beginning.

Still, as every long-term reader of science fiction knows, the current darlings in animal communication stories are not rats or dogs or chimps, but dolphins, and it is to those creatures that we now turn.

II Over the past twenty years, stories using the moon and Mars as locales for alien creatures greatly declined in number as we learned more and more about our nearest celestial neighbors. Similarly it is my impression that the number of stories using talking chimpanzees and other primates declined over the same period, while dolphin stories rose dramatically. I think we see the result of the same process in both kinds of stories: as what was formerly strange grows familiar, writers bring ever more exotic material to their work. The theme of human-dolphin communication is especially popular now, so popular that some stories (e.g., Lawrence Yep's "The Selchey Kids," 1968; rpt. D. A. Wollheim and T. Carr, eds., *World's Best Science Fiction 1969*) simply assume that in the future we will converse with dolphins and go on from there.

Talking to dolphins as a theme is a textbook case: it has seldom been possible to trace so clearly the transmission of an idea from its first appearance in public until its transmutation into art as science fiction. The starting-point for human-dolphin communication was 1961, in the work of the experimental psychologist, John C. Lilly. That year saw the publication of his *Man and Dolphin*, a work certain to attract the attention and interest of science-fiction enthusiasts, right from its dramatic "Preface: A Prediction":

> Within the next decade or two the human species will establish communication with another species: nonhuman, alien, possibly extraterrestrial, more probably marine; but definitely highly intelligent, perhaps even intellectual.
> . . . If no one among us pursues the matter before interspecies communication is forced upon Homo sapiens by an alien species, this book will have failed in its purpose.[10]

Lilly continued to justify his project in terms of its utility for developing a methodology for communicating with extraterrestrials: six years later in his *The Mind of the Dolphin*, one chapter, titled "The Importance of Interspecies Communication," cited the space program and Project Ozma (discussed in chapter 6) as projects with objectives similar to his.[11]

Reviews of Lilly's *Man and Dolphin* were curious: the less informed the reviewer, the more favorable the reception the book received. Popular and semipopular magazines found the work credible and convincing in a way not matched by learned journals. Some reviewers in science fiction, such as Ben Bova, mirrored the skepticism of the better informed. Bova, later editor of *Analog*, judged that dolphin studies showed "no really impressive evidence for an intelligence comparable to man's."[12] But other reviewers in the field of science fiction made claims more extravagant than any Lilly had made, demonstrating the degeneration of information from one field to another, and helping to create a modern legend about dolphins.

I am not talking about writers of fiction—at most, their work needs to be plausible, not factual—but about writers of the nonfiction essays and reviews that appear in science-fiction magazines. If some of these reviewers met Lilly's ideas with diminished objectivity, it is understandable. It would be surprising, in fact, if some had not been dazzled by such a clear espousal of a cause they had supported for years. Here was a respected scientist saying that we needed to prepare for contact with intelligent, extraterrestrial creatures. In the chapter entitled "Implications," Lilly says,

Obviously the science of linguistics will benefit tremendously from these studies. Interspecies languages and new intraspecies languages will do much to push this science in new areas. . . .

The nonterrestrial, interplanetary and astral sciences, the so-called space sciences, will benefit from our having established contact here on earth with alien creatures that had an evolutionary development separate from ours in another kind of environment. I want to emphasize the fact that even if we are successful, we shall still not be fully prepared to encounter intelligent life forms not of this earth. (P. 222)

This was vindication from an unsuspected source, even if that source was not entirely unbiased.

John C. Lilly frankly admits at the beginning of his books that he firmly believes in the intelligence of dolphins, but readily distinguishes between what he believes and what he can demonstrate. *Man and Dolphin* is studded with comments like these: "In the present chapter I will try to describe and discuss the so-called 'mimicry' or 'copying' phenomena in more detail. . . . This method of describing results has a high degree of subjectivity to it. It can be inexact, and even completely mistaken" (p. 196). "These are sounds which to me (but not to all of my colleagues) sound like human vocalizations" (p. 201). "Human words: These are the most subjective of all the judgments of the sounds emitted by dolphins" (p. 202). In addition, Lilly becomes more guarded in the years following 1961. One instance of this concerns an episode that began the false though widespread belief that dolphins not only talk but talk eight times faster than humans.

In chapter 5 of *Man and Dolphin*, Lilly recounts an instance of serendipity that occurred in his early studies: "When we replayed this first set of tapes we discovered that (in a very terse shorthand and quacking sort of way) this dolphin had been mimicking some of the things I had been saying while dictating technical data on my channel of the tape simultaneously with the experiment" (pp. 78–79). He then says that the animal had repeated "T R R" and "three hundred and twenty-three." The close reader will have some difficulty with these statements: in chapter 11, the repeated words are given as "Tee ar Pee" and "three-two-three," but in any case, the whole of chapter 5 is removed from *Lilly on Dolphins*, the 1975 reprint of his several publications, in which most of *Man and Dolphin* appears. Whatever Lilly thought the dolphin said, it is precisely this episode he referred to when he stated that not all of his colleagues recognized the dolphin sounds as mimicry.

It is in connection with this episode that the idea of slowing down the tape occurred to him: "Further studies of the tapes slowed down to half speed and to one-quarter speed revealed an additional unexpected factor. Apparently these animals are quite capable of taking a vocalization by a human and compressing it with respect to time. We found that most of the vocalizations [note: not *all*] made far more sense and their inherent complexity showed up much more easily when we extended their duration and lowered their pitch by slowing down the tape" (p. 80). Later, in chapter 11, he states that further studies used "tapes with much wider acoustic bands which recorded their whistles, creakings, squawks, etc. [which] were slowed down four, eight, and sixteen times to emphasize this speed in their dolphin to dolphin exchanges" (p. 200).

The fallibility of human-to-human communication sometimes makes one pessimistic about our chances with aliens: out of this variety of tape speeds, one-half, one-quarter, one-eighth, one-sixteenth, why is it that subsequent accounts of Lilly's work select one-eighth, giving it a prominence and authority that Lilly nowhere even suggests? All restraints disappear from the editor's blurb for Vincent H. Gaddis's "The New Science of Space Speech," in *Worlds of Tomorrow* (August 1963): "How to talk to Martians, dolphins and creatures from the farthest stars—not tomorrow, but now!" (p. 115). In the article, Gaddis retells the "T R R" episode in an account riddled with errors: he says "the doctor played back the recording and in order to more distinctly hear the sounds he decided to run the tape at one quarter its normal speed" (p. 118). Lilly says that he cut the speed only later, *after* he thought he heard the mimicry. Gaddis says "the dolphin immediately and clearly repeated the words in high-pitched whistles" (p. 118). On the contrary, Lilly sharply separates these dolphin sounds from their normal whistles. And, despite saying that other tape recordings were played "at half or quarter speed with the sound volume lowered," Gaddis concludes, "they were talking at a rate eight times faster than humans" (p. 118). Whereas Lilly says that he hopes to prove that dolphins have a language, Gaddis simply asserts "Dolphins have a complex vocal language" (p. 118).

Comments on dolphins, fictional and nonfictional, are riddled with a particular confusion for which Lilly must shoulder responsibility: a confusion between the amount of information a channel can carry, and the amount it does carry. This confusion shows up in a story by A. A. Attanasio,

"Interface" (1975; R. Elwood and R. Silverberg, eds., *Epoch*). In this story, an investigator has raised a boy and a dolphin together from childhood. He explains: "The dolphin has a cerebral cortex the size of a human's. But the parietal area, the silent zone linked to abstract thinking, is almost twice as large. When I began to study dolphin sounds, I found they had an immensely more complex communication system than we do. This is what led me to question whether we might establish interspecies communication. Our biggest problem right now is structural. The dolphin language is sonic, but it's waterborne and is therefore ten times faster than ours. We just think too slowly to talk with a dolphin" (pp. 294–95). The human subject is therefore given drugs to speed up his perception. If Attanasio has read chapter 9 of *The Mind of the Dolphin*, and not depended on a garbled retelling, he has misunderstood much of it, since it is there that the "ten times" figure occurs, but as I said above, the heart of the problem is in Lilly's misunderstanding, not in Attanasio's.

To begin with, the speed of sound in water is about 4.5 times as fast as its speed in air. After observing this, Lilly notes that dolphins have two sets of phonation apparatuses, multiplies 4.5 by two, gets nine, throws in an extra one for "stereo effect" and estimates "that the dolphin can put out ten times the sonic physical information per second that a man produces" (*Mind of the Dolphin*, p. 251).[13] While it is true that two men speaking can say twice as much in a given time as one, the relative speeds of sound in water and air are absolutely irrelevant to the question. A given message has a certain amount of information: that amount of information will not increase if you send the message through a faster channel. In addition, the sender of a message may be physically unable to utilize the whole capacity of a channel to carry information, since an additional factor is what we may call the speed of initiation: suppose two typists are sending the same message at teletypewriters; at two receiving consoles, the message arrives at a faster rate from the faster typist, although the speed of transmission is the same for each. Again, when we turn on the radio, we hear normal-sounding speech, even though the radio waves arrived at the set with a speed more than 16,000 times faster than that of sound in air. The fact, therefore, that the putative dolphin language is water-borne has nothing to do with whether or not a human could understand it; what is important is how fast the dolphin can "talk."

Lilly is apparently unaware of this distinction, and further complicates the matter by stating that "according to physical information theory, the higher the frequency of a signal, the more physical information it contains, i.e., the greater the number of bits transmitted per second" (*The Mind of the Dolphin*, p. 249). But the theory only asserts that the capacity of high-frequency channels is greater. A ten-inch pipe can carry more water than a three-inch pipe, but if two identical pumps with an output less than the capacity of either pipe are hooked up to each, you get the same amount of water from the ten-inch pipe as you do from the three-inch pipe.

Lilly's work, whatever its accuracy or final merits, was genuinely original, and stimulated thought among laymen and scientists alike. Its subject was a spur to creativity; it acted, to switch the metaphor, as a vehicle to carry many messages, even among those not generally given to writing fiction. "The Voice of the Dolphins" (*The Voice of the Dolphins and Other Stories*, 1961) was one of the first works to make purposeful fictional use of Lilly's theme. This parable of international scientific cooperation and universal disarmament came from Leo Szilard, the renowned atomic scientist, illustrating yet again the fitness of science fiction for political argument.

Professional science-fiction writers just as readily adopted Lilly's ideas. His direct influence is easily traced in dozens of stories; Robert Silverberg, for instance, sets his "Ishmael in Love" (1970; rpt. D. A. Wollheim and T. Carr, eds., *World's Best SF 1971*) in St. Croix in the Virgin Islands, the site of Lilly's experiments. The plot of the story, the unrequited love of a dolphin for his female human colleague, was surely suggested by Lilly's account of his female assistant's lengthy cohabitation with a dolphin.

The first well-done long story of talking dolphins came from the pen of Arthur C. Clarke: "People of the Sea" (*Worlds of Tomorrow*, April–June 1963). Perhaps the most remarkable feature of this story is its foreshadowing of a device that was later actually built for human-dolphin communication. The research professor in the story designs

> something like a very small adding-machine with twenty-five buttons arranged in five rows of five each. It was only about three inches square, had a curved, sponge-rubber base, and was fitted with straps and buckles. Obviously, it was intended to be worn on the forearm, like an overgrown wristwatch.
>
> Some studs were blank, but most of them carried a single word engraved in large, clear letters. . . . The words . . . were: NO, YES, UP, DOWN, FRIEND, RIGHT, LEFT, FAST, SLOW, STOP, GO, FOLLOW, COME, DANGER! and HELP! . . .

"There's a lot of solid-state electronics inside that," explained the Professor, "and a battery good for fifty hours operation. When you press one of these buttons, you won't hear anything except a faint buzz. A dolphin, however, will hear the word printed on the button, in its own language." (April, p. 52)

There are three points to be noted about Clarke's device: first, it assumes that a dolphin language exists and has been decoded; second, the human signal begins as an electrical impulse; and third, the signal is translated by the machine into the corresponding dolphin whistle.

The next year, 1964, saw Dwight W. Batteau, a researcher for the Navy, build a strikingly similar device. As Forrest G. Wood recounts the experiment,

> Wayne Batteau assumed . . . that of the various sounds made by porpoises whistles were the likeliest candidates for communication signals. If this were so, and one wanted to communicate with a porpoise, would it not be advantageous to put the signals in a form familiar to the animal?
>
> An imaginative and ingenious man, Batteau had, on the basis of this rationale, developed an electronic device that would translate human vocal sounds into whistles similar to delphinid whistles.[14]

Had Batteau been reading science fiction when he built this limited sort of automatic translator? Although we will never know (he died soon afterward), when we compare his device to Clarke's fictional one, we can see the truth of H. G. Wells's lament that reality sets itself to outstrip the writer of fantasy. First, since no dolphin language had been found, it was necessary to create one, or at least to create some command signals for them in a familiar medium. And it was to be a two-way conversation, too: the machine was designed to translate dolphin whistles to equivalent human words, although this capacity was never attained. Second, the input was a spoken word, and in this respect the machine was more ambitious and convenient than Clarke's. On the third point, though, Clarke was dead on center, for the device did just what he had envisioned the year before in using the whistles the dolphins were accustomed to.

All things considered, Clarke's serialization is a far more competent and insightful work than the longest story of dolphin communication, Robert Merle's *The Day of the Dolphin* (1967 [in French]; trans. 1970). Merle's fictional workers often mention real ones (such as Lilly), but are crowned with more success: they teach two dolphins, Fa and Bi, first to use words, and then sentences. Eventually, their fluent pupils are introduced to the public at a press conference. One question is settled quickly: "REPORTER: 'Do animals have a language of their own?' FA: 'Dolphins do. I do not know whether the other animals in the sea talk. I do not understand them'" (p. 161). A panel of psychologists concludes that the dolphins "possess the vocabulary, knowledge, and intelligence of the average American teenager, except that they do not know slang and express themselves in correct English" (p. 174). No doubt if the dolphins did hear slang, they would be as offended as Blood, the telepathic dog, was. But whatever their feelings about language, the two dolphins are unfailingly polite and full of good will, by far more interesting and appealing than any of the humans. One wonders if the English language is good enough for them.

Shortly after *The Day of the Dolphin* was published, final reports on government-sponsored cetacean research began to appear. One of the last of these contains a statement that casts some doubt on Fa's truthfulness: "The data strongly suggest that the message content of a dolphin whistle is simple and redundant rather than complex and specific. No evidence was found indicating a 'song patterning' or 'language.'" [15] The uniformly negative results of this and similar studies might suggest that the future will see a decline in dolphin stories, at least in those which have dolphins speak without surgery, mutation, or genetic tinkering—or perhaps not. It may be that the myth of the talking dolphin has already become entrenched too deeply to be removed by fact. A recent essay by the science-fiction writer Katherine MacLean supports the possibility; in it, she observes that "we are not sure that dolphins and whales are wise; we are only sure that their brains are larger and their language more complex than ours." [16] A few pages after this comment, she again attributes to dolphins "a complex and delicate language" (p. 157). MacLean's article is as reliable as a dollar watch, yet it is praised by Stephen Goldin in *The Bulletin of the Science Fiction Writers of America*, a professional journal for publishing authors in the field. [17] One is reminded of Ambrose Bierce's comments on what happens when truth confronts rumor: rumor slaughters it.

The stories discussed throughout this section amply illustrate the fascination talking animals hold for mankind, and this enduring interest goes far beyond the bounds of science fiction. Its source is twofold. As Le Guin implies in an afterword to "Mazes," animals are aliens; that very story originated as her example to a writing class of taking the alien viewpoint (*Epoch*, p. 83). Yet at the same time, animals are here, not set apart on a planet light-years away. In a special way, they are our wards and our partners; before history began they shared our work and our fate. As creatures they are paradoxically both strange and familiar. A recent wilderness adventure story ("Guardian Dragon of Sulphur Bottom," *Sports Illustrated* [26 July 1976]) most poetically expressed this tension; in it William Humphrey notes the goal the stories above approach—the wish that speech could bridge the enormous gap to creatures so close.

> Now every twist in the river carried one further from all that he knew and was. Even the occasional cries of the birds and the animals were strange— surely they came from creatures different from the ones in the alphabet book. And yet, along with the deepening sense of strangeness came a sense of familiarity, as though one had been here before, but in another life. Then the cries of the animals seemed parts of speech, and one was led on by the feeling that soon, perhaps around one more turn, that long-forgotten universal mother tongue would come back to him. Here, untended since our expulsion from it, was surely the garden that once was ours, where we had given the creatures their names. A little farther on, those names would recur to us, and they would all come meekly in answer to our call. (P. 38)

III The three categories of stories about "resident aliens" present sharp contrasts in their characteristic treatments. In the "dead language" category, the stories we have seen show nothing particularly science-fictional, since both good and bad examples (with the exception of "Omnilingual") rely on present knowledge of present methods: change the setting to Iran and the language to Elamite and we no longer have science fiction. With animals, we are on more accustomed grounds: we see extrapolation by diverse methods—surgery, radiation, genetic engineering—from what is now known, and extrapolation has always been considered legitimate for science fiction. But if decipherment stories show the present, and animal stories the future, machine stories show the past. Writers in the sixties and seventies seldom endow their robots with vocal capabilities that are now being approached or, in the case of machines with emotionless voices, surpassed by the current state of the art. And with this third category, we have a hint of something to be explored in more detail later: that writers of science fiction, despite many, many pronouncements to the contrary, will not hesitate to make scientific accuracy yield to artistic intention.

5

The Medium is the Message

Tall and knotty, his vocal chords were clamped within his gnarled body, and he spoke by curving his branches until his finest twigs, set against his mouth, could be blown through to give a slender and whispering version of language. (Brian Aldiss, "The Worm That Flies," p. 60)

In science fiction one can indeed talk to the trees—or the Martians, or the Xaxans, or the T'Worlies, or anything else the writer's imagination can provide. And in this linguistic freedom, the writer of fantasy or science fiction is set apart from his colleagues who write other kinds of fiction. Although a novelist of realistic or naturalistic bent will have to invent *what* his characters say, he will choose *how* they say it from a limited set of alternatives: the characters may speak, type, write with pen and ink, carve in stone, and so on. The possible messages are countless, but the possible media are not.

But the science-fiction writer frequently invents both message and medium. The conversations of his characters may not use lips and larynxes; they may not even use sound waves. What they do use is the present subject—the different media, or channels, science-fiction writers have employed whenever their stories present an intelligent extraterrestrial being.

The aliens in many stories furnish abundant evidence that their creators had human languages in mind when designing their nonhuman ones: communication is most often spoken, its channel the familiar one of sound. This predominant use of speech or something like it is hardly surprising, since, as Charles F. Hockett noted in a discussion of language universals, "the channel for all [human] linguistic communication is vocal-auditory." [1] In addition, it makes communication much simpler between the aliens and any humans who may appear in the story.

One of the chief appeals of the alien character, however, is his very strangeness, and the writer runs a risk if he makes his aliens resemble human beings too much. As the science-fiction writer Poul Anderson points out,

when a story does take its characters beyond Earth, [the reader] is entitled to
more than what he so often gets. This is either a world exactly like our own
except for having neither geography nor history, or else it is an unbelievable
mishmash which merely shows us that still another writer couldn't be both-
ered to do his homework. . . .

At the very least, a well-thought-out setting goes far toward adding artistic verisimilitude to an otherwise bald and unconvincing narrative.[2]

Part of that well-thought-out setting is the system of communication of the
natives, and if that system is similar to human speech, the writer can supply
the necessary touch of the exotic by making the method of producing that
speech different. Thus, although we frequently find aliens using sound for
communication (especially when dealing with humans), we occasionally
find that their organs for phonation are not lungs and larynxes.

The divergence from human physiology of the alien system may range
from minor to radical: in his story "Hostess," Isaac Asimov introduces an
alien who sounds no worse than a man with ill-fitting false teeth: "The
construction of his mouth, combined with an absence of incisors, gave a
whistling sound to the sibilants. Aside from that, he might have been born
on Earth for all the accent his speech showed" (1951; rpt. H. L. Gold, ed.,
Galaxy Reader of Science Fiction, p. 309). Asimov does not tell us what lies
behind that differently constructed mouth, but Gordon R. Dickson does, in
"The Christmas Present" (1958; rpt. *Star Road*). In this story, an alien much
like a jellyfish in form has a voice described as "croaky and unbeautiful, for
a constricted air-sac is not built for the manufacture of human words" (p.
83). But even with vast differences in the means of production, the aliens
may not be inept in their product.

Apparently, no one would mistake John Brunner's people of Yan for
human beings, yet they do well in sound production for speech purposes.
They have their lungs at their sides, "drawing air directly through spiracles
between the ribs; like a bagpipes, they had continual through-put. Sound
to talk with was generated by a tympanal membrane and relayed through
resonating chambers in the gullet, giving a rather pleasant, if monotonous,
timbre; in Kaydad's case, resembling a 'cello droning away on a single
note" (*The Dramaturges of Yan*, p. 44). Not nearly so good as it is a name-
less alien monstrosity in C. M. Kornbluth's "Friend to Man" (1951; rpt.
F. Pohl, ed., *Best of C. M. Kornbluth*), a creature who resembles a cello in

more than sound. This alien has rescued a human named Smith from an extraterrestrial desert, and brought him to its lair to recuperate:

> "Salt?" asked Smith, his voice thin in the thin air. "I need salt with water."
> The thing rubbed two appendages together and he saw a drop of amber exude and spread on them. It was, he realized a moment later, rosining the bow, for the appendages drew across each other and he heard a whining, vibrating cricket-voice say: "S-s-z-z-aw-w?" . . .
> It did better the next time. The amber drop spread, and "S-z-aw-t?" was sounded, with a little tap of the bow for the final phoneme. (P. 243)

The prize for virtuosity, however, must go to James Blish's Callëans: the narrator discovers "how the Callëans spoke: the sounds issued at low volume from a multitude of spiracles or breath-holes all along the body, each hole producing only one pure tone, the words and intonations being formed in mid-air by intermodulation—a miracle of co-ordination among a multitude of organs obviously unsuitable for sound-forming at all" ("This Earth of Hours," 1959; rpt. *Galactic Cluster*, p. 164). Aliens that resemble bagpipes or cellos or, as in the last instance, pipe organs, bring us close to the borders of music itself: obviously, the elements of rhythm and melody could have some speech function. For some reason, however, this device is not often used.

The use of music for communication brackets the history of science fiction: the first of two examples I have discovered is in Francis Godwin's *The Man in the Moone* (1638). In this posthumously published novel, the hero, Gonsales, is carried to the moon by geese. He has some problems, though, with the language of the moon-people: "The Difficulty of that language is not to be conceived, and the reasons thereof are especially two: First, because it hath no affinitie with any other that ever I heard. Secondly, because it consisteth not so much of words and Letters, as of tunes and uncouth sounds, that no letters can expresse. For you have few wordes but they signifie divers and severall things, and they are distinguished onely by their tunes that are as it were sung in the utterance of them, yea many wordes there are consisting of tunes onely, so as if they list they will utter their mindes by tunes without wordes" (pp. 94–95). Godwin twice exemplifies the language by a sequence of notes on a musical staff.

Three hundred years later, the same theme was used in a science fiction story printed in an unusual place—*The Graduate Journal*, a publication of the Dean of the Graduate School of the University of Texas, 8:1 (December 1965)—by an unexpected author, W. P. Lehmann, Professor of German at Austin, and a well-known linguist. In his story, "Decoding of the Martian Language," we find out that Martian is a language of music, too, a highly complicated one, worked out in a detail too great to be fully explained here. One point may be noted, however. In English, both sounds and tones are used; the difference in their use is this: sounds such as *b, p, m, r, l,* distinguish utterances from one another—are phonemic—on what we might roughly call the word-level. But tone is used to distinguish utterances at the phrase-level: we recognize the difference between "My dinner is ready." and "My dinner is ready?" by tone—by the differing sequences of pitches at the ends of the two sentences. Lehmann reverses this relationship: for the Martians, tones are phonemic at the word-level, and sounds at the phrase-level: "The problems resulting from the early attempts to relate Martian vowels and consonants to those of Earth-tongue were dispelled when it was noted that these corresponded to variations of pitch in languages like English, and were signals of sentence structure. Alveolar fricatives, *s z,* for example, signalled finality; resonants, *r l m* and so on, indicated lack of finality, continuation of the music" (p. 270). Although Lehmann's story is mighty short on plot, its science is impeccable.

Stories have also dealt with sounds inaudible to humans. We do not hear sound waves with a frequency lower than 20 cycles per second, although if they are strong enough, we may feel them. An alien character in Henry Kuttner's "The Big Night" (1947; rpt. *The Best of Henry Kuttner*) uses subsonics to communicate with his own kind, but wears a machine that converts his speech for human ears to higher frequencies. At the other end of the scale of audibility are those sounds too high for us to hear, those above about 20,000 cycles per second. In at least two stories, the aliens are capable of producing sounds at both audible and inaudible frequencies (as far as humans are concerned). In both stories, perhaps coincidentally, they conceal their special ability in order to deceive the humans in the tales. In Hal Clement's *Mission of Gravity* (1953), an alien "had long been sure that many of the sounds his vocal apparatus could produce were not audible to the Earthman" (p. 78). He can apparently send complete messages using only the high frequencies. Isaac Asimov's Diaboli ("In a Good Cause," 1951; rpt. *Nightfall and Other Stories*) have a specialized organ for their high-frequency sounds, separate from that which produces the speech humans can hear: "the skin between their horns could . . . vibrate rapidly. The tiny waves which were transmitted in this manner were too rapid to be heard by the human ear. . . . At that time, in fact, humans remained unaware of this form of communication" (p. 177).

Before leaving those stories that tell of aliens who use the vocal-auditory channel, we should note what these aliens' native languages (the ones that can be heard) sound like to human ears. The subject was first surveyed by John R. Krueger in "Language and Techniques of Communication as Theme or Tool in Science-Fiction." He discovered an interesting consistency: "contact with a non-earthly language can produce a pleasant effect, but is more often characterized as harsh, strident, grating, and invariably 'guttural.'" [3] I can confirm his observation: using Krueger's space-saving method, some phrases from typical descriptions are listed below, with slashes separating the extracts:

> a language rich in guttural sounds / I'm the only human . . . ever to master this clicking they do / the voice had a peculiar guttural quality / a guttural, hissing tongue / low-pitched, guttural and penetrating / a flowing language with many short vowels and shifts of pitch / the clicks and rattlings of the Xaxan communicative system / sounded like a catfight / clicks, groans, and diphthongs. [4]

Another comment of Krueger's is supported by the examples: "It seems clear that every s-f writer knows that exotic languages have clicks."

No account of alien speech would be complete without mention of that of the people of Proxima Centauri. According to Murray Leinster's 1935 short story, as human explorers near the star, their radio picks up a voice speaking "what were plainly words, without vowels or consonants, yet possessing expression and varying in pitch and tone quality" ("Proxima Centauri," rpt. I. Asimov, ed., *Before the Golden Age*, p. 662).

As mentioned above, Charles F. Hockett had noted that all the major human communication systems used the vocal-auditory channel; yet he was hesitant about proclaiming this feature a true universal. As he said, "one can imagine other channels—say light, or heat-waves—" that would just as well imply the features he considered definitive of language, such as broadcast transmission, directional reception, rapid fading, and so on. [5] In his hesitancy he was recalling his earlier doubts that an alien language would depend on analogues of vocal cords and ears. In an article entitled "How to Learn Martian" in *Astounding Science Fiction*, Hockett began by outlining the technique of classifying the phonemes of a language through differential meaning; he then considered the possibility of something more speculative: "Suppose that the Martians communicate with a system just as complex as human language and with much the same essential structure, but that instead of modulating sound they modulate a carrier at frequencies above the reach of human ears—or radio waves, or a light beam, or odors, or electrical flows, or some kind of energy transmitted through the 'sub-ether.'" [6] Such carriers fall into two groups: those that, like odors and light beams, would be perceptible to human senses, and those like radio waves and electrical current that would not, without mechanical aid, be accessible to us. The second kind seems to be relatively rare, for several reasons: first, since the channels would be closed, at least initially, to humans in the story, they would be an unnecessary impediment to communication unless the plot concerned alien deception or human decipherment. Second, and this is probably the more important reason, the channels likeliest to occur to the author are those he is most familiar with—the human senses, with the vocal-auditory being primary. Nevertheless, there are a few examples of the more exotic means: an early instance was John W. Campbell's story "Out of Night" (1937; rpt. L. del Rey, ed., *Best of John W. Campbell*), wherein his aliens, the Sarn, each possess "a sensory organ sensitive to radio waves, and a radiator of those waves" (p. 165). More recently, Judith Merril invented aliens, the Ullerns, whose hide is made of quartz and functions much like a crystal set ("Daughters of Earth"; 1952, rpt. *Best of Judith Merril*, p. 133). However, the most inventive use of unusual means of communication was made by John Brunner in *Total Eclipse* (1974), a novel that, as far as language is concerned, is a model of fresh invention, careful extrapolation, and sound linguistics.

   In the novel, a human expedition finds a planet with the remains of a dead civilization. The subsequent investigation finds that the extinct aliens "possessed . . . a sense we don't have, though many fishes do: the ability to perceive electromagnetic fields" (p. 8). The complaint of Poul Anderson cited above finds no target here: Brunner gives his planet both a geography and a history, even a prehistory, as his human characters reconstruct the evolution of the aliens. They note that "surviving species [on the planet] can actually imprint suitable rocks with a distorted trace of their own fields—leaving a false spoor, as it were, to mislead predators that are hunting them down" (p. 38). They interpret this ability as contemporary evidence of the survival value of what had eventually become the channel for communication, just as the warning and distress calls of gibbons show a prelinguistic use of the vocal-auditory channel.

The method of *Total Eclipse* has two consequences, one of them a subtle linguistic problem, but Brunner considers and accounts for them both. The first of these is the necessarily close link between the aliens' language and the states of their nervous systems, since they "imprinted their 'inscriptions' directly, so that language consisted of shared patterns of nervous impulses common to all individuals—in other words, they probably didn't use names because they identified themselves by simply being!" (pp. 79–80). As the hero-linguist points out, "They didn't have to invent a system of sound-to-symbol correspondence. Their symbols were a direct reflection of a real-time process going on in their nervous systems" (pp. 82–83). But this could be a problem. One universal of human languages is what is called displacement—that is, we can talk about things not physically present or experiences not actually occurring. Without the ability to lie, paradoxically, there could be little truth, since displacement makes it possible for us to have ideas about the past, to plan for the future, to formulate hypothetical statements, even to write fiction. Brunner's characters consider the system more deeply, and decide that the aliens must have had some way of labelling their statements to allow the necessary displacement.

The second consequence is that the aliens, the Draconians, "didn't have to invent writing—they evolved it. It was as natural to them as making mouth noises is to us. They merely refined and improved the materials" (p. 82). Brunner then combines these two notions—a system much like writing and one connected with states of the nervous system—to come to a logical conclusion; as an example of what he means by "referents to real-time events rather than arbitrary symbols like human words" the linguist offers this:

> Individual A wants to inquire whether Individual B is hungry. . . . a Draconian would—at least I suspect he would—ask by imitating the pattern associated with lack of food, and modulate it by imposing other patterns defining "ask" and direct what he was saying to the correct hearer by reflecting that other person's pattern. (P. 101)

An auditor notes a similarity between the units of the alien system and Chinese ideograms, and the hero confirms his suggestion:

Just as Chinese writing originally consisted of stylized pictograms, so the Draconian language would have evolved from a number of relatively simple root concepts most probably associated with bodily states. Naturally, over the centuries it would have grown to be tremendously sophisticated, and the same difficulty that a modern person finds in dissecting the original shape for "man" or "house" or "sun" from a contemporary Chinese symbol will no doubt be found as we try to analyze these imprinted patterns. (P. 101)

Linguistics in *Total Eclipse* is central to the story, and is used with competence and sophistication. The Draconians are not oddly shaped humans; they are truly different, and their "otherness" provides the novel with a powerful means of doing the job all literature attempts, showing us to ourselves through different eyes.

II *Total Eclipse* is comparatively rare in its use of an exotic channel, and even rarer in its detailed discussion of that channel. In the genre as a whole, this lack of inventiveness comes as something of a disappointment. Loren Eiseley, the biologist, mentions the possibility of using an imaginative channel, a possibility that most writers of science fiction fail to exploit.[7] In his introduction to David Lindsay's novel *Voyage to Arcturus*, Eiseley tells of walking along the beach of a West Indies island at low tide: "Now if I had chosen to walk through these tide pools with the mind and thirsty imagination of a David Lindsay, . . . its voices would have been equally dissembling in expressing their interpretations of the universe. . . . The multiple-personed Portuguese man-of-war might have had a philosophy, or the starfish some radial pure delight unknown to creatures of mere bilateral symmetry."[8] Had Eiseley followed his ruminations through to the point of committing them to paper in the form of a science-fiction story, he would have been taking a chance. When a writer tells us of starfish talking to one another, the first question likely to occur to the reader is "How?" But farther than the bare statement of communication, few writers go. Eiseley had either not read, or chose to ignore, Naomi Mitchison's *Memoirs of a Spacewoman* (1962) when he wrote his introduction. The heroine of that novel, a spaceship "communication specialist" who will be mentioned again later, in fact meets intelligent starfish; unsurprisingly, it is "quite a problem to get through to those radial entities" (p. 13). Although achieving communication is difficult and takes a long time, we never do find out just how the starfish speak to the heroine, or to one another, for that matter. The closest the author comes to discussing method occurs when her heroine is cautioned by a friend, "You've been with them too long. You're thinking radially" (p. 20). Of course, not all stories are like this, but in general those fictional channels that depart from the vocal-auditory more often than not simply employ some other sense accessible to humans—a far cry from Brunner's Draconians or the suggestions of Hockett.

After the vocal-auditory, the most obvious second choice for a channel might be the sense of sight—after all, humans already use it: all writing systems but Braille depend on sight, and the different sign languages of the deaf come to mind, as they came to the mind of Kilgore Trout,[9] in a novel that in large part satirizes the clichés and concerns of the genre. Some of the creatures in *Venus on the Half-Shell* (1974) are rather like wheels, with various appendages that can be extended from their hubs:

"What do they talk with?" Simon said to Chworktap.
"They use their fingers, just like deaf-and-dumb people."
. . . The eyes on the ends of the stalks rolled with fright as the jeep neared them, and the herd veered to the left. Their arms came out, the fingers wriggling and crossing and bending as they asked each other what in hell these strangers were and what did they mean to do? (P. 101)

It might be argued that writing and sign languages are secondary methods, and at least partially derived from the vocal-auditory system used by the mass of men. However, several stories describe languages that depend for their channels on specialized organs to produce effects that humans cannot duplicate; though the humans in these stories could conceivably learn to understand the language, they could not "speak" it without mechanical aid. One such story is James Blish's novel *VOR* (1958), in which the title character "communicates by color-shifts in the light spectrum [varying the colors on an organ in the front of his head]. As the particular colors denoting his name are Violet-Orange-Red, they call him 'VOR' for short."[10]

A British story of about the same time describes creatures with a system of much more grandeur: Rex Gordon's *First on Mars* (U.K. 1956 as *No Man Friday*) has a human marooned on Mars encounter aliens as big as freight trains, whose conversations are symphonies of color—"there simply has not been on Earth such a colloquy of light" (p. 158).

Talking with color can be enlisted in the service of humor, too. In Isaac Asimov's "What Is This Thing Called Love?" the aliens have "color patches" somewhere above the eyes, and, through the patches' change of hue, communicate with each other: "Botax felt warmly comfortable to be following color-changes once again, after months in a spy cell on the planet, trying to make sense out of the modulated sound waves emitted by the natives. Communication by flash was almost like being home" (1961 as "Playboy and the Slime God"; rpt. *Nightfall and Other Stories*, p. 314). Thus, for example, when one of the aliens feels embarrassed, his color-patch turns purple. M. J. E. Barnes is therefore led to comment that "through the changing hues, pure concepts are transferred from one person to another."[11] It is hard to say just what is meant by "pure concept" here, since, on one occasion, when an alien says "'I can prove it,' Botax's color-flashes turned intensely yellow-green" (p. 316).

Easily the most detailed description of such specialization is given in Michael Bishop's novelette "Death and Designation among the Asadi" (1973; rpt. D. A. Wollheim, ed., *1974 Annual World's Best SF*). The central character, an anthropologist,[12] is investigating an alien race. His task is complicated by the assumed low level of civilization among the Asadi: they have no permanent dwellings, no visible social organization, nor any apparent means of communication at all. Bishop describes the breakthrough that his hero makes after noticing what he calls "staring matches" between pairs of natives:

> As for the staring matches, they're of brief duration and involve fierce gesticulation and mane-shaking. In these head-to-head confrontations the eyes change color with astonishing rapidity, flashing through the entire visible spectrum—and maybe beyond—in a matter of seconds.
>
> I'm now prepared to say that these instantaneous changes of eye color are the Asadi equivalent of speech. . . . Three weeks of observation have finally convinced me that the adversaries in these staring matches control the internal chemical changes that trigger the changes in the succeeding hues of their eyes. In other words, patterns exist. And the minds that control these chemical changes cannot be primitive ones. Nor can I believe that the changes in eye color result from involuntary reflex. The alterations are willed. They're infinitely complicated. . . . The Asadi have a "language." (P. 175)

From Bishop's description, the language of the Asadi lacks one of the universals proposed by Hockett, the expansion of the signal in all directions from its point of origin—broadcast transmission; the aliens must necessarily be in rather close contact to "talk" to each other. Hockett argues that the broadcast transmission of speech has evolutionary advantages as well as disadvantages: "A warning cry may tell all one's fellows something of the location of the danger, but also, if the danger is a predator, it tells the predator where one is."[13] But the lack of this human universal does not make the Asadi language implausible: on their planet, they have no natural predators. One story, in which speech is considered from an alien viewpoint, presents broadcast transmission as a disadvantage: the aliens complain that communicating with humans is troublesome, "owing to the fact that the creatures employ a method of communication not heretofore found. Their range approaches zero and there is almost no directional factor" (Graham Doar, "The Outer Limit," rpt. G. Conklin, ed., *Big Book of Science Fiction*, p. 232).

III Using smell for communication challenges the science-fiction writer. The writer Hal Clement noted that "scent seems to have all the disadvantages and none of the advantages, as a long-range sense."[14] Nevertheless, olfaction has an incidental use in some few stories, and is centrally important in at least three. In "Doomship" by Frederik Pohl and Jack Williamson (rpt. D. A. Wollheim, ed., *1974 Annual World's Best SF*), the T'Worlies, vaguely batlike creatures, communicate through odors. As a human in that story comments, "The vinegary smell deepened. It was a sign of polite cogitation in a T'Worlie, like a human being's *hmmm*" (p. 42).[15] But to talk to other races, the T'Worlies have recourse to machines. If we examine more closely the possibility of a language based on smell, the question of universals again arises. For any kind of transmission of ideas, you must have some carrier and some way to modulate it. It would seem to follow, therefore, that communication based on smells would require the ability to emit at will several distinctly different odors (because of the persistence of scents, we can dismiss the possibility of an on-off modulation, like that of Morse code). But this presents two problems for face-to-face (or whatever) communication: first, how do you clear the channel? A story by Damon Knight, "Cabin Boy" (1951; rpt. H. L. Gold, ed., *Galaxy Reader of Science Fiction*), deals with the adventures of two humans who contact a species that uses scent. In their first attempt to communicate with the aliens, "there had been a series of separate odors, all unfamiliar and all overpoweringly strong. At least a dozen of them, Roget [one of the humans] thought; they had gone past too quickly to count" (p. 357). But the "conversation" has taken place inside the cramped quarters of the humans' spaceship, to which they have brought one of the aliens, and we are left wondering just where the odors went to. Perhaps the alien's equivalent of a full stop is a whiff of deodorant.

The second problem with using air-borne scents for communication is that even a casual breeze becomes "noise" in the system, blending the odors and distorting their original sequence. Colin Kapp neatly solves this problem in his story "The Old King's Answers" (*Galaxy*, September 1973). Here the planet-exploring human scientists are intrigued by what seem to be prearranged meetings between large bearlike animals. Since the scientists are surveying the planet for possible colonization, part of their task is ascertaining whether the world contains indigenous intelligent life. As one of them observes, "If the meeting were prearranged the fact would suggest the bears have the ability to make abstract communications at a reasonably high level. Frankly, they would need a developed language" (p. 165). The bears, it is discovered, have at least a "written" language, one which avoids the potential noise problem in their medium: they have

> scent glands in the pads of their feet. . . . They've settled on the flat faces of the crystal rocks when they really want to leave a message for the world. Using chromatography [says the head of the expedition], I've managed to identify three individual scent products, all of them remarkably persistent. They are combined together on the crystal faces in an amazing spectrum of complexity. In their scent-writing they have the capacity—though I'm not sure how much of it they utilize—to compress more bits of information in a given space than we humans can in our optical writing. (P. 167)

Kapp (or his character) goes overboard at the end of the quoted passage. Because the proper comparison of the scent-writing is not to human speech, which may involve only binary discriminations to distinguish sounds, but to human writing, it seems his claim is not only exaggerated, but flatly incredible. With twenty-six letters and a blank space as candidates for appearance at any given point in a sequence of written English, for example, the reader identifies a character by making a twenty-seven-way distinction. The area to which scent is applied in the bears' three-way system would have to be minute indeed "to compress more bits of information in a given space" than even the largest print or handwriting. And, of course, the smaller the areas and the closer they are together, the more acute the blending problem would become.

Finally, the bears would be hampered by the system's lack of another human universal: rapid fading. After a while, the signals would clutter the channel (Hockett's metaphor is a blackboard without an eraser). Smell may be fine for a written message like "There's a meeting here tonight," but it seems unable to handle an ordinary comment like "Look out below!"

Communication by scent is of central importance, and discussed at length, in John Norman's *Priest-Kings of Gor* (1968), where the problems associated with the medium have been carefully investigated and thoughtfully worked out. The Priest-Kings of the title are much like giant ants, a resemblance which allows the human narrator to allude to similar earth systems; as he says, "What in the passageways I had taken to be the scent of Priest-Kings had actually been the residue of odor-signals which Priest-Kings, like certain social insects of our world, use in communicating with one another" (p. 77), referring to the pheromone communication discussed in the last chapter. Norman is likewise aware of the problems that have been cited here: "Communication by odor-signals can in certain circumstances be extremely efficient, though it can be disadvantageous in others. For example, an odor can carry . . . much farther than can the shout or cry of a man to another man. Moreover, if not too much time is allowed to elapse, a Priest-King may leave a message in his chamber or in a corridor for another Priest-King, and the other may arrive later and interpret. A disadvantage of this mode of communication, of course, is that the message may be understood by strangers or others for whom it is not intended. One must be careful of what one says in the tunnels of Priest-Kings for one's words may linger after one, until they sufficiently dissipate to be little more than a meaningless blur of scent" (p. 78). The off-handed insertion of "tunnels" shows how Norman has obviated the problem of winds.

A simpler but more drastic way to forestall unwanted breezes is to do away with air altogether. Hal Clement took this approach to overcome the disadvantages he mentioned above: "In a story of my own some years ago ('Uncommon Sense,' *Astounding Science Fiction*, September 1945), I assumed an airless planet, so that molecules could diffuse in nearly straight lines. The local sense organs were basically pinhole cameras, with the retinal mosaic formed of olfactory cells" ("The Creation of Imaginary Beings," p. 270). The creatures in question are not intelligent, so their potential for communication remains unexplored.

IV No one, to my knowledge, has written of creatures who use taste as a language; if we limit our scope to observable uses of human senses, this leaves only motion and touch. Kinesics, the use of motion as part of a system of communication, is one of the youngest branches of linguistics, but the study of one of its parts, gesture, is hundreds of years old. Actors of the eighteenth and nineteenth centuries learned a large number of gestures having rather specific meanings within the conventions of the day. Most of the gestures we use in everyday life, like their dramatic counterparts, are as arbitrary in their meanings as any spoken word: they depend for their intelligibility on the prior agreement by the members of the community. We see this codelike aspect of gesture in Piers Anthony's *Orn* (1971), in which manta-shaped flying fungoids snap their tails once for yes and twice for no in answer to questions from their human companions. Communication gradually improves, and eventually the mantas can initiate conversation "with that combination of gesture and tail snaps they had gradually worked out as their code" (p. 147).

Science-fiction writers often use motion in combination with some other channel. The Loarrans, creatures in a story by Terry Carr, illustrate this point; they communicate by "wave-dancing," and a conversation is not just communication but an art-form: "The dance he went through to give the description was intricate and even imaginative. . . . It used motion and color and sound and another sense something like smell" ("The Dance of the Changer and the Three," 1968; rpt. D. A. Wollheim and T. Carr, eds., *World's Best Science Fiction 1969*, pp. 261–62). Less flashy but still complex is the use of gesture by the nildoror, aliens in Robert Silverberg's *Downward to the Earth* (1969), a work that coincidentally makes a point about the human use of gesture—what we would do if we couldn't use our hands. Humans, thanks to an upright method of locomotion, have hands and arms available for gestures, but the nildoror are large elephantlike creatures, and all four of their limbs are fully occupied in walking. They therefore use other appendages: "The spiny crest down the middle of the alien's broad skull began to twitch. . . . The nildoror had a rich language of gesture, employing not only the spines but also their long ropy trunks and their many-pleated ears" (pp. 8–9). The novel does not discuss the gesture system at length, but we do find out that it provides information on the speaker's attitude toward what he is saying. At one point, a nildor says he remembers the human hero, but the alien's speech "did not reveal whether [he] remembered Gundersen fondly, bitterly, or indifferently. Gundersen might have drawn a hint from the movements of [the] cranial crest, but it was impossible for someone seated on a nildor's back to detect any but the broadest such movements. The intricate nildoror system of nonverbal supplementary communication had not evolved for the convenience of passengers" (p. 21).

In human society, the use of gesture is closely related to the use of the sense of touch. Any tactile language would lack the quality of broadcast transmission, just as the Asadi's color language did, yet in two works the authors remedy this defect by contriving a sort of dual-channel system, supplementing the tactile channel with a vocal-auditory one. In the first of these (Ursula Le Guin's "The Word for World Is Forest," H. Ellison, ed., *Again, Dangerous Visions* [1972]), we might not want to call the tactile system a full-fledged language, although we are assured that it is:

> Touch was the main channel of communication among the forest people. Among Terrans touch is always likely to imply threat, aggression, and so for them there is often nothing between the formal handshake and the sexual caress. All that blank was filled by the Athsheans with varied customs of touch. Caress as signal and reassurance was as essential to them as it is to mother and child or to lover and lover; but its significance was social, not only maternal and sexual. It was part of their language. It was therefore patterned, codified, yet infinitely modifiable. (Pp. 79–80)

The few usages described offer nothing of more linguistic interest than a pat on the back. The story supplies insufficient evidence to let us determine if the touches have associated meanings, however loose, and are therefore merely gestures, or lack meaning in themselves. If the latter were true, and meaning resided in combinations of touches, they would then be something we could call "tactemes," units that could be combined into indefinitely many morphemes, and hence units of a true language.

A fully tactile language does appear in Naomi Mitchison's remarkable *Memoirs of a Spacewoman*. The title character, narrator of the novel, is the "communication specialist" on a spaceship. Her reticence about her methods with starfish has been noted, but she is more voluble about the fascinating Martians, who "rarely speak. . . . They communicate through the highly educated tactile senses. This started in their subterranean [sub-martian?] days, in the original darkness in which they lived for so many millennia" (p. 55). There are attendant drawbacks to their method: for one, the Martians must disrobe to talk.[16] After the narrator has gained the confidence of Vly, a Martian member of the crew, the alien begins "communicating all over with his tongue, fingers, toes, and sexual organs" (p. 55). Other members of the expedition are understandably reluctant to witness a Martian conversation, let alone participate, and the narrator takes pains to dispel this provincial attitude: "I went on to explain how the uncovered and mobile sexual organs, which Olga had barely brought herself to look at, were not unnaturally particularly sensitive, and could communicate fine shades of meaning" (p. 57). Indeed they do. During one conversation, the heroine gets pregnant.[17]

In this short survey, the communication systems discussed must first have been observable, and second, the channel must have been natural. By means of these limitations, two venerable and widespread science fiction themes were ruled out. The requirement that the system be observable excluded telepathy, a plot device of unparalleled utility to the writer who must establish communication between a human character and a really bizarre yet intelligent being. If that being is a large, sentient mass of roots like the Plant-Grandfather in Gordon R. Dickson's "Twig" (J.-L. del Rey, ed., *Stellar 1* [1974]), the presupposition of telepathic powers avoids some knotty problems. The requirement that the system be natural excluded the mechanical translator, a device that, like telepathy, avoids similar difficulties that the author may not wish to deal with. Neither telepathy nor the translation machine is without linguistic interest, but their frequent use warrants a separate discussion later.

With these two exclusions, some generalizations can be made about alien channels of communication. First, the channel for alien communication is overwhelmingly likely to be accessible to human sense. Second, of those senses, the language will most likely employ the vocal-auditory channel. Third, and finally, the language will most probably sound unpleasant to the humans in the story, consisting in large part of clicks, hisses, and assorted noises. All of the above characteristics are more likely to occur in run-of-the-mill science fiction, which, like the majority of any branch, is undistinguished. Science fiction is generally considered so bizarre by the uninitiated that it comes as a surprise that in matters of language it should be so commonplace. Seldom do we meet really different alien channels, and almost never do we read of creatures like Jme, a little alien in S. Kye Boult's "The Safety Engineer" (S. Goldin, ed., *The Alien Condition* [1973]), who can communicate by touch or with "infra-red, high frequency, sonics, or any of the other sensory frequencies her body could put out" (p. 121). Yet as Charles F. Hockett has noted, and some writers have shown, the possibilities exist; consider Theodore Sturgeon's "The [Widget], the [Wadget], and Boff" (1955; rpt. A. Boucher, ed., *Treasury of Great Science Fiction*, vol. 1):

> Subtle differences in nuclei, in probability shells, and in internal tensions were the coding, and fields of almost infinite variability were used to call up the particles in the desired combinations. These were channeled in a way beyond description in earthly mathematics, detected by a principle as yet unknown to us, and translated into language (or, more accurately, an analog of what we understand as language). Since this happened so far away, temporally, spatially, and culturally, proper nouns are hardly proper." (Pp. 308–9)

It is in the work of those writers of talent and imagination, some of whom have been mentioned here, that we read of communication systems that expand the definition of language, and make the term "language universal" sound insular indeed.

6

"Take Me to Your Leader"

An illustration from John Wilkins's *The Discovery of a World in the Moone* (in a 1751 edition) shows an eighteenth-century gentleman seated on a chair watching winged, humanlike creatures battle with sword and spear in the sky.[1] Readers of the thirties and forties (and later, in some cases) can remember the typically lurid covers of the pulp, depicting in four-color detail a lecherous monster leering at or fumbling with a nubile maiden.[2] From Cyrano de Bergerac and Bishop Godwin to Samuel R. Delany and Larry Niven, the alien—the intelligent extraterrestrial being—endures as a staple of science fiction. "The exploration of another world, the encounter with alien forms of life," as the science-fiction writer Thomas M. Disch argues, is the theme that "more than any other defines sf."[3] In the last chapter we saw some representative alien communication systems; in this chapter we focus specifically on the "alien encounter," examining how writers depict their characters preparing for it, and the methods those characters use when it comes to attempting communication.

Within the category of alien-encounter stories lies the subcategory of the "first contact," the initial meeting of intelligent beings, each previously unaware of the other's existence. As Frederik Pohl has said, first contact "is clearly a probable event somewhen in Man's future. Sf writers have so considered it for a long time. H. G. Wells told us that the essence of first contact might be invasion and exploitation (in *The War of the Worlds*), on the highly defensible assumption that since that had been the way it had usually been in earthly affairs, interplanetary affairs would likely be the same. Murray Leinster, Hal Clement, and a hundred other writers have expanded on this assumption and investigated specific areas contained within it."[4]

By definition, a first contact is not something that one knows in advance will come at a certain place and a certain time. If a spaceship's complement is being pondered for a voyage of exploration, one knows that an astronomer and a geologist will be needed, but whether the services of a linguist will come in handy depends on chance. Thus, the crew of the exploring vessel in Stanley G. Weinbaum's "A Martian Odyssey" (1934; rpt. R. Silverberg, ed., *The Science Fiction Bestiary*) consists of an engineer, an astronomer (who is also captain of the ship), and a chemist. In the course of their adventure on Mars, they meet Tweel, one of the most celebrated aliens in science fiction, and their attempts at communicating are a hit-or-miss affair. But the same crew realizes its limitations in a sequel, "Valley of Dreams" (1934; rpt. *Best of Stanley G. Weinbaum*). As the narrator remarks, "The next expedition to this golf ball ought to carry an archeologist—and a philologist, too, as we found out later" (p. 34). Thirty years later, in 1965, crews were still coming up short in communication skills: Norman Spinrad asserts, "There were three basic specialties needed to make a preliminary evaluation of a planet: geology, ecology, and xenology" ("A Child of Mind," rpt. *The Last Hurrah of the Golden Horde*, p. 51). Perhaps the xenologist, a specialist in alien animal life, doubles as a linguist.

Alien crews are often better prepared. One such is sent to Earth to end a centuries-old quarantine of humanity: "It was, therefore, decided that a party consisting of Commander Rappan, Navigator Zinin, Communicator Phrnnx, a philologist, a xenologist, and of course, the Professor, would take a ground car down to the structure and attempt a First Contact" (Alan Dean Foster, "With Friends Like These," 1971; rpt. D. A. Wollheim, ed., *1972 Annual World's Best SF*, pp. 183–84). The usefulness of having a linguist along finds confirmation when the party meets its first human: "'Uh,' began the philologist, straining over the guttural syllables, 'we come in peace, Terran. Friends. Buddies. Comrades. Blutbruderhood. We good-guys. You comprende?'" (p. 185).

There is, of course, the odd story (odd in more ways than one) in which the job of a linguist is handled by some other specialist, not by necessity but by design. James Blish, in "This Earth of Hours" (1959; rpt. *Galactic Cluster*), sends a poet. Although this is precisely the same as sending a sculptor to do the work of a geologist, the characters in Blish's story seem satisfied: "It had to be admitted that assigning 12-Upjohn, a poet, as an interpreter on this mission had not been a wholly bad idea. . . . Getting along with these people on the first contact would be vital, and yet the language barrier might well provoke a tragedy wanted by neither side, as the obliteration of Nagasaki in World War II had been provoked by the mistranslation of a single word. Under such circumstances, a man with a feeling for strange words in odd relationships might well prove to be useful, or even vital" (p. 161).⁵ The most incomprehensible choice, however, comes on a mining expedition in Terry Carr's "The Dance of the Changer and the Three" (1968; rpt. D. A. Wollheim and T. Carr, eds., *World's Best Science Fiction 1969*). To negotiate with and translate the language of the aliens on Loarr, Earth sends a public-relations man, which must be the most confidence ever reposed in someone of that profession.

What happens when the crew, whatever its composition, meets the aliens? At first glance, it would seem that for communication to take place, the beings involved must have at least one language in common, however the result is achieved. It might be the result of sheer good luck, as in S. P. Meek's "Submicroscopic" (1931; rpt. I. Asimov, ed., *Before the Golden Age*). The hero of this early story, born in Honolulu, "the only child of the richest sugar planter in the Islands" (p. 66), goes to war in World War I, returns to study at the University of Minnesota, takes a science degree, and, in the face of scoffers, sets out to experiment on his own in a valley "in the most inaccessible crags of the Timpahute range in southern Nevada" (p. 68). He builds a machine to shrink him to "submicroscopic" size. He finds a miniature world, and meets a girl whom he rescues from apelike creatures. "Her speech was beautifully liquid and hauntingly familiar. I couldn't understand her, but I was sure that I had heard that language before. Presently I caught a word and like a flash I knew. She was speaking some dialect of Hawaiian. Desperately I strove to recall the speech of Leilani, my old nurse" (p. 75). One must admit that this is a stroke of extraordinary good fortune; perhaps the hero's submicroscopic world lies in some earlier prospector's discarded pineapple can. But the sequel to this story illustrates a surprising theme in alien encounter stories: often a writer asserts that a character does not understand an alien language, but communication takes place nevertheless. In Meek's "Awlo of Ulm" (1931; rpt. I. Asimov, ed., *Before the Golden Age*), the same hero meets apelike villains, the leader of whom "spoke in a strange guttural voice and while his language was not that of Ulm [the Hawaiian noted above], I was able to understand it" (p. 99). One does not resolve a contradiction by asserting it, but many stories use this nonmethod of achieving communication.

The first way, then, that science fiction deals with the language gap is to fall into it. In Ward Moore's "No Man Pursueth" (rpt. A. Boucher, ed., *Best From Fantasy and Science Fiction*, Sixth Series), a woman from present-day

America finds herself in the midst of a Nazi concentration camp, due to a "warp in the space-time continuum": "Most frightening of all to Hesione was the realization that though she knew no more than a few words of his [German], yet she understood everything [the Nazi guard] was saying perfectly, even when he used colloquialisms" (p. 188). Perhaps the silliest story of this kind is Stephen Tall's "The Bear with the Knot on His Tail" (1971; rpt. D. A. Wollheim, ed., *1972 Annual World's Best SF*). Humans in a spaceship approaching a planet hear a strange music radiating from it. Although they are unable to understand the words of the choral music coming from their radios, the humans have no trouble perceiving the messages in the singing. As the narrator says, "We could hear the exultant questions in them: '*Who are you? Where are you? Speak to us again!*'" (p. 75). How the humans know that the music is not just the aliens' top forty is anybody's guess; rational analysis fails here. Eventually the ship lands on the planet, which will be destroyed in a few hours when its sun becomes a nova. In the short time they have after making contact, they are naturally unable to puzzle out the alien language, nor can the aliens decipher the earthmen's language. But all is not lost; they establish rapport with the aliens by playing a guitar at them. A woman in the crew takes her instrument: "She plucked single, somehow questioning notes. They responded with a flood of sound" (p. 86). To make herself clear, apparently, she includes gestures: she "swept her hand in a wide arc to indicate the ship. She plucked a single sharp inquiring note on the A string. And the visitors grew completely quiet. There was no way to substantiate it, but to me they seemed appalled" (p. 86). The reader may share the aliens' feelings.

This mystical method depends on presumption, and its dangers are clearly shown in Miriam de Ford's "The Apotheosis of Ki" (1956; rpt. J. F. McComas, ed., *Special Wonder*). In her story, an alien crashes near a wandering Neanderthal. The alien crawls from the burning spaceship; he speaks, but the Neanderthal, Ki, does not understand. He tries gestures, indicating that he is hungry, but Ki takes him to refer to the tribe's need for better hunting grounds. Thinking that the space traveler is a god demanding Ki's death as a ritual sacrifice for better times, Ki advances toward the alien with his club raised, offering himself willingly. Now it is the alien's turn to misunderstand, and frightened, he tosses away his weapon and approaches Ki, holding his hands out: as Ki thinks, "in his tone, had he been a man and not a god, was what would have seemed a note of plead-

ing" (p. 121). Finally, Ki thinks he understands the stranger: he strikes the
alien dead, roasts him, and eats him. As he later explains to his tribe, an-
nouncing that he has been appointed by the gods to be their medicine man
and lead them to good hunting grounds, "All this the god told me without
words, before he commanded me to strike him dead" (p. 121).

Should the parties to the first contact avoid problems like those outlined
above, they can attempt to learn one or the other's language, always assuming that they have a common channel of communication. In that case,
they will probably start with ostension. Edgar Rice Burroughs's hero, John
Carter, begins this way frequently, setting an early example of sensible procedure: "I commenced in the usual way that one learns a new language. I
pointed to various articles in the room and to various parts of our bodies,
repeating their names in my own language. My companion seemed to
understand immediately what I was attempting to do; and pointing to the
same articles himself, he repeated their names" (*Swords of Mars*, 1934;
rpt. *Swords of Mars and Synthetic Men of Mars*, p. 122).

The eponymous forefather of the theme, Murray Leinster's "First Contact" (1945; rpt. G. Conklin, ed., *The Best of Science Fiction*) avoided the
inanity satirized by de Ford, while providing an alternative to Burroughs's
method. In Leinster's very reasonable account, a ship full of humans meets
an alien ship in outer space. They do not try to learn one or the other's
languages; instead they find a sensible compromise, devising a third language: "We agreed on arbitrary symbols for objects . . . by way of the
visiplates, and worked out relationships and verbs and so on with diagrams
and pictures. We've a couple of thousand words that have mutual meanings" (p. 570), reports the communications officer to his captain. But, as
has been demonstrated, Leinster's successes are not always matched.

The examples above may give the impression that the first contact is
always face to face. Not so. Although the personal confrontation appeals
to the writer's sense of the dramatic and therefore tends to monopolize the
theme, the first contact may be a meeting of minds separated in body by
light years. If we send a message, we don't have to have a particular recipient in mind; anyone out there will do. A message like this has indeed
been sent, fixed to the Pioneer 10 spacecraft. A six- by nine-inch plate
carries an etching that its designers, Frank Drake and Carl Sagan of Cornell,
hope will be interpretable to an intelligent alien. Some parts of the message
seem, a priori, much clearer than others, if we divorce ourselves from

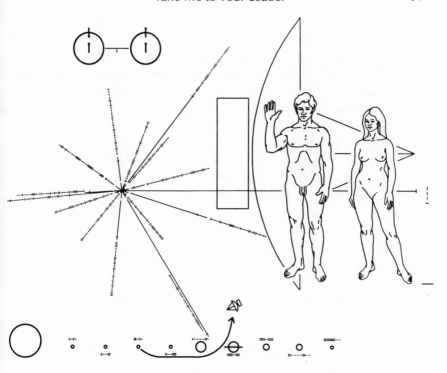

human preconceptions. First of all, we must assume that the aliens have the requisite organs to see the plaque; the chapter on alien channels of communication should caution us against taking this for granted. But suppose the aliens do have eyes. They should then be able to identify the time and place of the launching of Pioneer 10, assuming that they have astronomical knowledge of pulsars and chemical knowledge of hydrogen. But the figures of the man and the woman to the right of the plaque say very little, it seems to me.

Critics of the plaque have pointed out how much of its interpretation depends upon knowing the conventions of line drawings. Because we, looking at the picture, know what humans look like, we can sort out the various lines and dots, and identify them as symbols of the parts of the anatomy they are intended to represent. But an alien, looking at the plaque, has no way of telling that some dots are eyes, some nipples, and some belly-buttons. Moreover, what is the alien to make of all those lines on the body intended to represent musculature? It is sobering to note how little agreement there was among humans of Drake's and Sagan's own culture about the intent and meaning of the drawing. Articles such as John P. Wiley's column in *Natural History* (August 1972), pp. 72–73, or that in *Time* (5 June 1972), p. 60, show how little commonality of symbolism we can expect from our own kind; how much less would there be among aliens! Isaac Asimov was perhaps more optimistic about the message than it deserves when he said that advanced aliens could read it (Introduction to Carol and Frederik Pohl, eds., *Jupiter*). Zach Hughes, in his *The Legend of Miaree* (1974), has a similar drawing broadcast as the first contact between two alien cultures, but in that case, the beings are much like each other (and like us) as is evident from their understanding of the picture: "A planet circled the sun, a rim sun, position indicated by a superimposed drawing of the galactic wheel. Picture two was three figures. Biped. Different, yet near the Artonuee form. A larger figure, naked, male genitalia evident. A medium-sized figure, the male identification absent. A small figure with smaller male genitalia" (p. 32).

The trouble with pictures is that they are worth a thousand words—in fact, any number of words. Hughes's fictional picture and Drake and Sagan's real one show an enormous number of ambiguities; it is possible to design messages that have far fewer, and some science-fiction writers have done so.

Frank Drake, one of the designers of the Pioneer 10 plaque, is also one of the founders of Project Ozma, an enterprise of the National Radio Astronomy Observatory at Green Bank, West Virginia, which has been searching for radio signals from space since 1960.[6] A story published that same year, Winston P. Sanders's "The Word to Space" (rpt. M. Mohs, ed., *Other Worlds, Other Gods*), takes place at Project Ozma, and outlines the difficulties involved with interstellar radio communication:

> Communication has always been tough. After the project founders first detected the signals, fifty years must pass between our acknowledgement and their reply to that. Of course, they'd arranged it well. Their initial message ran three continuous months before repeating itself. In three months one can transmit a lot of information; one can go all the way from "two plus two equals four" to basic symbology and telling what band a sonic cast will be sent on if there's an answer. Earth's own transmission could be equally long and carefully thought out. Still, it was slow. You can't exactly have a conversation across twenty-five light years. All you can do is become aware of each other's

existence and then start transmitting more or less continuously, meanwhile interpreting the other fellow's own steady flow of graded data. (Pp. 76–77)

Isaac Asimov takes the same tack in his story of radio communication, "Not Final" (1941; rpt. D. Knight, ed., *Toward Infinity*). Writing twenty years before "The Word to Space," Asimov emphasizes the difficulty of the task, and the use of mathematics as a beginning (the story concerns radio communication between humans in orbit around Jupiter and creatures on its surface, so long time-lags do not complicate matters): "It was a heartbreaking job. It was five years before we got past the elementary clicks of arithmetic: three and four are seven; the square root of twenty-five is five; factorial six is seven hundred and twenty. After that, months sometimes passed before we could work out and check by further communication a single new fragment of thought" (p. 202).

But even Asimov's story was not the first to explore the technique and difficulty of this approach. In 1965, Derwent Mercer, a lecturer in physics at the University of Southampton, discussed how we might go about contacting people on other planets; he begins, "But how should we start to communicate? Obviously there is no point in flashing English messages in Morse code."[7] One of the earliest and best stories dealing with interplanetary radio communication does in fact use Morse code, and makes that method seem very plausible indeed. That story is Raymond Z. Gallun's "Old Faithful" (1934; rpt. I. Asimov, ed., *Before the Golden Age*), a fine tale about a Martian astronomer who sees light signals emanating from the Earth and attempts to establish communication. When Earth responds, it is through light signals in Morse code. The Martian, referred to as Number 774, receives his first message: "'Hello, Mars! Hello, Mars! Hello, Mars! Earth calling. Earth calling. Earth calling,' the message spelled, and Number 774 was grimly in the midst of the colossal task he had set for himself" (p. 593).

Number 774 has no idea what the message means, and Gallun does not make things easy for him: "In the first place, the messages that were coming to Number 774 were the code representations of alphabetical letters standing for various sounds which, when taken in groups, made up words of vocal speech" (p. 594). But sound, had the Martian encountered it, would have been wasted on him: "Number 774 had no idea of sound except as an interesting phenomenon recorded by his scientific instruments. . . . He had no ears; neither did he have well-developed vocal organs" (p. 594). But this is not the greatest handicap under which he works: "Strange as it may seem to us, prior to his experience with the light, he had not the faintest idea of what a word was, either a vocal word or a written word, or a word represented in the form of a group of signals. Because Martian methods of communicating with one another, and of recording knowledge, are so different from ours that a word would have been as great a mystery to him as it would have been to a newborn kitten" (p. 594).

Despite these many drawbacks, Number 774 sets to work. He easily distinguishes the dot-and-dash symbols for the letters of the alphabet from the ones for the numbers 0 through 9. Although he does not understand the significance of any of these symbols, the number sequence eventually gives him the clue he needs to go on:

> It was when the counting proceeded above nine, and numbers of more than one digit appeared, that Number 774, after a long period of association with the riddle, had received his first faint glimmer of understanding. . . . He had noted that there were but ten separate signals in this strange system, which was apparently quite distinct from that other mysterious system of twenty-six symbols, for the two had never yet been mixed in one signal group or word; and that, as the flashing of the signals proceeded, each symbol seemed to bear a definite relationship to the others. (Pp. 595–96)

After 774 notices the sequence of numbers, his counterpart on Earth begins to transmit arithmetic problems, just as Asimov's philologist does in "Not Final." From equations like "7 and 2 are 9," 774 finds out the meaning of *and* and *are*. The meaning of the question mark comes next. From 774's errors and their correction by his earthly respondent, he discovers the meaning of *no*. In the same way, he comes to understand *times*, *divided by*, *plus*, *minus*, and so on.

Once he has grasped the number system, those numbers can then be used to increase the vocabulary by ostension, that is, by pointing at something and naming it. The "pointing" must be figurative, of course: " 'Earth, Planet 3, Mars, Planet 4,' was a message he was able to guess the meaning of correctly. . . . Aided by the message, 'Earth, Planet 3, has 1 moon. Mars, Planet 4, has 2 moons,' he had been half able to clinch his guess" (p. 597). In this manner, he adds *moon*, *planet*, and one sense of *have* to the words he knows. 774's telescope is very powerful; he can see earthly meteorological conditions, and when those conditions are discussed by radio, he adds *snow*, *clouds*, *storm*, etc., to his list. Gallun generalizes about the method in a good description of 774's progress: "And so the process of his Earthly education had gone on, slowly, depending to a large extent upon brilliant though not very certain guesswork, and demanding a degree of patience in instructor and pupil for which teaching a person to talk who had been deaf, blind, and dumb since birth is but a feeble and inadequate analogy" (p. 598). When a comet enters the solar system, the occasion is taken advantage of to explain the verbs *come* and *go* by means of messages like "Comet coming toward sun, Mars, and Earth" (p. 603).

A judgment is made by his superiors that 774's work is unproductive; his project is to be ended, and his life along with it. He therefore decides to leave Mars, and sends word of that decision to Earth: "Comet coming. Yes. Comet coming. Yes. Comet coming of Man of Mars. Comet Man of Mars coming toward Earth. Comet coming Man of Mars. Man of Mars. Comet. Man of Mars. Comet. Man of Mars. Comet. Yes, yes, yes. Man of Earth. Yes, yes, yes. Signing off. Signing off" (p. 607). Earlier in the story, the curious message is explained: "For a full three minutes, . . . Number 774 continued to send, repeating the same phrase over and over again, changing certain words each time, in the hope of hitting the right combination that would convey his meaning" (p. 601). And come he does, though he dies of injuries received in the crash on Earth, but not before giving Earth the information needed to build a spaceship.

Gallun's story, which Damon Knight has called one of the "most vivid and memorable stories about aliens ever written," [8] remains a model treatment of the theme, a carefully thought-out depiction, step by step, of the conquest of the difficulties of communication between different beings. Many stories on the topic followed it; few equalled it, and none excelled it.

Communication by radio has inherent limitations, however; assuming that earthman and alien have a channel in common, a face-to-face encounter entails fewer problems and more opportunity for improvisation. The first thing necessary is to get the alien's attention: the characters of Poul Anderson's "The Serpent in Eden" (in R. Elwood, ed., *Omega* [1973]) try using Polaroid snapshots. Many times, though, the humans suffer from an excess of attention, not a lack of it. In P. Schuyler Miller's "Tetrahedra of Space" (1931; rpt. I. Asimov, ed., *Before the Golden Age*), the tetrahedra, giant intelligent crystals, land in South America. Quite by accident, a museum expedition (joined by a downed aviator) encounters the hostile tetrahedra, and is immediately besieged by them. The aviator ponders how communication might be established: "I thought of stories I had read of interplanetary communication—of telepathy, of word-association, of sign language. They had all seemed far-fetched to me, impossible of attainment, but I resolved to try my hand at the last" (p. 185). He cuts a diagram of the solar system in a soft rock, with grooves for the orbits and pebbles showing the planets. The diagram is useful when communication is later achieved.

The quotation from "Tetrahedra of Space" illustrates a general practice of science-fiction writers: they mine earlier stories for themes and approaches, frequently making reference to what they regard as flaws or virtues in the works of their predecessors. Anthony Boucher refers to the "solar-system drawing" as a method in his "Expedition" (1945; rpt. G. Conklin, ed., *Best of Science Fiction*): Martians land on Earth, specifically intending to contact intelligent life; after a few failures, they run into a human being, and attempt "the fifth approach, the one developed for beings of a civilization roughly parallel to our own" (p. 743). After some initial shock on the man's part, the contact specialist, Halov, settles down to work: "The stick in Halov's digit traced a circle in the dirt with rays coming out of it, then pointed up at the setting sun. . . . Then Halov drew a series of concentric ellipses of dotted lines about the figure of the sun. He drew tiny circles on these orbits to indicate the first and second planets, then larger ones to indicate the third and our own. The biped was by now following the drawing with intense absorption" (p. 745). Miller's "Tetrahedra" method, which must have been used in at least a hundred first-contact stories, works well here. But other authors are not so sure the method is practical.

The diagram method fails the humans of Poul Anderson's "Epilogue" (1962; rpt. R. Silverberg, ed., *The Ends of Time*), who return to the earth of the far future after the machines have taken over. The robots, who have forgotten their creators, capture three humans in spacesuits, and are unaware that their captives are intelligent, free agents. The humans are likewise unaware that the robots have developed volition; after they understand the free will of the robots, the humans still cannot communicate with them, since the robots "talk" on radio frequencies. One of the humans tries to demonstrate his intelligence by the use of pictures; a robot observes that "all at once it squatted and drew geometrical shapes in the sand, very much like the courtship figures drawn by a male dune-runner" (p. 181). The robots then conclude that the humans are some sort of domesticated, semi-conscious robot.

Lack of understanding hampers the characters in Anderson's story at every turn. Arthur C. Clarke has one of his characters in a similar situation reflect: "Communication was practically impossible, and Jan realized bitterly that getting in touch with an alien race was not as easy as it was so often depicted in fiction. Sign language proved singularly unsuccessful, for it depended too much on a body of gestures, expressions and attitudes which the Overlords and mankind did not possess in common" (*Childhood's End* [1953], p. 192). In science fiction's recycling of themes, stories like "Tetrahedra of Space" and "Expedition" themselves become part of the background for later stories, making possible, among other things, satire of weaker representatives of the field, as in the next example.

The rise of descriptive linguistics was contemporaneous with the rise of pulp magazines in science fiction (though there seems no obvious causal connection either way, I should think). From the early 1930s, American linguists and anthropologists developed a methodology for the investigation of exotic languages. This methodology specified a step-by-step process—called a discovery procedure—for the investigation of linguistic problems, including those of languages unknown to the analyst. Theoreticians and practitioners of descriptive linguistics dominated the discipline until the late fifties; during that decade, discovery procedures were introduced to the science fiction public in two articles, G. R. Shipman's "How to Talk to a Martian" (*Astounding Science-Fiction* [October 1953], pp. 112–20); and Charles F. Hockett's "How to Learn Martian" (*Astounding Science-Fiction* [May 1955], pp. 97–106). The two essays illustrate the methods used to determine the sound-system of a language, and these methods found an outlet in fiction in Chad Oliver's *The Winds of Time* (1957).

Oliver did not need Shipman's or Hockett's articles to introduce him to the subject. At the time of the writing of the novel, he was an anthropologist at the University of Texas at Austin, and is now chairman of the Department of Anthropology. As might be expected, his novel is one of the soundest expositions of linguistics in fiction.

It is not without humor, either. It deals with aliens who, as a result of parallel evolution, are identical to humans. A ship of the aliens crashes on

Earth in the Stone Age. Realizing the hopelessness of trying to repair the
ship, they put themselves into a life-preserving sleep, determined to revive
only when humans have developed the space travel that will allow them to
return to their own planet. Wes, an American of the twentieth century,
encounters one of the aliens who has awakened to find out if the time has
come to call the rest of the crew to activity. Wes's attempt to overcome the
language barrier satirizes works such as "Tetrahedra of Space" and popular
misinformation at the same time:

> Wes borrowed the man's tablet and the writing instrument. *Let's see now*,
> he thought. *How do they do it in the movies?*
> He started with the sun, drawing a circle in the center of the page. So far, so
> good. But what came between the sun and the Earth? Wes had never had time
> to bother with a course in astronomy, and he was neither more nor less igno-
> rant of such matters than the bulk of his fellow citizens.
> Well, eliminate some of the outer planets. Pluto, that was the little one way
> out on the edge; throw that one away. But what else? How many planets were
> there, anyhow? Eight? Nine? Ten? He shook his head. Mars was the one he was
> after; that was where aliens always came from in the movies, so there must be
> *some* reason behind the choice. But which side of the Earth was Mars on?
> Toward the sun or in the direction of Pluto?
> "Hell," he said.
> He drew ten planets in a straight line out from the sun and handed the tablet
> to Arvon. Arvon looked at it with blank incomprehension. After all, it was just
> a series of circles on a piece of paper. Arvon studied it solemnly, and finally
> folded it up and put it in his pocket.
> So much for *that*. (Pp. 41–42)

Luckily, communication does not depend on Wes. Arvon, the alien, is
competent in the field methods of descriptive linguistics, well able to carry
out the task by himself, and in the doing, capable of illustrating those
methods.

One of the principles of the methodology is the necessity of working
with a native informant; Wes serves to fill that position though he "didn't
know a phoneme from a hole in the ground" (p. 37). A second principle
requires that the investigator begin with the phonology of the language,
and at that level Arvon begins. He "made no attempt to teach Wes his own
language, whatever *that* might have been, but concentrated on mastering
English. He started with nouns, things that could be pointed to: cave, shirt,
shoes, meat, candy. He kept a list of words, writing them down on a curious
sort of tablet, and Wes soon caught on to the fact that Arvon was not so

much after the words themselves as he was interested in the significant sounds that went into them" (p. 38). Arvon is searching out the distribution of sounds into English phonemes.

The phonemic principle holds that human languages group the large number of possible sounds into classes of sounds, and speakers of a language do not distinguish between members of a single class. For instance, the first sounds of English *cool* and *keel* are from our viewpoint the same sound, although the tongue touches the palate further back for the sound of *cool* than for that of *keel*. No words in English depend on the contrast between a front-palate stop and a back-palate stop to signal a difference in meaning, so speakers of English are free to consider these two sounds as the same phoneme. In contrast, speakers of some dialects of Arabic do depend on just this difference to distinguish pairs of words from one another. Therefore, for these Arabic languages, the front-palate stop is a member of one phoneme, and the back-palate stop a member of another. When the linguist confronts a new language, this organization of sounds is unknown to him, so he must first of all attempt to transcribe every distinction of sound he can. The next step is to classify those sounds into phonemes through the use of what are called "minimal pairs"—pairs of utterances that differ by only a single sound. Thus the alien, speaking to his English informant, will try to manipulate suspected contrasts: "Is this table made of *pique*?" In this case, the contrast being tested is that between *p* and *t*. When his pronunciation is corrected by the informant—"No, that's pronounced *teak*"—the alien has a pretty firm idea that *p* and *t* can be classified as members of different phonemes. On the other hand, if his utterance "That boat has a deep keel" (pronouncing the word *keel* with a back-palate stop) goes generally uncommented-on, he classifies back-palate and front-palate stops as members of the same phoneme, and uses only a single phonetic symbol to record them both. These phonemes are the "significant sounds" that Oliver speaks of in the portion quoted above.

We next see Arvon (through Wes's uncomprehending eyes) going through the second part of the task, grouping the phonetic distinctions he has recorded into phonemic classes: "He used recording symbols Wes had never seen before, but he assumed that they were phonetic marks of some type. He started with hundreds, marking every tone and pause and inflection, but rapidly whittled his alphabet down to a realistic series of marks as he discovered what counted in English and what didn't" (p. 38). We may presume that Arvon, in orthodox descriptive linguistic fashion, goes next to morphology, the changes in the forms of words determined by grammatical function, and finally to syntax. Although Oliver much condenses this process, we have hints that Arvon proceeds according to these steps: "Then he went on to the structure of the language, the way the word units were strung together. When he got the hang of the agent-verb-object series, his progress was rapid" (p. 38). In like manner, the progress of the reader in linguistic sophistication is rapid, as he reads the pages of this well-written, plausible novel. *The Winds of Time* sets a high standard of excellence for the use of linguistics.

Many of the staple themes of science fiction are deeply pessimistic— dystopias, apocalypses of one kind or another—but alien encounter stories in general sharply contrast with these gloomy themes. Surely it was a reader of science fiction who wrote the thesis "An Attempt at Devising a Program of Language Instruction for Hypothetical Aliens" in Lester del Rey's story "Natural Advantage" (1976; rpt. D. A. Wollheim and A. W. Saha, eds., *1977 Annual World's Best SF*). The thesis comes in handy when the aliens arrive at Earth. Like the thesis, most first-contact stories are enspirited by the optimistic discovery that communication is possible, regardless of whether or not that communication leads to agreement. And in this respect science fiction (much of it, at least) is set apart from other twentieth-century literature, in which the impossibility of communication is one of the now-unchallenged axioms. Therefore, when an attempt at communication with aliens is a total failure, as has more often been the case in the last decade, we have still another sign of the disappearance of barriers between the genre and literature as a whole, even though we might have wished that influence to have proceeded in the other direction. It would be pleasant if some of the optimism about communication in science fiction had spread to the rest of literature, rather than having the characteristic twentieth-century failure of nerve panic writers of science fiction.

We should not forget, though, that stories like Sydney J. Van Scyoc's "Deathsong" (1974; rpt. D. A. Wollheim and A. Saha, eds., *1975 Annual World's Best SF*), stories in which no real communication takes place, are in the minority. That story shows human explorers trying to establish communication with some primitive natives on another planet, and failing. Van Scyoc equips his linguists with the best tools human learning can provide, but without success: "When Young Nevins squatted and uttered the humanoid universals he had learned in the American University system the response was further repose on the part of the aborigines" (p. 64). In the story the methods that served the characters of Miller, Boucher, and Oliver well are tried and found wanting: "Heller and Nevins initiated a valiant effort involving the humanoid universals, hand language, body language and finally slashing in the moist soil with finger and pointed stick" (p. 88).

Similar doubts about the possibility of human-alien communication are expressed by the writer Joseph Green, in the afterword to his story "Encounter with a Carnivore" (in R. Elwood and R. Silverberg, eds., *Epoch* [1975]); there he suggests "that it will be impossible for human and alien to have truly meaningful communications, due to totally different cultural backgrounds" (p. 196).[9] The most notorious fictionalization of this attitude in recent times is Stanislaw Lem's *Solaris* (1961). In that novel, the alien is an oceanlike being covering a whole planet. The humans in the story are not certain the ocean is sentient, but it is capable of invading their minds while they spin in orbit about the planet. For years, the novel relates, humans have been crashing against the communication barrier constituted by the difference between the parties, with no breakthrough whatsoever. The activities of the ocean, brilliantly described in the story, are absolutely incomprehensible to its observers. The novel is studded with aphorisms of the problem: "Where there are no men, there cannot be motives accessible to men" (p. 142); "no experiences in common, no communicable notions" (p. 180). The thesis of the novel is that "transposed into any human language, the values and meanings [of the alien] involved lose all substance; they cannot be brought intact through the barrier" (p. 180).

Some critics have proclaimed, on the basis of this single work, that "science fiction has come of age as never before,"[10] yet Lem's contention is not original with him: in arguing that man suffers from anthropocentrism and is channeled in his thinking by human linguistic categories, Lem repeats the thesis of many earlier science fiction stories, some of which we will examine in detail in chapter 10.

It is surely no coincidence that *Solaris* is written by a Middle European; its pessimism suggests hundreds of years of experience with problematic communication between humans. An American opinion, expressed by a writer with one of the longest careers in the field, appears in Clifford D. Simak's *Shakespeare's Planet* (1976). Simak's novel is also about communication, and can be read as a reply to Lem's *Solaris* by American science fiction. One character in Simak's work is again a sentient, world-covering ocean, but it has no great trouble making its desires understood to humans who, far from being engaged in its conscious study, are unaware of its existence. If the method Simak uses—telepathy—is somewhat open to quibble, it is nonetheless the method found in *Solaris*, and therefore allowable under the ground rules of the game.

A similar answer came in 1978 from someone familiar with both linguistics and science fiction: Justin Leiber, son of the eminent writer Fritz Leiber, and at that time visiting professor in the Department of Linguistics and Philosophy at MIT, the birthplace of transformational theory. Leiber considered the worst possible case, one in which humans try to communicate with beings whose methods of communication depend on no sense possessed by humans:

> What do we have going for us when we try to communicate with a sightless, squid-shaped Siliconian? My beginning answer is that we share the notions *sentence, word, rule of grammar, truth, falsity*; logical notions like *negation, conjunction, implication, proof*; basic scientific notions like *electron, atom, force, electro-magnetism, star, planet, organism*. In the end, what we really need for translation is a shared scientific grasp of the basic character of the universe and of the logic and mathematics required in understanding it. . . . That is why I may hope . . . for a shared understanding and respect, and love, with the Siliconian, though it may wholly lack the rough mammalian range of immediate emotion and sensation.[11]

Given the popularity of the alien encounter in science fiction, and the manifold opportunities the alien offers for comment on human affairs from a fresh perspective, I doubt that the impossibility of human-alien communication will ever be a theme of more than minor importance. Difficulties will abound, of course, as they do in human-to-human communication; those difficulties will be of many kinds, arising from different codes and different channels and different cultures; but probably few works will surrender (as few do now) to the self-fulfilling prophecy that those problems cannot be solved. Alex, a human in Phyllis MacLennon's "Thus Love Betrays Us" (1972; rpt. D. A. Wollheim and A. Saha, eds., *1973 Annual World's Best SF*) has many obstacles in his path in his dealings with the alien Sessiné, but he persists: "Slowly, in halting steps, he learned to communicate with 'him,' as language-bound to sex identification, he thought of his outwardly genderless companion. He had no hope of ever reproducing the half-whispered, bubbling sounds made by the Deirdran, but Sessiné picked up a smattering of Galactic and enriched it constantly as Alex talked to him; and talk he did" (p. 264).

To assume the impossibility of communication is to ask the writer to throw away a most effective tool. And the insistence of the genre as a whole that communication must be attempted is a good thing, worthy of preserving. It shows, if any more proof were needed by now, that science fiction is not just the western in outer space. A vanishingly small percentage of the genre is of the "shoot first, ask questions later" school. Indeed, most frequently the characters ask questions as their first priority. As Dr. Frederic Wertham says in *A Sign for Cain*, as important a book as has been written in our generation, "Communication is the opposite of violence. Where communication ends, violence begins." [12] Science fiction presents examples in great number of sane and tolerant responses to the most unexpected and frightening situations; anyone concerned with the social dimensions of literature will find much in the genre to praise.

7

Berlitz in Outer Space

Language teachers are usually thought of as crabs and drudges, but their successful pupil, the polyglot, shimmers in an aura of ineffable sagacity. If you say you can speak several languages, people regard you as godlike indeed. Yet given the proper motivation, learning to speak a natural language is commonplace, even universal, in its attainment. After all, everybody has learned at least one. What, then, causes people to fear having to learn a second language? For Americans, the argument could be made that this dread is caused by the size of the United States and the relative homogeneity of its language population, and the importance of English as a second language throughout the world. And people hate to invest their time and energy in something they judge of doubtful utility. The merit of this attitude (it is surely a harmful one) is not the question; simply grant its existence and we go a long way toward explaining what we find in science fiction concerning the learning of language.

In the middle of a dull paradigm, even the most skillful of us have, I suppose, wished for an easier way. Irrational as it may be, we put a new record on the phonograph and wish we could switch languages that easily. In science fiction, machines often have just this capability. In several of his stories, Clifford D. Simak has used a device called a "transmog," a snap-in section of a robot brain that contains all the information needed for a particular competence. By changing transmogs, a robot can change from a French chef to a neurosurgeon. In his "Installment Plan" (1959; rpt. *All the Traps of Earth*), a man explains to his mechanical companions that they have been equipped with "basically sales transmogs, of course. They will provide you with the personality and all the techniques of a salesman. But, in addition to that, they contain as well all the data pertaining to the situation here and the language of the natives, plus a mass of planetary facts" (p. 210). The human himself, however, has to learn the native language the usual way, and finds it a hard job: "For a fleeting moment, he wished that there were some sort of transmog that could be slipped into the human brain" (p. 215).

Besides the general desire that Simak's character shows, there are more specific reasons that contribute to the search for an easy way out. For instance, the genre relies heavily on the short story form, which has little room for extended descriptions of elaborate processes. But a more important reason, I think, is that so little is known about the mechanisms of learning and memory that the field is a fertile one for invention. With not much known for certain, a writer can improvise with fair confidence that he will not be offending against plausibility. And since the genre is very often marked by a belief in progress in technology, it is not surprising that writers should assume that some faster way will be found to bring their characters to fluency.

In the course of this chapter, we will look at some examples of each of several approaches, beginning with the method we all know and dislike— study.

I As a character in Kilgore Trout's *Venus on the Half-Shell* (1974) says, "A planet that had its own version of a Berlitz school of language couldn't be all bad" (p. 117), but science-fiction writers seldom send their characters to language classes. The genre has worked out a half-dozen or so substitutes for the task: Beverly Friend, science-fiction editor of the Chicago *Daily News*, numbers among them

1. telepathy and automatic translators (to be discussed in detail later)
2. "He spoke faultless Anglic"
3. "We call it Amer-English. I happen to be a student of dead languages"
4. "It was in a curious slurred English that I could barely understand"
5. "The whole galaxy operated on an English basis. It's the court language of the Mother Planet, you see."

With the exception of the first item, all of these consist of having the alien learn the human language, and, as Friend comments, "these are cop-out approaches."[1] Sometimes a little ham-handed chauvinism is mixed with anti-intellectualism, as exemplified by a human explorer in Stephen Tall's *The Ramsgate Paradox* (1976); "With primitives I try to teach them our language rather than learn theirs, mainly because I can take the initiative. My objective is communication, not language study. We leave that to the etymologists. Further, good old English is much more versatile than any speech they are likely to have" (p. 53). An earlier student of the problem found many of the same flaws operative through the whole history of science fiction. J. O. Bailey concluded, however, in his pioneering work *Pilgrims through Space and Time*, that "travellers through space in intellectually better disciplined books have to learn the language."[2] It is to those works that we now turn.

There are two simple ways of smoothing the road to fluency, both of long and widespread usage in science fiction. First, make the traveler adept at learning new languages; Swift endowed Gulliver with this facility, and Edgar Rice Burroughs gave a similar talent to his voyager of worlds, John Carter. Carter's skill is equal to the demands he places on it, even when (i.e., in *Llana of Gathol* [1941; rpt. *Llana of Gathol and John Carter of Mars*]) he is under the pressure of deadlines:

> "Your education is to commence at once," he said, with a wry smile.
> "What do you mean?" I asked.
> "During this voyage you are to learn the language of the Morgors," he explained.
> "How long is the voyage going to last?" I asked. "It takes about three months to learn a language well enough to understand and make yourself understood."
> "The voyage will take about eighteen days, as we shall have to make a detour of some million miles to avoid the Asteroids. They happen to lie directly in our way."
> "I am supposed to learn their language in eighteen days?" I asked.
> "You are not only supposed to, but you will," replied U Dan.
> My education commenced. It was inconceivably brutal, but most effective. My instructors worked on me in relays, scarcely giving me time to eat or to sleep. U Dan assisted as interpreter, which was immensely helpful to me, as was the fact that I am exceedingly quick in picking up new languages. (P. 270)

It makes much sense to select first-contact teams for this quality, as Henry Kuttner does in "The Iron Standard" (1943; rpt. *Best of Henry Kuttner*): "All the Earthmen had learned Venusian quickly; they were good linguists, having been chosen for this as well as other transplanetary virtues" (p. 232).

Second, make the language to be learned a simple one. Bailey cites Percy Greg's *Across the Zodiac* (1880) as an early example. The voyager in this work finds no trouble with Martian: "My time was occupied, for as great a part of each day as I could give to such a task without extreme fatigue, in mastering the language of the country. This was a much simpler task than might have been supposed. I soon found that, unlike any Terrestrial tongue, the language of this people had not grown but been made—constructed deliberately on set principles, with a view to the greatest possible simplicity and the least possible taxation of the memory. There were no exceptions or irregularities, and few unnecessary distinctions; while words were so connected and related that the mastery of a few simple grammatical forms and of a certain number of roots enabled me to guess at, and by and by to feel tolerably sure of, the meaning of a new word." [3] There is probably evidence here, too, of a shift in our ideas of what makes a language simple, because Greg describes a language totally Indo-European in structure, with the customary two numbers and four cases in the noun, and three persons, two numbers, and six tenses in the verb.

While a simple language does turn up from time to time in more modern works, John R. Krueger noted that "the author usually cannot resist the temptation to make it difficult in structure and filled with impossible sounds." [4] C. J. Cherryh's *Hunter of Worlds* (1977) contains not one but three alien languages, one of them difficult indeed. But the difficulty is well motivated: the aliens, the Iduve, differ radically from humans (and some other alien races, as well) in their philosophy and culture, and their language differs accordingly. Rather than segmenting reality into noun and verb, into solid and action, the Iduve have as basic categories Tangibles and Ethicals, two concepts that differ "from both kalliran and human speech to such a degree that translation cannot be made literally if it is to be understandable. Paraphrase is the best that can be done" (p. 208). While the language is described and a glossary provided, we do not have the chance to see a character in the process of learning Iduve, as we do in the example Mildred Downey Broxon provides from her "Stones Have Names" (T. Carr, ed., *Fellowship of the Stars* [1974]). Here an Earthman named O'Rourke is struggling with the difficult structure of a language an alien is teaching him. The story is told from the alien's viewpoint, with O'Rourke speaking first:

> "What's that?"
> "A *tial*. A mass ancestral grave."
> "What's two of them?"
> "*Tal*."
> He shook his head. "And three?"
> "*Talona*."

"You mean you have a different case of noun for each number?" [Note that O'Rourke's terminology is sometimes deficient.]

"Sometimes. . . ."

O'Rourke . . . pointed to a rock. "What's that?"

"*Nar.*"

"And two of them?"

"*Nar.* It's an exception. . . . And the pronunciation makes a difference."

"*Na-ar.*"

I twitched my ears. "No, the way you said it means *sky*. It's the timing and a falling tone." I repeated the word. . . . I flipped a stone into the water. "*Nari.* One stone, in water."

"I thought stones had no number."

"Well, when they're in the water they are active. It's an exception to the exception." (Pp. 64–65)

Clearly, O'Rourke has his work cut out for him. And he will have to do just what we all have to do with Latin or Spanish or French in high school.

When we turn to those writers who assume the discovery of some better method, we find that they fall into two classes: those who check for the latest technical developments in the field, and those who bluff their way with some high-sounding but meaningless word, by means of which the reader is expected to infer an unexplained breakthrough in language learning. Before looking at examples of each kind, it should be noted that in none of the stories cited is learning a language a central concern. In each case, the target language represents a minor obstacle to be overcome before the main action of the plot can unfold. Therefore, one group of stories shows that its authors have attended to detail, whereas the other group shows authors who have not.

While those details may have been extracted from professional and academic journals, they are more likely to have come from general sources. Gordon R. Dickson, discussing how information comes to the science-fiction writer, points first of all to those sources the informed layman would turn to, such as *National Geographic, Science Magazine,* and *Science News-Letter.*[5] Titles such as these can be surveyed quickly for their content in the *Reader's Guide to Periodical Literature.* There we find a variety of methods listed in articles grouped under the headings "Learning" and "Memory." And we can trace the rise to popularity of the different methods and the decline from it if we look at the number of articles listed for each method over almost twenty-five years:

Method	47–49	49–51	51–53	53–55	55–57	57–59	59–61	61–63	63–65	65–67	67–69	69–71
				Biennial Period								
Hypnosis			1	1								
Neural Changes			1									
Sleep-Learning	3	2	1		5		1	2				
Electric Shock				1		1				1		
Chemical Means								1	5	4	10	5
DNA or RNA									1	6	3	2

Science fiction closely follows the changes in scientific notoriety of the different methods of learning language and of memory and learning in general. We will see, especially in the work of Poul Anderson, the close attention to detail that marks the careful writer.

The first method on the chart is the oldest; since Mesmer's discoveries in the eighteenth century, writers have been fascinated by hypnotism. In Edward Bulwer-Lytton's subterranean adventure, *The Coming Race* (1877), a book dedicated to the philologist Max Müller, the hero undergoes what he calls mesmerism; as he says, "while I had been placed in the state of trance, . . . I had been made acquainted with the rudiments of their language" (p. 47). After his second trance, he can "converse with comparative ease and fluency" (p. 49). Hypnosis also aids learning in George du Maurier's *Trilby* (1894), but in that book Svengali still has Trilby take voice lessons. She does not become an opera singer as fast as one of John W. Campbell, Jr.'s characters becomes bilingual: in "The Brain Stealers of Mars" (1936; rpt. I. Asimov, ed., *Before the Golden Age*), an Earthman is assaulted by a Martian who knocks him down and shakes his head around. But it has been done for his own good. As the human says immediately afterward, "That old bird just opened up my skull and poured a new set of brains in. Hypnotic teaching—a complete university education in thirty seconds—all done with hypnotism and no mirrors used. . . . The worst of it is, it works. I know his language as well as I know English" (pp. 844–45).

There was a spurt of stories using hypnosis immediately following the Second World War, probably for a reason that one of them hints at: "I guessed now that the canopy was part of a hypnotic teaching machine, something like those the Navy tried to use to teach Morse Code," says a character in John Wyndham's "Pillar to Post" (1951; rpt. H. L. Gold, ed.,

Second Galaxy Reader, p. 427). The character emerges with some knowledge of a new language. Even ten years later, Cordwainer Smith, in his "Alpha Ralpha Boulevard" (1961; rpt. R. Silverberg, ed., *The Ends of Time*), has people in the far future learn foreign languages by "hypnopedia" (p. 4).

Near the start of his career, Poul Anderson had recourse to this method; in "Inside Earth" (1951; rpt. H. L. Gold, ed., *Galaxy Reader of Science Fiction*), one of his characters has more success than the limited gains of Wyndham's. He tells us that "several of the Earth's languages were hypnotically implanted in my brain" (p. 210). Six years later Anderson used it again, this time with chemical aid, in the aptly titled "Memory" (1957 as "A World Called Maanerek"; rpt. *Beyond the Beyond*): "I and some others went down on ethnic survey in the Island region. I suppose you've heard something about the techniques. Kidnap a native, use accelerine and hypnosis to get the language and basic cultural information" (p. 23). The fact that hypnosis works here to extract rather than implant linguistic information perhaps shows time catching up with the theory. Certainly, since 1955, as the chart shows, hypnosis has had no advocates for its utility in language-learning, although it has turned up in fiction from time to time, the most recent, I think, being Larry M. Harris's "Lost in Translation" (*Analog*, August 1961). In that story, "drug hypnosis" made what may have been its final bow.

The next method on the chart, neural changes, refers to the doubtful theory that memories exist as physical changes in the brain. E. Roy John, in *Mechanisms of Memory*, summarizes the theory: "The concept of 'neurobiotaxis,' enunciated many years ago by Kappers (1917), concretized [the] common-sense argument [that memories are somehow 'made' and stored] with the proposition that new neural processes grew between active cells as they responded to stimuli: new synaptic connections were formed, new boutons laid down, better contact was achieved, and the storage of experience was mediated by such structural changes."[6] One term for the hypothetically altered nerve tissue is "engram." The word is probably better known to long-time readers of science fiction as part of the jargon of the pseudo-science (or perhaps pseudo-religion) of Dianetics, the invention of the former science-fiction writer, L. Ron Hubbard.

This confusion of terminology makes it impossible to be certain which of the two meanings Tak Hallus intends in "The Linguist" (*Galaxy*, February

1975), but most probably he uses the word in the first sense, as a technical term from an obsolete theory of memory. "The Linguist" (by which he means 'polyglot,' not 'language scientist') supposes not only that engrams are formed, but also that they can be surgically removed, and transplanted in the brains of others. The operation, an "engramectomy," has been outlawed on the grounds that "it allowed the rich to become not only richer but smarter" (p. 90), but there are criminals who will do it for the right price. The central figure of the story, Eberly, is an engram donor, a quick learner of foreign languages, who has seven times learned Spanish, only to have his engrams removed for sale. Like Simak's transmogs, the engrams can carry the knowledge of any subject. The operation costs $5,000, which explains why "Liberal Arts seldom become economically interesting enough to transplant, except foreign languages, Eberly's specialty" (p. 91).

Hallus's story is a rarity; neurobiotaxis has not attracted much attention. But a discovery of the twenties burgeoned forth in scores of stories. In 1929 Hans Berger introduced the electroencephalograph, the machine that measures the brain's changes in electric potential. More than one writer must have reasoned that if thought consists of electric impulses and a machine can detect them, similar machinery might eventually be able to transmit as well as receive. One of these was Nat Schachner, who envisioned the "Inducto-Learner" in "Past, Present, and Future" (1937; rpt. I. Asimov, ed., *Before the Golden Age*). In this story, Sam Ward and Kleon, whom we first met in chapter 2, are to be instructed in the language of the future. Their tutor shows them "a metal helmet suspended at the end of a long, transparent tube, whose other end entered the ceiling and disappeared." He explains that "short waves, oscillating at high speeds, and automatically attuned to the wave length of your particular brain, pulse through the tube. The latter leads to the cubicle of the chief Technicians. At the signal, the proper Technician adjusts his own sending unit. He concentrates on the subject of which knowledge is desired. His thoughts, converted into current, are transmitted inside your skull, make the necessary impress on your neurone paths. Behold, you have learned, well and painlessly" (p. 936). A similar method turns up ten years later in Edmund Hamilton's "The King of Shadows" (1947; rpt. *What's It Like Out There?*), in which a character receives "a direct transmission of thought-currents" (p. 40).

The chart shows that by 1967, articles on memory and neural changes had disappeared from the popular magazines, but the method is so quick and therefore so useful in plotting that it did not disappear from science fiction. Poul Anderson illustrates the writer's understandable reluctance to give up a good thing: twice in 1967 he wrote stories that implied the method. In "Starfog" (1967; rpt. *Beyond the Beyond*), the hero undergoes "re-encoding [of a language] into his own neurones," giving him "a working knowledge of the tongue" (p. 219). A similar event occurs in "Supernova" (*Analog*, January 1967). Note the similarity to Schachner's "Past, Present, and Future" of the language-learning in Anderson's *The Dancer from Atlantis* (1971): here the helmets, provided by a time-traveler from the future, are "twin two-foot hemispheres of bright metal upon which were several tiny studs, plates, and switches" (p. 26). The traveler tells an American of our era that the machine scans the speech center in the brain, takes the language information, and passes it to the receiver's brain (p. 30). It's harmless, but stressful, "seeing as how . . . the data patterns aren't just scanned, they're imposed" (p. 30). The method could well turn up in a novel published tomorrow.

The next method on the chart, sleep-learning, enjoyed a vogue from the late forties to the early sixties; the science-fiction magazines themselves often carried full-page advertisements making extravagant claims, among them the learning of languages, for the method. Like hypnotism, sleep-learning addresses itself to a subject in a lessened state of consciousness, so perhaps it was inevitable that a story should suggest a combination of the two. In Charles W. Runyon's "Sweet Helen" (1969; rpt. E. L. Ferman and R. P. Mills, eds., *Twenty Years of the Magazine of Fantasy and Science Fiction*), the hero "threaded a tape into the reader, swallowed a narco-hyp capsule, and lay down on the bunk. He awoke a half hour later with a 2,000-word Eutrian vocabulary etched in his mind" (p. 166).

The final three methods represent new aspects of the topic, innovations that had excited scientific interest in the late fifties and sixties. The first of these involved electric currents which, paradoxically, in some techniques inhibited but in others facilitated the formation of memory traces. The second was the discovery that chemicals such as puromycin and Metrazol had an effect on learning and memory. Anderson was quick to pick up on the new approaches and combined the two in "Eutopia" (H. Ellison, ed., *Dangerous Visions* [1967]); in that story, a parallel-worlds traveler receives "electrochemical inculcation" in the languages necessary for his trip (p. 278).

At almost the same time that drugs made news in memory research, an enormous stir was created by experiments that seemed to demonstrate a molecular basis of memory. Several experimenters claimed proof in studies in which flatworms were trained to respond in certain ways; the trainees were then ground up and fed to a second group of flatworms, which were then supposed to have shown the same responses without training. RNA was as much a term to be conjured with as chlorophyll had been twenty years before, so it was speculated that memory was somehow coded in the RNA of the cells. New scientific ideas of whatever validity quickly find their way into science fiction, and this one was no exception. In Larry Niven's "Rammer" (rpt. L. del Rey, ed., *Best Science Fiction Stories of the Year*), a man frozen two hundred years is revived. He says to the defroster, "Hasn't the language changed at all? You don't even have an accent." He is answered, "Part of the job. I learned your speech through RNA training" (p. 251). One hopes it was not necessary to grind up a philologist to supply the RNA.

The RNA-DNA theory was at the same time aided by a linguistic confusion over an ambiguous use of the word *code*. If the learned responses of flatworms were somehow carried in the ribonucleic acids of their nervous systems, and that information was carried over to the recipient flatworms, it seemed reasonable to say that the learning was "encoded" in that RNA. Several Nobel prizes were awarded in the fifties and sixties for research on DNA and RNA that showed the role of nucleic acids in the determination of inherited characteristics, and the possible combinations of the four chemicals that transmitted those characteristics were universally referred to as "the genetic code." Thus, award-winning research on the genetic "code" appeared at first glance to support speculation on the flatworm learned-response "code," although in actuality these are two very different undertakings. Nevertheless, the role of RNA in learning and memory-transmission was much emphasized in science fiction of the late sixties and early seventies. Alan Burt Akers's *Transit to Scorpio* (1972) provides us with an example of the confusion of the two "codes" when an alien hands an Earthman a pill and says, "When the pill has dissolved and its genetic constituents habilitate themselves in your brain, you will have a complete understanding, both written and oral, of the chief language of Kregen" (pp.

38–39). The Earthman later learns about "the genetic code, and of DNA and the other nucleic acids, and of how imprinted with information they can be absorbed into the brain" (p. 39). Nothing could show more clearly the confusion between the two codes. When the "genetic code" was "cracked," we discovered how information such as blood type, eye color, and the like is preserved in cell division, and how it is altered in reproduction. To put linguistic information into this category means that the people of Kregen would never need to learn a language; they would be born knowing one, even knowing how to write it.

The genetic transmission of languages is not theoretically impossible, as far as I know, but it would have predictable consequences. How could there be different languages on Kregen ("the *chief* language of Kregen")? Only in the same way that there could be different blood types; in this case, the chief language might correspond to Type O blood: a language that lacked certain features in the other types, and was therefore comprehensible to speakers of "Type A," "Type B," and so on. The reverse, however, would be impossible: speakers of Type O could not fully understand "Type A" or "Type B." Also, language change would be impossible except through spontaneous mutation. If not flatly impossible, the genetic transmission of particular languages seems *extremely* improbable.

In any case, Larry Niven, among present science-fiction writers, characteristically uses this method of language learning: his "The Ethics of Madness" (1967; rpt. *Neutron Star*); "The Fourth Profession" (1971; rpt. D. A. Wollheim, ed., *1972 Annual World's Best SF*); and "Rammer" (1972; rpt. L. del Rey, ed., *Best Science Fiction Stories of the Year*) all refer to the encoding of memory in nucleic acids.

By 1969, reviewers of research in the field were saying things like this: "In the face of some of the negative evidence we have reviewed, to hold to a strictly molecular view of memory requires something of an act of faith." [7] But obviously something was happening, and experimentation continued. Thus in 1975 appeared John Shirley's "Uneasy Chrysalids, Our Memories" (R. Elwood and R. Silverberg, eds., *Epoch* [1975]), in which a character says, "Experimenting on rats, Lawrence and I found that the memory of the sound of an electric bell was chemically recorded into an eight-segment chain of amino acids. When the chemicals were isolated from the brain and injected into other rats that were not trained to the sound, the untrained animals acted as if they had been conditioned to the bell. My husband simply extrapolated it into humanity" (p. 482). Studies published in the late sixties by G. Ungar and others lie behind this story: the experimenters showed some transfer of memory, and "suggested a basic peptide with 6–10 amino acids as a probably effective substance." [8] Of course, *simply*, in the last sentence quoted from Shirley's story, is a monumental understatement.

An expert should have the last word on these various means of learning, and it should be one familiar with science fiction, as well. Dr. John Chalmers of the Baylor College of Medicine summarized the present scientific opinion on these topics in a letter written to *Analog* and published in the January 1975 issue. He says,

Very few molecular biologists still take the RNA hypothesis seriously because of the poor repeatability of the early flatworm and rat studies. Much of the flatworm data can be explained by the fact that flatworms leave slime trails, and when the apparatus used to train the donor worms is cleaned with chromic acid, the recipients no longer seem to be able to learn the maze. In the case of the rats, radioactively-labelled RNA extracted from the brains of trained rats is rapidly degraded and excreted without crossing the blood-brain barrier at all. The same fate occurs to RNA injected directly into the brains of naive rats—it simply isn't incorporated into their brains. In all fairness, though, the experiments did not rule out the possibility that RNA injected directly into the brain is copied either by an RNA replicase or a reverse-transcriptase through a DNA intermediate. However, there is no evidence for these enzymes in normal brain tissue.

There is somewhat more support for the idea that protein synthesis is involved in memory. While it is true that an injection of puromycin, or other protein-synthesis-inhibiting drugs will prevent fixation of short-term memory, these drugs have also been found to inhibit electrical activity itself, so these experiments don't really distinguish between facilitated conduction and more purely electrical models. A peptide has been isolated from the brains of rats trained to avoid the dark. This small protein molecule has been named "scotophobin" and has also been chemically synthesized. Although it has been claimed that an injection of this compound transfers "fear of the dark," the experimental design doesn't rule out the explanation that scotophobin merely causes hyperactivity.

It is highly unlikely that memory is transmitted genetically through DNA, although that would be an attractive model for instincts and the mysterious racial memories. . . . The most generally accepted view is that the genes determine the overall design of the nervous system, the basic hardware and

wiring, as it were, and that memory involves the facilitation of certain
neuronal pathways by the laying down of new proteins at the synapses. Since
protein synthesis requires RNA, the three factors—RNA, protein, and electrical activity—are all related. (Pp. 175–76)

II Hypnosis, sleep-learning, neurobiotaxis, electric shock, chemicals,
DNA and RNA—whatever the effectiveness or rigor with which these
methods were used in the stories cited above, their appearance still demonstrates that the authors of those stories at least connected their treatments of language-learning with what was known about the process,
however tenuous that connection. Such is not always the case.

There are writers, well-known ones among them, who will pull a name
out of the air to account for the rapid achievement of fluency by their
characters. Two stories in James Blish's *Anywhen* (1970) show this failing.
In "And Some Were Savages" (1960), we find out that "current heuristics
can get a man through a language in about eight hours, but it's a deadly
technical process, an ordeal to the student and absolutely unendurable to
the bystander" (p. 94). Likewise, a character in "A Dusk of Idols" (1961)
undergoes "a twenty-four hour delay during which he could be force-fed
the language of the nearest city-state by a heuristics expert" (p. 113).
Heuristics is meaningless here; it is just a fine-sounding word that might as
well be *magic*. A similar but even less ingenious reliance on the reader's
ignorance occurs in W. Macfarlane's "Quickening" (*Galaxy*, September
1973), a story that has a tough enough job as it is, attempting as it does to
justify mass murder. In a passage reminiscent of Schachner's "Past, Present,
and Future," an alien is given "the English language under a helmet" (p.
98). When he asks the visitors how they learned his language so fast, they
answer "computer analysis and rationalization" (p. 99). Maybe there was
just a bit of heuristics, too.

I mentioned earlier that contraints of the form may account for the author's not having complete freedom in what he wants to do with details. A
short story's limited size may often require the DNA tablet or an electrochemical cocktail. Jack Vance in "The Moon Moth" (1961; rpt. *The
Worlds of Jack Vance*) uses the abracadabra method: a character learns
"the Sirenese language by subcerebral techniques" (p. 41), but in a longer
form, the novel *City of the Chasch* (1968), a character takes advantage of a

convalescence to learn a language in the usual way over a period of probably six to eight weeks.

The root of all this concern with language learning is the author's perception of how difficult it is to learn a foreign language. In *Childhood's End* (1953) by Arthur C. Clarke, in my opinion the most overrated science-fiction novel of all, there is abundant evidence that Clarke thinks that job is on a level with building the pyramids. The first section of the novel concerns the appearance of the Overlords, aliens who assume control of the affairs of Earth. The central figure is Stormgren, a Finn by birth, Secretary General of the United Nations, through whom the Overlords deal. At one point Stormgren is musing about the Overlords, and decides they must have a great civilization behind them, "one that's known about man for a very long time." He decides that the Overlord who seems to be in control, Karellen, "must have been studying us for centuries." His evidence? Karellen has a good command of idiomatic English! Karellen has learned a second language well—this argues that he is at least as intelligent as Lemuel Gulliver. More evidence of Karellen's powers: "English is the only language he understands completely, though in the last two years he's picked up a good deal of Finnish just to tease me. And one doesn't learn Finnish in a hurry!" (p. 25). If the Overlord has picked up "a good deal of Finnish" in two years of conversations with a Finn, I think we would have to give the edge here to Gulliver.

Perhaps the best way is to always have an interpreter handy. Roger Zelazny supplies his hero in *Doorways in the Sand* (1976) with a semi-sentient information processing device that enters his body and thereafter translates for him. This being possesses all the benefits of a transmog, and provides conversation besides.

Writers of science fiction seldom spare their characters: they may slam their heroes' ships into planets or send their heroines to kill tigers with knives; they may freeze them into statues on Pluto or shoot them through exploding suns. Hardly any degradation or suffering is spared—with the exception of exposing them to the rigors of learning a foreign language. Off hand, one might think that mastering a planet is a task beside which memorizing a paradigm becomes insignificant, yet writers freely exercise their ingenuity in creating means of achieving instant fluency. In doing so, they have preserved the fads of language-learning and memory in general of the last sixty years.

8

Plausibility vs. the Automatic Translator

Certain devices, unexplained and probably unexplainable in their operation, are familiar to readers of fantasy—the *Tarnkappe*, a flying carpet, seven-league boots. Science fiction also has such devices, one of which figures largely in alien-encounter stories: the automatic translator. In this chapter, the automatic translator is considered in some detail as a test of a centrally important idea in criticism of the field, the idea that plausibility is the determining criterion in evaluating science fiction.

The words *automatic translator* have two possible meanings in science fiction: the first denotes a machine that translates from one known language to another. At present, nothing like this capability is possible, although the prospects seemed rosy only a decade ago. At that time, both government and private agencies aimed at the machine-translation of scientific and technical Russian into English. A typical program might have guided the computer through the parsing of the Russian sentences down to the level of individual words, at which time reference to dictionary-like material occurred. When faced with several alternatives in the target language, the machine did one of two things, depending on the particular program: it might make a random choice among the available translations, leading to some strange results indeed. Or, the machine might simply print out all the alternative translations for the word at hand. Philip K. Dick burlesques the first method in *Galactic Pot-Healer* (1969), in which some characters play a game based on the ambiguities that result from the machine's random choices. A player reads the title of a book or song or play into a computer which translates it into a foreign language. Then a second translation is made of the result, back to the original language. The result is presented to another player, who has to guess what the original title was. Given "The Lattice-Work Gun-Stinging Insect," one of the characters successfully guesses that the original input was *The Great Gatsby* (p. 7). The second method has its problems, too. If the machine prints all the alternatives, then a bilingual human has to go over the result, striking out the inappropriate translations. Although the technical term for this second kind is "machine-aided translation," workers in the field have been known to refer to it as "machine-impeded translation."

Even though machines cannot now make good translations, it is almost certain that they will someday, perhaps in the very near future. But it is doubtful that we will ever see a machine with the capability asserted for the second meaning of *automatic translator*, the ability to accept *any* language as input and translate it into a known language. Both kinds of translators, "known-to-known" and "unknown-to-known," are omnipresent in science fiction; they appear so frequently that a faithful reader of the genre can tell you everything about them but their prices.

Devices of the first kind, "known-to-known," are small affairs in science fiction, typically worn as a pendant or pinned to the shirt: "'Good to see you again, gentlemen,' said the Jhan, through the mechanical interpreter at his throat" (Gordon R. Dickson, "Jackal's Meal" [1969; rpt. *The Star Road*, p. 178]). They work the other way, too, from English to alien: "The vocalizer on his breast rendered the sounds he made into soprano cadenzas and arpeggios, the speech of Lenidel" (Poul Anderson, "A Little Knowledge" [1971; rpt. L. del Rey, ed., *Best Science Fiction Stories of the Year*, p. 180]).

Jack Vance goes into more detail in "Brains of Earth" (1966; rpt. *The Worlds of Jack Vance*), in which an alien's voice comes "in discrete and distinct words from an apparatus hanging over the alien's chest: a muffled unnatural voice accompanied by hisses, buzzings, clicks and rattles, produced by vibrating plates along the creature's thorax. . . . The box seemed to find difficulty with l's and r's, pronouncing them with a rasping and rattling of the glottal mechanism" (p. 210). Vance has exploited the automatic translator as fully as any other writer; for example, it is from him that we learn that "robot brains, automatic translators, psychoeidetic analogues, and the like" are produced by Palladian Micronics ("The Dogtown Tourist Agency," in R. Elwood and R. Silverberg, eds., *Epoch* [1975], p. 490). His name will appear frequently in this section.

Our concern here, however, is the second kind of automatic translator, which, to distinguish it from the first, I will call "the magic decoder." In a first-contact situation, the magic decoder does all the work. Perhaps as a consequence, it is bigger, sometimes mounted on wheels for mobility. In comedy, where our disbelief is suspended a little more willingly, the magic decoder works instantaneously: in James Tiptree, Jr.'s "I'll Be Waiting for You When the Swimming Pool Is Empty" (1971; rpt. L. del Rey, ed., *Best of Science Fiction Stories of the Year*), a character lands on a planet picked more or less at random and sees a battle going on. "Without pausing to think, he switched on his Omniglot Mark Eight voder and shouted 'Stop that!'" (p. 46). And they do. Maybe Omniglot makes a better machine than Palladian. Tiptree's model has a switch marked "Semantic Digest"; when set to this position, the decoder will boil down the input speech and give you just a summary of what is being said, rather than a sentence-for-sentence translation, although it can do that too.

In stories that are not intentionally comic, the magic decoder takes only a little longer: Stuart, a linguist, is the hero of Robertson Osborne's "Contact, Incorporated" (1949 as "Action on Azura"; rpt. G. Conklin, ed., *Big Book of Science Fiction*). after his data is collected, "such was the tremendous power of the cephaloids [his machines], and the delicate, almost intuitive skill of his handling, that the major part of the analysis was complete in little more than an hour. He switched the controls to 'Translate, Univ[ersal] Sp[eech] to Other'" (p. 446). In Horace Fyfe's "Ransom" (1952; rpt. J. F. McComas, ed., *Special Wonder*), the human explorers both gather and analyze data in a few hours; as they tell the master of the properly impressed slave who has reported their landing, "We analyzed the speech of your companion this morning. . . . The machine translates as we speak into it" (p. 211).

An odd characteristic of magic decoders is that the bigger they are, the slower they are. In Larry Niven's *Ringworld* (1970), a ship's autopilot serves the purpose (although why an automatic pilot should have this capability is never explained), but is not quite as fast as Osborne's cephaloids. Of course, the cephaloids had Stuart's help; Niven's autopilot does the job by itself. His characters meet an alien, who makes a speech: "That was luck. The autopilot would need data before it could begin a translation. . . . Presently the discs were filling in words and phrases" (p. 170). A ship-based computer also appears in Joan C. Holly's "The Gift of Nothing" (R. Elwood, ed., *And Now Walk Gently Through the Fire* [1972]), and again, although it has an "Alien Contact Officer" to help, takes longer than the wheeled, portable models: "Tuned to the language-computer on the *Wasp*, the speaker-transmitter hookup helped whenever a conversation demanded more fluency than any of the crew possessed. But he seldom needed it anymore. He had "taught" the computer at first and then learned from it as fast as it could extrapolate" (p. 60). Largest of all, presumably too large to be transported, is the computer at the California Institute of Technology: "There was no telling how long the translation plan would take. It involved three steps: sending pictures of the writings on the crematory wells and other artifacts to Earth, so that computers could translate the language" (Larry Niven, "How the Heroes Die," 1966; rpt. *The Shape of Space*, p. 33), and as the quotation shows, it is the slowest of all. In taking an extended, indefinite amount of time, it shares that stigma with the magic decoder in Katherine MacLean's "Unhuman Sacrifice" (1958; rpt. D. Knight, ed., *A Century of Science Fiction*). MacLean's "translator machine was built to assimilate a vast number of words and sentences in any tongue, along with fifty or so words in direct translation, and from that construct or find a grammatical pattern and print a handbook of the native language. Meanwhile, it would translate any word it was sure of" (p. 155).

With these examples before us, let us investigate the plausibility of the magic decoder. Tiptree's Omniglot Mark Eight is flatly impossible: it translates with no data at all; but the story is comedy, and science-fiction comedy typically edges toward fantasy. Just as impossible, though, are the *Ringworld* autopilot and the Cal Tech computer of "How the Heroes Die." As was pointed out in chapter 3, languages are closed systems: unless you have some entry into the system, you can examine an infinite amount of data and get absolutely no results. Two others, the Holly model and the MacLean model, depend on extrapolation from a small amount already known. But as Charles F. Hockett notes, deriding the idea that "everything in a language could be inferred logically from some small sample," "acquiring a language demands thousands of unrelated individual acts of learning; it just *isn't* a logical system that grows from elementary premises."[1] The truth of his statement is astonishingly easy to demonstrate; just ask a friend who knows no German this question: "Given that the German word for goat is *die Ziege*, extrapolate the German word for necktie." If you give a computer "a vast number of words and sentences in any tongue, along with fifty or so words in direct translation," what you will get back is fifty or so translated words and a lot of undeciphered sentences.

In fact, the magic decoder is such a confidence game that it is even satirized in the genre. The most succinct burlesque appears in Jack Vance's *The Eyes of the Overworld* (1966); a magician hands a device to the hero-picaro, Cugel, saying, "In order to facilitate your search, I endow you with this instrument which relates all possible vocables to every conceivable system of meaning" (p. 104). A middle-sized satire is found in Michael Moorcock's *An Alien Heat* (1972), which has to show an alien using the magic decoder, since the humans in the story have language-learning pills of the sort described in chapter 7:

> "Greetings, people of this planet," began Yusharisp. "I come from the civilisation of Pweeli"—here the translator he was using screeched for a few seconds and Yusharisp had to cough to readjust it—"many galaxies distant. . . ." Again a pause and a cough while Yusharisp adjusted his translator, which seemed to be a mechanical rather than an organic device of some kind, probably implanted in his equivalent of a throat by crude surgery—"I see you are shocked, skree, skree, skree," said the alien. "Perhaps I could have (roar) put the news more tactfully, but I, skree, skree, have so little time. There is nothing we can do, of course, to avert our fate. We can only prepare ourselves, philosophically, skree, skree, for (roar) death." (Pp. 32–34)

The most extended satire is book-length, David Gerrold and Larry Niven's *The Flying Sorcerers* (1971), the most detailed account to date of the operation *in situ* of the magic decoder. *The Flying Sorcerers* takes place on a planet with a pretechnological society; one earthman, in what is apparently a first contact, sets up his device, which begins communicating with the natives. The machine has no mechanical failures, as Yusharisp's does from time to time; its problems are linguistic. The earthman, who has acquired the nickname Purple, tries to work through the headman of the native village, the local magician, Shoogar. Shoogar wants Purple to teach him to fly (he has seen the earthman land in his ship), but in the argument that ensues, Purple is handicapped by having his words translated by the decoder. The decoder (the speakerspell, as Shoogar calls it) apparently cannot paraphrase; it uses the native words with the native meanings, and since Shoogar uses the word *magic* to mean any organized body of knowledge, so does the decoder; so Purple tries to explain that he can't teach Shoogar how to fly:

> "No, no—I meant that I would teach you my—" the speakerspell seemed to be having some trouble with the word, "—*magic*; but I can't teach you my flying spell."

Shoogar shook his head, as if to clear it, "Your flying spell is not magic then?"

"No, it isn't. It's—" Again the device hesitated, "—it's *magic*." (P. 28)

Magic decoders leave much to be desired.

Their undesirability has been pointed out time and again, too. Possibly no device in science fiction has been subjected to such continued, withering scorn, beginning (as far as I have been able to find out) with G. R. Shipman's article, "How to Talk to a Martian" (*Astounding*, October 1953). Shipman places the magic decoder high on his list of irritants, deriding "the Martian [who] has a walkie-talkie translating machine that picks up his native garglings, whirls them around for a few microseconds in its electronic insides, and sends them out of its loudspeaker in pure United States" (p. 113). A more devastating attack occurred in Kingsley Amis's *New Maps of Hell*, one of the most important and widely read works of science-fiction criticism: "The idea of a translation machine, . . . usually introduced by phrases like 'He set up the translation machine,' . . . [presents] a direct affront to common sense, for such a machine would clearly be foiled even by an utterance in Portuguese unless it had been 'taught' Portuguese to start with."[2] Three later studies, appearing in more specialized journals, continued the attack: in 1964 G. D. Doherty counted the magic decoder among "the hoary old conventions . . . constantly served up with a dash of gimmick sauce to add a little piquancy to yesterday's cold meat."[3] In 1968, John R. Krueger labelled the device "another kind of convention, and a very unsatisfactory one it is too."[4] And finally, in 1973 Beverly Friend listed it among the "cop-out approaches" to language problems.[5] Throughout all this litany of abuse, there was no apparent diminution in the popularity of the magic decoder, the machine that represented, of all the linguistics in science fiction, what C. F. Hockett called "the most unsoundest of all."[6]

II The magic decoder is science fiction's immovable object, apparently. Let us turn now to the irresistible force, the idea of "plausibility." "There is no question that plausibility—that writerly art of making a story worthy of belief—in science fiction makes a different and extra demand upon its author in comparison, for example, to that which an equivalent piece of historical or contemporary fiction makes upon its creator."[7] This quotation from Gordon R. Dickson is typical of many writers and critics who give a special role to plausibility in the assessment of science fiction. Like any other, the theory of plausibility has a history; however, it cannot be considered apart from the larger history of science fiction in the early twentieth century. And this history, too, will involve linguistics, since it is itself part of the still greater account of the attitudes and emotions evoked by the word *science*. But whatever its origin, adherents of the plausibility theory at present are divided into two camps.

The first of these, which maintains what we may call the strong form of the theory, holds plausibility to be a necessary condition for good science fiction (whether it is also a sufficient condition is a question that further subdivides the group). For these writers and critics, science fiction aims "to offer an experience outside of ordinary reality; and it undertakes to make this particular experience believable—however unfamiliar or bizarre—or fails as a story" (Dickson, p. 295). In other words, science-fiction writers have a special duty not to violate our understanding of the world; their success is to be primarily judged on whether or not their work maintains an internal plausibility, the ingredients of which are authority and extrapolation. One of the most hard-line advocates of the strong form is the writer Joanna Russ. In a recent article in *Science-Fiction Studies*, she argues that standards of plausibility "must be derived not only from the observation of life as it is or has been lived, but also, rigorously and systematically, from science." [8] Here is the first characteristic of the strong form: it invokes the authority of science, especially the physical sciences, and sees science fiction as a commentary on these sciences, or at least on their effects on humans. And deviation from that authority invalidates the work: as Russ says, "Science fiction must not offend against what is known" (p. 114). Secondly, science fiction, according to the strong form of the theory, is extrapolative: "Only in areas where nothing is known—or knowledge is uncertain—is it permissible to just 'make it up.' (Even then what is made up must be systematic, plausible, rigorously logical, and must avoid offending against what is known to be known)" (p. 114). In her second stricture, Russ paraphrases Samuel R. Delany, another writer.

The strong form of the theory of plausibility is not new, of course; Donald A. Wollheim stated it in an article he wrote for a fan magazine in 1935, when he offered his definition of science fiction, calling it "that branch of fantasy, which, while not true of present-day knowledge, is rendered plausible by the reader's recognition of the scientific possibilities of it being possible at some future date or at some uncertain period in the past." [9]

If I understand him correctly, Darko Suvin adopts the strong form as a critical stance, or at least outlines how it is used in evaluation:

> Significant modern SF, with deeper and more lasting sources of enjoyment, also presupposes more complex and wider cognitions; it discusses primarily the political, psychological, anthropological *use and effect of sciences, and philosophy of science*, and the becoming or failure of new realities as a result of it. The consistency of extrapolation, precision of analogy and width of reference in such a cognitive discussion turn into aesthetic factors. (That is why the 'scientific novel' discussed above [he has cited as examples Verne's *From the Earth to the Moon* and Wells's *The Invisible Man*] is not felt as completely satisfactory—it is aesthetically poor because it is scientifically meager.) Once the elastic criteria of literary structuring have been met, *a cognitive—in most cases strictly scientific—element becomes a measure of aesthetic quality, of the specific pleasure to be sought in SF*. [Author's italics.] [10]

Science fiction, then, as has so often been asserted, is about ideas above all, and those ideas must be sound and rooted in scientific knowledge.

The strong form of the plausibility theory has two corollaries: because it depends on authority, it must be historically oriented, and because it is extrapolative, it must be conservative. First, what science tells us about the world changes from day to day; since science fiction must not offend against what is known, and since what is known is known at a given time, then the evaluation of science fiction requires that we place a given story against a historical reconstruction of what was known at the time the story was written. Otherwise, we have the bizarre result of a scientific experiment in, say, genetics changing a generic classification of a literary work. More specifically, as I write this, photographs are daily being received from the surface of Mars. If we find out that there is no life on Mars and never has been, what happens to all the science-fiction stories with Martians? Do they suddenly become fantasy, regardless of how carefully researched they were to avoid offense against our more meager knowledge at the time of their composition? This is absurd; hence the strong form of the plausibility theory requires that the authority on which a given story depended must be rediscovered through historical research before the story's merits can be fairly judged.

The second corollary, that the strong form of the plausibility theory is conservative because it is extrapolative, has frequently been discussed, and I will not repeat those arguments here. Suffice it to say that extrapolation is inherently conservative, since it depends on the assumption that the way things have gone is the way they will continue to go, for greater or lesser expanses of time in each case.[11]

The strong form of the plausibility theory works best with those writings sometimes called "hard-core" science fiction, and writers such as Robert Heinlein, Hal Clement, Larry Niven, and Isaac Asimov are usually cited as noteworthy examples of its producers.

III Let us now consider the magic decoder as a touchstone for the validity of the strong form of the plausibility theory. If we accept the theory, then the stories that incorporate the magic decoder, no matter how peripherally, are bad science fiction. They offend against what is known, and, as the long line of scorching criticisms of the decoder demonstrates, they offend against what is known to be known. We have two choices at this point: first, we can judge that authors like James Tiptree, Jr., Larry Niven, Katherine MacLean, and Joan C. Holly are ignoramuses incapable of correction. But this would leave us with the inconsistency that one of these writers, Larry Niven, who together with David Gerrold wrote *The Flying Sorcerers*, is in one of his works satirizing himself! Obviously, no writer as aware of the shortcomings of magic decoders as are the authors of *The Flying Sorcerers* would use the device in a serious story if he felt that the device was a cardinal sin against his art. We are forced to the second alternative, which has much evidence in its favor: that no writers seriously practice or practiced the plausibility theory in its strong form, whatever they may say they do or did.

Yet it seems we must hold onto the plausibility theory in some form, since, if we do not, science fiction disappears as a genre, and becomes indistinguishable from fantasy in general except by arbitrary ruling. Some critics and writers, therefore, have been led to what we may call the weak form of the plausibility theory; several arguments for this reformulation have been made, not all of them tenable. Gregory Benford in 1974 noted that "few major 'hard science' sf works are rigorously correct scientifically; fictional imperatives often make this impossible." He went on to argue that "a reasonable standard, then, would not fault a story unless the scientific or technical errors were visible to the lay reader (remembering, however, that the typical science fiction reader is relatively sophisticated in scientific matters and not easily fooled)."[12] We might call this the "abracadabra form": as long as it sounds good, it is good. As illustrious a writer as H. G. Wells supported this form of the theory, as he stated in 1933:

> For the writer of fantastic stories to help the reader to play the game properly, he must help him in every possible unobtrusive way to *domesticate* the impossible hypothesis. He must trick him into an unwary concession to some plausible assumption and get on with his story while the illusion holds. And that is where there was a certain slight novelty in my stories when first they appeared. Hitherto, except in exploration fantasies, the fantastic element was brought in by magic. Frankenstein even, used some jiggery-pokery magic to animate his artificial monster. There was trouble about the thing's soul. But by the end of the last century it had become difficult to squeeze even a monetary belief out of magic any longer. It occurred to me that instead of the usual interview with the devil or a magician, an ingenious use of scientific patter might with advantage be substituted. That was no great discovery. I simply brought the fetish stuff up to date, and made it as near actual theory as possible.[13]

As these quotations demonstrate, the "abracadabra" weak form has the disadvantage of tending to classify the reader rather than the work. Benford's argument, especially, puts things backward: usually the critic presumes the ideal reader, not the average one, as the hypothetical audience of a literary work. To accept his argument, we would have to agree that in science fiction, and only in science fiction, it is often necessary *not* to know something to appreciate a particular story.

More recently, Ursula K. Le Guin has joined the abracadabrans, beginning an address by observing that science fiction and fantasy are alike in that the writer of each gets to create his own world. As she puts it, in fantasy "you get to make up the rules, but then you've got to follow them. Science fiction refines upon this: you get to make up the rules, but within limits." She follows with the familiar canon that a science fiction story "must not flout the evidence of science, must not . . . deny what is known to be known." So far Le Guin sounds like a defender of the plausibility theory in its strongest, hardest form. But she continues by saying that when a story does deny what is known to be known, "the writer must . . . defend the liberty taken, either with a genuine hypothesis or with a sound, convincing fake. If I give my spaceships [faster-than-light] speed, I must be aware that I'm contradicting Albert Einstein, and accept the consequences—all the consequences." [14] For an example of "a sound, convincing fake," we may turn to a communication device that appears in several of Le Guin's novels, the ansible.

Nothing in Le Guin's novels moves faster than the speed of light. Since inhabited planets are sprinkled through several solar systems, this restriction makes travel and communication span a matter of years. Or rather, it would make communication span a matter of years were it not for the ansible, which is "a device that [permits] communication without any time interval between two points in space. The device will not transmit messages, of course; simultaneity is identity. But to our perceptions, that simultaneity will function as a transmission, a sending. So we will be able to use it to talk between worlds, without the long waiting for the message to go and the reply to return that electromagnetic impulses require. It is really a very simple matter. Like a kind of telephone." [15] It seems strange to speak of a fake as "sound," and how convincing it is turns us again away from the work to the reader, some of whom will be convinced by almost anything.

Rather than judge whether the fake is convincing enough or the use of scientific patter is ingenious enough, we may prefer to recognize that the writer's art comes first. Science fiction is, after all, a branch of literature and uses literary techniques. Much of the genre has suffered critical disdain for putting the exposition of its scientific content ahead of literary values like characterization. It would be a foolish irony if things were now reversed, and authors faulted for putting first things first. In fact, science-fiction writers have very frequently sacrificed scientific accuracy for the sake of the literary element of plot, as Alexei Panshin, among others, has recognized:

> The common appearance of the time-travel theme is added evidence that the name "science fiction" indicates the origins of the field and not its true nature. Time travel is a philosophical concept, not a scientific one. It is, in fact, as has often been pointed out, scientific nonsense. Science fiction, developing in its modern guise out of the radio magazines of Hugo Gernsback in the early years of the century, kept insisting it was about science. That s-f writers, knowing this, and believing this, kept returning just as insistently to the scientifically unsensible theme of time travel indicates that their viscera knew something that their minds did not. [16]

Panshin, himself a writer, points us to the "usage" variant of the weak plausibility theory, which seems to me the most sensible reconciliation of the different claims and arguments that have been advanced on the subject. A second writer takes the same approach, noting that science fiction has always had recourse to conventional usage. Thomas N. Scortia observes that scientific justification "is not always considered necessary when the device has become through frequent use a convention of the genre. . . . It suffices that the story may not move without the assumption that faster-than-light travel is possible, and the convention 'space-warp' solves the problem without slowing the story for a long-winded explanation." [17] Scortia also observes that such conventions often reduce notions of plausibility to rubble, and cites time-travel stories as an example.

In its weak form, then, the theory of plausibility, together with the idea of conventional use, would go something like this (altering Joanna Russ's words slightly): science fiction must not offend against what is known to be known, unless there is some overriding artistic reason. When the work cannot be fully realized unless plausibility is violated, then the writer has license to sacrifice plausibility. Thus, to take the most obvious example, in the compass of one hour on the television program *Star Trek*, the aliens had to be encountered, a conflict discovered and intensified, and a resolution achieved. The demands of the genre left very little scope for long-term scholarly research. As a result, the program depended heavily on a "Universal Translator," specifications for which may be found in the *Star Trek: Star Fleet Technical Manual*. [18]

But even with our revised standard for evaluating plausibility, things do not always go smoothly. In fact, the implied use of the weak plausibility theory led to one of the most startling reviews I have ever seen: like many others, it involved a difference of opinion between a critic and an author about the worth of the author's book, but in this case, the critic, Stephen H. Goldman, thought better of the book than the author, John Brunner. The full account may be read in "The Polymorphic Worlds of John Brunner: How Do They Happen?" in *Science-Fiction Studies*, 3:2 (July 1976). Briefly, what occurred was this: Goldman reviewed *The Happening Worlds of John Brunner* (ed. J. de Bolt, Kennikat Press, 1975), a work which brings together essays by specialists in several fields, all of whom discuss aspects of Brunner's writing. One of those essays showed Brunner to be in error in an episode from one of his novels; Goldman, however, demonstrates that the incident in question functions as an essential part of a larger pattern of similar incidents through the novel, and argues that the error is justified by its symbolic value for the work as a whole. Clearly, for

Goldman the purpose of the incident is of primary importance, and its scientific accuracy is secondary. But he quotes John Brunner's confession that he would have changed the incident had he been aware of the error.

Perhaps the more hard-line critics and writers, those who espouse the strong form of the plausibility theory, would prefer to have the writer's freedom cover only clearly specified subjects, defining those subjects as conventions. The conventions would obviously include those two frequently cited above, time-travel and faster-than-light travel, but a strong case can be made for the magic decoder, too, in view of its long and frequent use. The danger here is the possible bankruptcy of the strong form: "convention" becomes an elastic bag into which anything can be stuffed that disturbs the theory.

9

Avoiding the Boring Stuff

As we have seen through the last several chapters, the science-fiction writer has many arrows in his quiver when the language barrier is the target. But after all the RNA pills have been swallowed and all the automatic translators consulted, there still remains a method so characteristic of science fiction that the investigation of how it works is often the theme of the story all by itself. I refer to telepathy.

The usefulness of telepathy has long been recognized as a solution to linguistic problems. A very full and early account appears in H. G. Wells's *Men Like Gods* (1923), in which a group of modern Britons is transported to the far future. At first, the time-travelers are unaware that their hosts in that distant time are not just speaking to them in the normal way. Gradually, it dawns on them that when one of the natives speaks, they do not all hear the same words:

> Another of their hosts, Serpentine, . . . called himself something that Mr. Barnstaple could not catch. First it sounded like "atomic mechanician," and then oddly enough it sounded like "molecular chemist." And then Mr. Barnstaple heard Mr. Burleigh say to Mr. Mush, "He said 'physio-chemist,' didn't he?"
>
> "*I* thought he just called himself a materialist," said Mr. Mush.
>
> "I thought he said he weighed things," said Lady Stella. (P. 46)

Serpentine does not long leave them in the dark. He soon explains that the people of his time have perfected telepathic transmission, but its precision is limited by the state of awareness of the receiver: "When I think to you," Serpentine says, "the thought, *so far as it finds corresponding ideas and suitable words in your mind,* is reflected in your mind. My thought clothes itself in words in your mind, words which you seem to hear—and naturally enough in your own language and your own habitual phrases. Very probably the members of your party are hearing what I am saying to you, each with his own individual difference of vocabulary and phrasing" (p. 59).

Through his character's mouth, Wells expresses with admirable candor just how handy telepathy can be to the writer of science fiction: "And all things considered, it is really very convenient for us that there should be this method of transmission. For otherwise, I do not see how we could have avoided weeks of linguistic bother, first principles of our respective grammars, logic, significs, and so forth, boring stuff for the most part, before we could have got to anything like our present understanding" (p. 60). One could not wish for a clearer statement of why telepathy turns up so frequently in science fiction. The method has been popular for over a hundred years with undiminished vigor at the present, as almost any of the space-opera novels of A. Bertram Chandler illustrate, for instance. The spaceships in Chandler's universe carry a telepath as a matter of course; in *The Hard Way Up* (1972), Chandler's hero, Commander Grimes, says to his ship's Psionic Communications Officer, "Perhaps you don't know the code, the language—" He is answered, "Codes and languages don't matter to a telepath" (p. 208). In later works, Grimes can explain the situation himself. He and the other nontelepaths in *The Way Back* (1978) cannot use a radio at one point to communicate because "We're up against the language barrier, Ruth. Ken and Clarisse [the psionic communications officers], working with ideas rather than words, aren't" (p. 140).

As useful a device as this could be expected to have a long history, and indeed the beginning of comments on mind-reading of one sort or another are probably found in antiquity. The word *telepathy*, however, is of more recent origin, and not difficult to trace. The *OED* lists an 1882 citation from Frederic W. H. Myers, *Proceedings of the Society for Psychical Research*, as its first use: "We venture to introduce the words *Telaesthesia* and *Telepathy* to cover all cases of impression received at a distance without the normal operation of the recognised sense organs." Both the word and the concept were in vogue over the next twenty years, as the subsequent citations indicate. David Lindsay, in his 1920 novel *Voyage to Arcturus*, endows his central character with telepathic powers without any hint that the notion might be new to his readers. In the process, he gives one answer to a question that concerned many later writers on the topic—how telepathy works. His hero wakes one morning to discover on his forehead "a fleshy protuberance the size of a small plum, having a cavity in the middle, of which he could not feel the bottom" (p. 45). This entirely new organ, which he calls the *breve*, allows him to read others' thoughts.

Although the British Society for Psychical Research, and its American counterpart founded by William James, were active from before the turn of the century, the study of telepathy attained new respectability in 1934 with the first publication by Joseph B. Rhine of the results of his research at Duke University. That work aroused a flurry of interest in psychological circles: "As a stimulant to experimental research, Rhine's work had unprecedented influence. For the first time a common methodology was adopted and employed on a large scale by a number of independent and widely separated investigators. . . . During the period between 1934 and 1940, approximately 60 critical articles by 40 authors appeared."[1] Rhine's studies used Zener cards, a deck of twenty-five cards, five each of which are imprinted with stars, circles, squares, plus-signs, and wavy lines. Typically, a subject was asked to guess the figures on the cards as they were turned by an experimenter out of sight of the subject. This guessing procedure is a far cry from the transfer at will of complex messages from one person to another, which is what we usually think of when science fiction mentions telepathy. Still, a message is a message, the writers must have thought, and Rhine became for telepathy what Lilly would be for talking dolphins thirty years later—a cloak of authority for the inventions of fiction. Thus, in "Who Goes There?" by John W. Campbell, Jr. (as Don A. Stuart, 1938; rpt. B. Bova, ed., *The Science Fiction Hall of Fame*, vol. 2A), the dreams of a monster—"a sort of telepathic muttering in its sleep"—influence the dreams of a human in the story, so much so that he perceives that the monster can change the structure of its body, down to the cellular level, to that of any living being. Two other humans discuss their failure to receive the dreams:

> "I guess you and I, Doc, weren't so sensitive—if you want to believe in tele-pathy."
> "I have to," Copper sighed. "Dr. Rhine of Duke University has shown that it exists, shown that some are much more sensitive than others." (P. 63)

Campbell was as much a true believer as his character, Copper, as this early story testifies. As editor of *Astounding*, his interest almost became a compulsion, and the fifties saw issues of the magazine in which the majority of stories dealt with what he called "psi" powers. Donald A. Wollheim observes that his policy affected other magazines as well: "for a number of years his magazine . . . read like an educated and literary version of the bulletin of the Society for Psychic Research. Dowsing, telekinesis, telepathy, clairvoyance, pyromancy, and all the rest of the paraphernalia of the Victorian seances and mediums was paraded out in new forms, labeled 'mutant' powers, and his readers were urged to look with an open mind upon these marvels of the psychic." [2] We should note, though, that at least his interest in telepathy dated from the days of his own writing, before he became editor of *Astounding*, from soon after the first publications of Rhine.

Rhine's reputation was to lend legitimacy to many another story in the years to follow 1938, and continues to do so: Joe Haldeman's *Mindbridge* (1976) shows characters being tested for sensitivity to extrasensory perception "with a standard Rhine test: a deck of fifty cards, ten each of five easily visualized symbols" (p. 40), in the year 2051. But much more often, the stories that invoke Rhine's name do not confine their characters to predicting the fall of cards or influencing the roll of dice. They use extrasensory powers to justify a wide variety of activities. A series of works beginning even earlier than Rhine's research exemplifies our interest in this chapter: the linguistic side of telepathy.

Edgar Rice Burroughs's much-loved and much-scorned novels of John Carter on Mars use telepathy from time to time and may even imply that the method retards language change. This conclusion, if it is indeed present, is a thought of some sophistication, and suggests that Burroughs is at least sometimes capable of subleties he is seldom given credit for. The people of Mars,[3] we are told, are all naturally telepathic, and at least the red men among them possess a second power: "They can shut their minds so that none may read their thoughts" (1912; *The Gods of Mars*, p. 86). John Carter, the Virginian hero of the series, learns the first ability, but has no need of the second since he seems naturally immune to the telepathic prying of the Martians. Moreover, the Martians, with perhaps some mechanical amplification, can detect at least the presence of conscious thought, if not the content, on Earth, Mercury, and Venus. This information appears in *The Master Mind of Mars* (1927, p. 23), in which thought is specifically described as a wave-phenomenon, a conclusion that will frequently reappear.

Our principal concern, as I stated above, is the effect of telepathy on language, and particularly here on language change. I think a good case can be made that a universal telepathic power would slow down, and perhaps even halt change altogether, if (and this is an important condition) change in language results from normal but inevitable variation in speech forms. Burroughs implies that telepathy stimulates the speech centers of the brain; the implication is stated explicitly in many later works, e.g., Ursula K. Le Guin's *The Left Hand of Darkness* (1969). But what does that mean? If we assume that linguistic information is stored in some form in the brain, research in aphasia suggests that concepts (whatever they are) and words are stored in separate, localized places. Yet if telepathy is received as words—a frequent assertion which we will explore in more detail later— then telepathy must stimulate the associations between concepts and words, and not just one or the other alone. This assumption has one important consequence which, as far as I know, has been noticed only by Le Guin: expectant mothers could converse with their unborn children (*Left Hand of Darkness*, p. 179). In fact, the child would be well on its way to learning language by birth, and need only practice the motor skills involved to join the linguistic community. These unborn children would learn the associations between concept and word, together with the concepts and words themselves, in an environment protected from the normal variation of speech.

Or consider the question from another standpoint: examples of historical change in words are omnipresent, but examples of change in concepts are much harder to come by. To supply just two examples, Latin *cantus*, through well-described sound changes, has one of its forms become French *chanson*; Latin *mensa* is entirely replaced by French *table*; but it seems unlikely that the concepts of "song" or "table" changed much over that period. If telepathy requires the close connection between concept and word that writers have suggested, then the stability of concepts should insulate words from change, at least to some extent. Zach Hughes reaches this conclusion in *The Legend of Miaree* (1974); he says of his insect-like race, the Artonuee, that "it was thought in University circles that a primitive Artonuee female, from the early days of self-spun nests, would be able to converse with a modern-day Artonuee in basic terms, leaving out the additions to the language caused primarily by technological development" (p. 57), and he is here talking about a period of three hundred thousand years.

Now to return to the point about Burroughs's Martian novels: writers are often chastised by commentators (and rightly so, in most cases) for endowing a whole planet with just a single language. Burroughs does not just assume that Mars has a single language, he insists on it again and again. For example, in *A Princess of Mars* (1912), the first of the series, he connects the universal Martian language with telepathy:

> Like the animals upon which the warriors were mounted, the heavier draft animals wore neither bit nor bridle, but were guided entirely by telepathic means.
>   This power is wonderfully developed in all Martians, and accounts largely for the simplicity of their language and the relatively few spoken words exchanged even in long conversation. It is the universal language of Mars, through the medium of which the higher and lower animals of this world of paradoxes are able to communicate to a greater or less extent, depending upon the intellectual sphere of the species and the development of the individual. (P. 34)

Should the single language of Mars be considered the defect in Burroughs's works it is usually assumed to be in others? Not if we assume (1) that language on Mars is the result of a single evolutionary event, (2) that variation in speech forms is the source of historical change in language, and (3) that the accumulation of historical changes in isolated groups results in separate languages. These assumptions, while by no means proven for Earth, let alone Mars, are at least tenable. If we adopt them, and allow Burroughs's contention that all Martians are telepathic, then it is hard to see how more than one language would be possible, and the criticism of this single-language planet by analogy with Earth would be misplaced. It should be pointed out in fairness to those critics who are harsh on Burroughs that I have nowhere found this line of reasoning specifically stated. But in any case the conclusion follows from considerations that are explicit in the Martian novels. It should be noted, too, that the history of writing on Earth is not similar to the history of speech. Writing was invented independently at least twice, in the Near East and in China; its association with speech is more tenuous (especially so in the case of Chinese); and it is not a universal accomplishment, as speech is. Thus, there is no reason to believe that telepathy would protect writing from variation as it would the spoken language, and Burroughs often mentions that Mars has several forms of the written language.

Burroughs's use of telepathy implies, as we have seen, that telepathy transmits linguistic constructions. But such a transmission presents obvious problems when transmitter and receiver do not share a common language; if I do not speak Finnish, my comprehension is not improved if I am conscious of Finnish sentences without hearing them. Yet all first-contact situations assume that the human-alien contact is not smoothed by a common language. Even if the telepaths involved take some trouble to learn which linguistic concepts their languages share, there are still lexical problems: speakers from two linguistic communities may both be acquainted with distinctions like singular/plural, completed action/continuing action, definite/indefinite, and the like, yet their communication may still founder on those terms deeply rooted in one's culture but not the other's, for example, *self-reliance, machismo, savoir faire*. Margaret St. Clair carries this facet of the problem to its absurd conclusion in "Prott" (1953; rpt E. Crispin, ed., *Best SF: Science Fiction Stories*). A telepath in her story is sent to establish contact with the prott, creatures living in deep space who look like big poached eggs. Over a long time, the telepath carries on fifty-two interviews with the prott, and numerous informal conversations, yet he reflects bitterly that he has learned nothing of value. Not linguistic but cultural barriers have brought him to this conclusion: "Out of the welter of material presented to me, I have at least succeeded in forming one fairly clear idea. That is that the main topic of the prott's communication is a process that could be represented verbally as ——ing the ——. I add at once that the blanks do not necessarily represent an obscenity. I have, in fact, no idea what they *do* represent" (p. 194). But the prott are keen on the subject; they eventually find their way to Earth, where they float about, plaguing humans with interminable monologues on ——ing the ——.

So the language barrier is not just one wall, but several: get past the word problem, and the concept problem remains. Paul A. Carter points out that these complications were understood almost forty years ago:

"Interpreters May Still Be Needed," John W. Campbell concluded in one of his typically speculative editorials (*Astounding*: June 1941). The Indo-European languages might be able crudely to get along with each other on a word-for-word basis, making the telepathic translation from *dog* to *perro* to *hund* to *chien*; and of course such things as the names of the chemical elements are uniform in most of the Earth's languages. But beyond that point, in situations demanding discernment of the cultural context of words, there might be trouble: "Most of our words have background references that we know so well we tend to overlook them."[4]

These cultural blocks to understanding suggest the problem basic to Stanislaw Lem's Solarian theories, and perhaps to overcome it, a considerable number of writers have suggested that pictures, not words, are transmitted in telepathy.

Such is the case in Judith Merril's "Whoever You Are" (1952; rpt. *Best of Judith Merril*), in which a human describes his encounter with an alien telepath this way: "They want to be friends. He keeps saying it different ways, but it's the same feeling all the time, with different—pictures, I guess, to go with it. . . . He says the pictures I get for meanings are all my own, so I might get his meaning wrong sometimes. He makes a picture in his mind, the way he'd visualize a thought on his world, but I see it the way it would be on mine" (p. 73). The mention of "feeling" typifies this sort of telepathy, because the pictures are characteristically accompanied by some emotional comment on the scene depicted. For example, the content of telepathy in Michael Elder's *Flight to Terror* (1973) is described as a display of "pictures. Three squat, tubby ships standing together in a hollow. Trees nearby. The frond trees of Roker II. The picture dislimns and reforms. This time there are four ships" (p. 186). But Elder also indicates the emotions of relief, dismay, sorrow, gratitude, etc., by the simple inclusion of the word. In addition, sentence elements such as "Question," "Affirmative Answer," and "Negative Answer" are capable of being transmitted. It appears, therefore, that despite the author's contention that pictures, not language, are being used, we really have linguistic structures in a hidden form. The pictures are used as substantives in sentencelike constructions of which the emotions transmitted are the predicates.

It is difficult to divorce the transmission of information in whatever medium from predications; introspection, if we can rely on it, seems to confirm that we think in linguistic structures. There is no denying that the composer sometimes thinks in notes or the artist in forms and colors, but these are more specialized activities, carried on in particular, almost predictable contexts. But if sentences are the normal messages of thought, then the science-fiction writer is right back in the dilemma stated earlier: how is telepathy to be accomplished between beings that do not share the code of a common language? Several writers have attempted a solution by making a division of the mind into parts more and less accessible to telepathy. An early instance was supplied by the innovative Stanley G. Weinbaum in "The Lotus Eaters" (1935; rpt. *Best of Stanley G. Weinbaum*); in this story the humans meet a partly telepathic alien: he can receive but not transmit. Moreover, the alien cannot read the words stored in the humans' lexical memory; it must wait until the words are brought to their conscious minds in syntactic structures, after which it can apparently read the links between the words they use and the concepts represented by those words. Only after the man and woman have used some words in its presence can it put them into sentences of its own. This leads the man to question it: "How do you know English?" to which the alien replies, "I isn't know English." The man then asks,

> "Then—uh—then why do you speak English?"
> "You speak English," explained the mystery, logically enough.
> "I don't mean why. I mean *how*!"

The woman, who has a quick mind, sees what is happening, and explains, "It uses the words we use. It gets the meaning from us!" The alien agrees with her guess: "'I gets the meaning from you,' confirmed the thing ungrammatically" (pp. 252–53).

That telepathy is limited to what we might metaphorically call the surface of consciousness is a relatively rare idea. A recent novel, Roger Zelazny's *To Die in Italbar* (1973), provides one of the few examples I have been able to find. A human and a telepathic alien are looking for a third character, and at one point they see a figure in the distance that they suspect may be the object of their search. The human asks the alien if this is the man they want, and she answers, "Quite possibly." The answer surprises the human: "Possibly? . . . You're the telepath. Read his mind." But she explains, "It is not that simple. People do not generally walk about concentrating on their identities—and I have never met the man" (p. 163).

Perhaps the most convincing argument that words, not pictures, are transmitted telepathically appears in Robert Heinlein's *Time for the Stars* (1956). In that novel, sets of twins with the talent are recruited for Earth-to-space communication, and in their training have ample opportunity to discuss the details of the medium. Two particular twins do indeed try to read each other's mind without the use of words, but as one of them remarks, "the silly, incoherent rumbling that went on in [the other's] mind in place of thought was confusing and annoying, as senseless as finding yourself inside another person's dream" (p. 28). As their training progresses, a psychologist assigned to direct their efforts explains why they habitually perceive each other's thoughts as language:

> You don't hear with your ears, you hear with your brain; you don't see with your eyes, you see with your brain. When you touch something, the sensation is not in your finger, it is inside your head. The ears and eyes and fingers are just data collectors; it is the brain that abstracts order out of a chaos of data and gives it meaning. . . . How would you expect to "hear" what your twin says to you telepathically? As little tinkling bells or dancing lights? Not at all. You expect words, your brain "hears" words; it is a process it is used to and knows how to handle. (Pp. 28–29)

But with language as the code of the telepathic message, we are once again caught in the trap of language barriers implicit in any first-contact situation, and telepathy helps not at all in that context.

It is not surprising, of course, to find no consistency of treatment from one writer to another in the use of telepathy; it would be odd, in fact, if we did not encounter this variety. But if *telepathy* means different things to different people, then one is entitled to ask what expectations are aroused in a long-time reader of science fiction when the word is used without explanation in a story. As we have seen, the word is not a reliable guide to what will be transmitted; as we will see, it is not a reliable guide to how the transmission occurs.

II So many explanations of the mechanism of telepathy have been offered in fiction that one sympathizes with the scientist in Isaac Asimov's "Blind Alley" (1945; rpt. *The Early Asimov*, vol. 2) who exclaims, "Telepathy! Telepathy! Telepathy! Might as well say by witch brew. Nobody knows anything about telepathy except its name. What is the mechanism of telepathy? What is the physiology and the physics of it? (p. 178). Characters who achieve telepathic communication in stories often put these very questions to one another in their attempts to understand their powers. A character of Walter M. Miller, Jr.'s ponders what is happening in "Command Performance" (1952; rpt. H. L. Gold, ed., *Second Galaxy Reader*): "It must be some sort of palpable biophysical energy-form, analytically definable—if we had enough data" (p. 326). He later considers the effect of distance on telepathy and concludes that if extrasensory perception exists, "it certainly involves transfer of energy from one point to another. What *kind* of energy I don't know. Possibly electromagnetic in character. But it seems likely that it would obey the inverse square law, like radiant energy-forms" (pp. 329–30). The characters in the story can rest content with this tentative explanation since none of them is in a position to put it to the test. They are all in the same city when transmitting and receiving, and if the speed of transmission is that of the propagation of a wave in the electromagnetic spectrum, it is in effect instantaneous for them. Over a few miles, even within the same country, no appreciable time-lag will occur.

Two authority figures, a professor and a doctor, argue precisely this point in Fritz Leiber's "Deadly Moon" (1960; rpt. *Ships to the Stars*). The professor begins by rejecting the notion of thought-waves: "You know, doctor, even if there is such a thing as telepathy or extrasensory perception, the chances are it takes place instantaneously, altogether outside the world of space and time. The notion of thought-waves similar to those of light and sound is primitive." But the doctor counters with an argument drawn from history: "'I don't know,' the doctor said. 'Galileo thought that *light* moved instantaneously too, but it turned out that it was just too fast for him to measure. The same might be true of thought-waves—that they go much faster than light, that they *seem* to move instantaneously. But only seem— another century may refine techniques for measuring their speed'" (p. 78).

The doctor will win the argument in "Deadly Moon," partly because the assumption that telepathy is a wave phenomenon is a convenient and useful one for writers. Poul Anderson uses it to account for a number of things in his "The Queen of Air and Darkness" (1971; rpt. L. Biggle, Jr., ed., *Nebula Award Stories Seven*).

Anderson's story involves the contact between humans and telepathic aliens on the aliens' home planet, and the range of their transmission is several miles at most. The mechanism of the ESP is the generation by individuals of "extremely long-wave radiation which can, in principle, be modulated by the nervous system" (p. 26). Telepathy as a system of communication is such an attractive idea that a species capable of it would obviously be better off practicing it than neglecting it, but equally obviously, we are not all telepathic. Accounting for this discrepancy is a tricky problem, and wisely avoided by most writers, but Anderson finds a satisfactory answer in his treatment here. The signals, he says, are very feeble, "elusive, hard to detect and measure." Hence, he argues, humans learned early on as a species to depend on their more reliable sight and hearing. This thought is another confirmation of Anderson's wide reading and careful researching of background for his stories, since the idea was first proposed by Sigmund Freud in 1933:

> One is led to a suspicion that [telepathy] is the original, archaic method of communication between individuals and that in the course of phylogenetic evolution it has been replaced by the better method of giving information with the help of signals which are picked up by the sense organs. But the older method might have persisted in the background and still be able to put itself into effect under certain conditions.[5]

Here is part of the answer to the question of why Poul Anderson is a better writer than, say, Jeff Sutton. In Sutton's *Alton's Unguessable* (1970) there are telepathic humans, specialists on an exploration crew. Why are they specialists? Why isn't everyone telepathic if some are? After all, everyone can see and hear and smell (with the obvious exceptions): why is not telepathy a general capacity as the other senses are? Sutton never explains, but Anderson does. In *Alton's Unguessable*, telepaths are quite limited: most can "only grasp the essentials of thought, and then only at a very short distance and under the most favorable conditions" (p. 64). Sutton never says why this should be, but Anderson does; nor does he toss in some off-the-wall explanation. Rather, he locates his answer in a conjecture by an authority of considerable prestige.

In "The Queen of Air and Darkness," the weakness of human telepathy makes it a chancy means of communication; but the aliens transmit more powerfully than we, because their evolution took a different turn, and they can put a correspondingly greater trust in telepathy. (Incidentally, Anderson assumes that language is involved: the only human language known to the aliens is English, and their mind-reading efforts can be frustrated by one of the humans simply by his thinking in French.) At one point in the story, it becomes crucial to have telepathy be wave-like in nature, because the humans resort to a jamming device as a defense.

Anderson is quite ready, though, to discard the above explanation of telepathy when it interferes with the narrative. In "Kyrie" (1968; rpt. D. A. Wollheim and T. Carr, eds., *World's Best Science Fiction 1969*) a character says, "Telepathy is not a wave phenomenon. Since it transmits instantaneously, it cannot be. Nor does it appear limited by distance. Rather, it is a resonance. Being attuned, we two may well be able to continue thus across the entire breadth of the cosmos; and I am not aware of any material phenomenon which could interfere" (pp. 42–43). Anderson here utilizes the results of several studies that, as Rhine notes, suggest that telepathy is not affected by physical barriers or distance.[6] Perhaps even more support was to be added some years later when the astronaut Edgar Mitchell was "able to successfully 'transmit' Zener signs or symbols to acquaintances on Earth during his trip to the moon and back."[7] These are some of the ideas behind "Kyrie," which comes close to being a perfect short story by any set of standards in or out of the genre. Everything in it is directed toward the achieving of a single effect, an effect which occurs with overwhelming power and pathos. Yet Anderson's insistence that telepathy is bound neither by time nor distance is not a matter of gilding, pasted on to make the story sound scientific; it is crucial to the story. If telepathy is transmitted in waves which become attenuated over time and space, then the plot of "Kyrie" does not just diminish, it vanishes. Anderson is wise, therefore, to get his explanation of telepathy in early, in order to forestall the arousal of unwanted assumptions about the mechanisms of telepathy, assumptions that stories like "The Queen of Air and Darkness" have helped to propagate.

No subject matter of science fiction seems to me more misunderstood than telepathy. A glance at a survey of nineteenth- and early twentieth-century science fiction, like J. O. Bailey's *Pilgrims through Space and Time*, will reveal dozens of works that dealt with telepathy before Rhine draped it with ivy. Yet some critics persist in thinking of its use as an innovation of the sixties and seventies: "In the so-called 'New Wave' of science fiction writing of the past decade, science fiction has become overtly and even belligerently antiscientific, especially in its obsession with mental telepathy, parapsychology, psychedelia, the occult, and other nonempirical phenomena that have all but replaced those old-time mechanical marvels."[8] This quotation, from an article by James Stupple, contains so many inaccuracies it is difficult to know where to begin. Putting aside the question of whether science fiction is antiscientific for the moment, we still find major errors. There is first of all the strange lumping together of "mental telepathy, parapsychology, psychedelia, the occult," etc. Second, if science fiction was ever "obsessed" with the first two of these (and I would have thought telepathy was included in parapsychology) it was during the heyday of John W. Campbell in the fifties, as we have seen. Finally, Stupple's use of *nonempirical* in connection with ESP shows only that he does not know what the word means. *Webster's New Collegiate Dictionary* (8th edition) defines *empirical* as "1: relying on experience or observation alone without due regard for system and theory, 2: originating in or based on observation or experience (~ data), 3: capable of being verified or disproved by observation or experiment (~ laws)." This definition, in all its parts, could not more accurately describe the post-Rhine treatment of telepathy had it been framed with solely those experiments in mind; the problem with ESP has never been one of experimental data, but rather one of theoretical support, as science fiction clearly reflects in the many explanations invented to account for ESP. And the reader need not rely on my assertion: compare what the staid *Encyclopedia Britannica* has to say:

> Can it be said that the existence of psi has been proved? . . . In the sense that there is much experimental evidence, collected under sound and well-controlled conditions and properly analyzed statistically, which supports such a view, the answer must be that ESP certainly and [psychokinesis] probably, does exist. If to prove the existence of psi it is necessary to have replicable phenomena that can be demonstrated with certainty and that behave according to certain well-known laws, the answer must be in the negative.[9]

Consider again the definition from *Webster's New Collegiate* in the light of this comment: it is difficult to conceive of a subject with more empirical arguments in its favor than telepathy. As far as the second part of the *Britannica* quotation is concerned (that ESP cannot be demonstrated with certainty and has no theoretical support), the article goes on to say that

> this position is not unusual in science, particularly in the initial phases of research; stellar parallax was searched for but not definitively discovered for over 200 years, although it formed an essential part of Copernicus' heliocentric theory. Neutrinos, having no charge and hardly any mass, were difficult to find and pin down; antimatter has a similar shadowy existence.

I will go still further: subjects like telepathy are perfect for science fiction. We feel pretty sure about some parts of our universe—e.g., how fast matter can travel in it—and when science fiction finds it necessary to contravene those parts—faster-than-light spaceships—it is antiscientific in a clear but not necessarily derogatory meaning of the word. But in those parts of the universe about which the scientific establishment has little or nothing to tell us, speculation is surely legitimate. ESP is one such part, and to complain that science-fiction writers speculate about it shows little understanding of either science or science fiction.

To be sure, there are inept as well as artistic treatments of telepathy in science fiction—what else would we expect? But there is no question that writers find the subject a fertile one for an array of linguistic functions.

10

A History of Linguistics in Science Fiction: I

This work has so far detailed many uses of language as a means in science fiction. And if many of those uses were wrong or misleading, still, a good number were well informed and artistic. Beginning with this chapter, we examine those works that represent the highest use of linguistic methods in the field, those stories and novels in which problems of language are not just means but ends, in which problems of language are at the heart of the plot and inform our perception of the work as a whole. In these works is mirrored the history of linguistics since the mid—eighteen hundreds, and it is with the monumental labors of historical linguistics in the last century that we begin.

I The giants of nineteenth-century thought, men of the stature of Darwin and Pasteur, were matched by those philologists whose collective efforts culminated in the reconstruction of prehistoric Indo-European, the language from which modern tongues as diverse as Gaelic and Hindi derive. Their tool was the comparative method, a procedure in which attested forms from several related languages are set side by side, and a form is hypothesized from which the modern ones are traced, in accordance with principles abstracted from a vast amount of accumulated experience. Although Rasmus Rask, Jacob Grimm, and Karl Verner are not as well known to the public as Karl Marx or Sigmund Freud, their importance in their field was as profound as, and indeed longer lasting than, the effect of Freud on psychology or Darwin on genetics. As Otto Jespersen, the great Danish linguist, expressed it, it was reserved for the nineteenth century

> to apply the notion of history to other things than wars and the vicissitudes of dynasties, and thus to discover the idea of development or evolution as pervading the whole universe. This brought about a vast change in the science of language, as in other sciences. Instead of looking at such a language as Latin as one fixed point, and instead of aiming at fixing another language, such as French, in one classical form, the new science viewed both as being in con-

stant flux, as growing, as moving, as continually changing. It cried aloud like Heraclitus "Pánta reî," and like Galileo "Eppur si muove." And lo! the better this historical point of view was applied, the more secrets languages seemed to unveil, and the more light seemed also to be thrown on objects outside the proper sphere of language, such as ethnology and the early history of mankind at large and of particular countries.[1]

How simply Jespersen phrases a task—"to apply the notion of history" to language—that constitutes one of the largest collective intellectual efforts of humanity. Gangs of scholars worked like Pharoah's slaves for a century, and if our present understanding of modern Indo-European languages is the capstone of the pyramid they built, one of the largest foundation stones was the compilation of the *Oxford English Dictionary*, "A New Dictionary on a Historical Basis." To trace the growth to completion of the *OED* is to trace a scholarly genealogy that begins with dons and deans and ends coincidentally with elves and hobbits.

In the eighteen fifties, the Philological Society of England considered publishing a supplement to Johnson's and Richardson's dictionaries, but that idea was discarded in 1858 when, in response to a paper by Dean Richard Chenevix Trench, the Society resolved "that instead of the Supplement to the Standard English Dictionaries now in course of preparation by the order of the Society, a New Dictionary of the English Language be prepared under the Authority of the Philological Society."[2] In the course of fulfilling that resolution, seventy years were to pass. Literally hundreds of early English manuscripts were to see print for the first time just to provide raw material for the dictionary, and hundreds of man-years' worth of research were completed by hundreds of workers—Sir James Murray, one of the editors, worked on the *OED* for thirty-eight years. Its originators planned to create a dictionary that would show the historical development of the language through most of its written history. And they succeeded: 'The present work aims at exhibiting the history and signification of the English words now in use, or known to have been in use since the middle of the twelfth century."[3]

Through the seventy years of its preparation to its completion in 1928, the dictionary enjoyed the services of a number of editors. One of these, William Alexander Craigie, came to Oxford in 1897 to assist Dr. Henry Bradley, who had been working on the dictionary since 1888. In time, Craigie was raised from the position of assistant: in 1901, he became an editor in his own right, although that task did not occupy all his time. He continued to tutor undergraduates at Oxford, and in that capacity he directed the work of a student who came up to the University in 1911, John Ronald Reuel Tolkien. When Tolkien returned to his studies after World War I, it was at Craigie's invitation that the young man accepted a position for two years as a junior editor of the dictionary. According to Tolkien's biographer Daniel Grotta-Kurska, Craigie provided "Tolkien's greatest impetus to transform Elvish from an experiment to a life-long pursuit."[4]

Tolkien has not been shy in admitting that his great narrative was written to provide a source and a setting for the Elvish language he had been building since his childhood. In his later years he seems to have developed a dislike for literary critics, and his answers were often guarded and occasionally contradictory. Yet the main outline of his work is now clear. *The Silmarillion*, an account of the Second Age, which covers a period prior to the action of *The Lord of the Rings*, was his first work, although it was published only posthumously. As Tolkien himself tells us, *The Silmarillion* was "primarily linguistic in inspiration and was begun in order to provide the necessary background of 'history' for Elvish tongues."[5] Only after this earlier work was rejected by a publisher did Tolkien return to *The Lord of the Rings*. The genesis of the whole connected work, then, was his desire to incarnate his mythical language.

Some commentators, even among Tolkien's most complimentary, have found his account of the source disturbing, as if it were somehow unworthy of the narrative to spring from material like that which now forms its appendices. William Ready, one of these, rejects the notion that a tail could grow a dog: he quotes Tolkien's plain statement that "the invention of languages is the foundation. The 'stories' were made rather to provide a world for these languages than the reverse," but refuses to believe it. Ready concludes, "That is just nonsense, and serve them right who believe it, if any really do."[6] Many really do believe it, myself among them, and think it not at all incredible. As Robley Evans argues, Tolkien's assertion "may sound either whimsical or pedantic on the author's part, but it is neither. This 'rationale' for *The Lord of the Rings* argues instead for its author's respect for the word as a beautiful and powerful instrument for 'realizing wonder.' . . . This identification of man and his creation means, too, that man reveals himself through his 'art,' and is particularly himself when he uses words."[7] As the academic heir, through Craigie and others, of the nineteenth-century tradition of historical philology, Tolkien would shape his narrative to fit not just one language at a particular time, but a whole world of languages in earlier and later stages, some related and some not, all molded by principles of historical change.

Paul Kocher has noted that the principles governing the evolution of the tongues of Middle-Earth are the same as those in the history of the Indo-European languages,[8] and the editors of the *OED* knew that when talking about language, one is also talking about culture. As if this were not enough, Tolkien himself, speaking of fairy-tales, argued that a language demands to be embodied in a story if it is to be fully understood:

> I feel very strongly the fascination of the desire to unravel the intricately knot-
> ted and ramified history of the branches of the Tree of Tales. It is closely con-
> nected with the philologists' study of the tangled skein of Language, of which I
> know some small pieces. But even with regard to language it seems to me that
> the essential quality and aptitudes of a given language in a living monument is
> both more important to seize and far more difficult to make explicit than its
> linear history.[9]

Given a man of Tolkien's interests and education and profession, the Elvish language leads naturally to the building of the story.

Tolkien openhandedly scatters hints of the centrality of language throughout his books: for example, primacy of place among the intelligent beings of Middle-Earth belongs to a race whose name Tolkien renders as "Elves," but the word he so translates, the *Quendi*, means literally "the speakers" (Appendix F, *LR*, 3:415), and their language, *Quenya*, can be translated simply as "speech." It was the Elves who, as the Ent Treebeard tells us, went through the world ages past, waking creatures to consciousness and giving them speech—"a great gift that cannot be forgotten" (*LR*, 2:76). Or again, we find that the High-Elven word for "name" is *esse* (*LR*, 3:401), and through this Latin-Elvish pun we have as clear a statement as could be wished that a part of the language, the name, reflects a part of reality, the essence. As Treebeard puts it, "real names tell you the story of the things they belong to in my language" (*LR*, 2:68).

The Lord of the Rings achieves much of its effect by its richness of linguistic detail. Its world is like our world in that we feel, while reading the work, that an abundance of experience, more than we will ever encounter, lies beyond the pages of the book. The feeling is more like reading history, during which we know that the author has not exhausted the subject in the discussion of it. The languages of *LR,* to use the useful abbreviation, are responsible for much of this feeling, I believe. We know of the existence of a realm of perception beyond our experience when we travel in a country whose language we do not speak. All around us we hear unknown yet articulate sounds, and we know that a culture lies behind them, a culture to which we can be admitted with patience and study.

It is much the same with *LR;* yet there we travel not in a foreign country, but in a foreign world, for the languages we encounter are many. Only the hobbits are transparent to us; their speech (with the exception of a word or two) is rendered in English, and they therefore become the fixed point to which all else is referred. But elsewhere Tolkien lavishes his skills: the dwarves speak a tongue of their own; the riders of Rohan speak a language archaic by comparison to that of the hobbits, and their speech is therefore exemplified by Old English in slight disguise; even the orcs have a language with several different dialects; and finally, there is the language of the elves, obviously Tolkien's first and greatest love. The language of the elves has not only completeness, it has history.

To begin with, there are two forms of Elvish, Quenya and Sindarin. The two are somehow related: it may be that Sindarin is derived from Quenya, but more probably both are derived from an older form, which Quenya more closely resembles, just as German and English both are derived from a common source, some features of which German has preserved but English has lost. We can appreciate the intricacy and capaciousness of Quenya by applying the methods of descriptive linguistics to a sample of it, "Galadriel's Song" (*LR,* 1:394). To the right is the translation given in the text; I have numbered the lines for reference.

1	Ai! laurië lantar lassi súrinen,	Ah! like gold fall the leaves in the wind,
2	Yéni únótimë ve rámar aldaron!	long years numberless as the wings of trees!
3	Yéni ve lintë yuldar avánier	The long years have passed like swift
4	mi oromardi lisse-miruvóreva	draughts of the sweet mead in lofty halls
5	Andúnë pella, Vardo tellumar	beyond the West, beneath the blue vaults
6	nu luini yassen tintilar i eleni	of Varda wherein the stars tremble in the

7	ómaryo airetári-lírinen.	song of her voice, holy and queenly.
8	Sí man i yulma nin enquantuva?	Who now shall refill the cup for me?
9	An sí Tintallë Varda Oiolossëo	For now the Kindler, Varda, the Queen of
10	ve fanyar máryat Elentári ortanë	the Stars, from Mount Everwhite has uplifted her hands like clouds,
11	ar ilyë tier undulávë lumbulë;	and all paths are drowned deep in shadow;
12	ar sindanóriello caita mornië	and out of a grey country darkness lies
13	i falmalinnar imbë met, ar hísië	on the foaming waves between us, and mist
14	untúpa Calaciryo míri oialë.	covers the jewels of Calacirya for ever.
15	Sí vanwa ná, Rómello vanwa, Valimar!	Now lost, lost to those from the East is Valimar!
16	Namárië! Nai hiruvalyë Valimar.	Farewell! Maybe thou shalt find Valimar.
17	Nai elyë hiruva. Namárië!	Maybe even thou shalt find it. Farewell!

We begin by identifying items in the original with items in the translation. *Ve*, for instance, appears in lines 2, 3, and 10. Lines 2 and 10 seem to have a fairly close clause-for-clause relationship with the translation, and the only element the translation clauses have in common is "like." Since "like" also appears in the translation of the long clause at lines 3–7, we tentatively list *ve* as "like," subject, of course, to future correction if warranted. "Like" appears in the translation of line 1, to which we will return later. In the same way, *sí* in 8, 9, and 15 is glossed as "now," and *ar* in 11, 12, and 13 as "and."

The poem ends with five short sentences. *Namárië* is obviously "farewell," although the possibility remains that it, like its English translation, is a compound. The answer to that question will have to wait further progress. The word *vanwa* is repeated in line 15, and the word "lost" is repeated in the translation. We gloss *vanwa* as "lost" and mark it as probably a past participle. This leaves, apart from proper names, only *ná* untranslated in line 15. At this stage, a good guess would be that *ná* means "is," based chiefly on the similarity in form between *ná* and *nai* in 16 and 17. If *nai* means "maybe," then we ascribe the difference in form to a difference between the indicative mood and a potential mood. Lines 16 and 17 have a compound form very much like two separate words: *hiruvalyë* and *elyë hiruva.* If we assume that personal pronouns are joined in an elided form to the end of the verb in Quenya, then we have the meaning of these forms, and we can give a word-for-word translation of the last three lines:

15　Sí　　vanwa ná, Rómello　　　　　　　　vanwa, Valimar!
　　Now lost　　is, to-those-from-the-East lost,　　Valimar!

16　Namárië! Nai　　hiruvalyë　　　　Valimar.
　　Farewell! Maybe find-shalt-thou Valimar.

17　Nai　　elyë hiruva.　　Namárië!
　　Maybe thou find-shalt. Farewell!

We are not interested in translating here (Tolkien has given us that), but in finding out something about Quenya. The work is yielding to analysis, but of course it is still too early to make generalizations.

We have isolated a verb form already, *hiruva,* and if we assume that verbs consist of a root plus a suffix, then looking for similar suffixes in the text gives us *enquantuva* in line 8 as "shall refill." We tentatively identify the suffix *-uva* as having to do with future tense.

Now we take a leap out of the poem itself and search for other, similar forms in *LR* that may shed light on the remaining elements in the last three lines. Two words in the poem begin with what may be the same morpheme, *oromardi* in line 4 and *ortanë* in 10; we find two topographical names in the book that are similar: *Orodruin* "Mountain of Fire," and *Orthanc* "Mount Fang." If we search the translation clauses corresponding to those containing *oromardi* and *ortanë* for some semantic similarity to the place-names, we find it in the idea of height—"lofty halls" and "uplifted hands." *Ortanë* therefore means something like *or-tan-ë* "up-move– present participle" (the meaning of the parts *tan* and *ë* depends on later analysis). Even more interesting is the gloss of *oro-mardi* as "high-halls," since it sheds light on the meaning of *Valimar* as a compound. The form *mar* occurs in a sentence in *LR,* 3:245, which is translated almost word for word by Tolkien:

Sinome　　*maruvan*　　ar　Hildinyar tenn' Ambar-metta!
In-this-place I-will-abide and my-heirs　until　the-ending-of-the-world!

Mar as a verb root, then, means something like "to dwell, reside," while as a noun it means "dwelling, home," confirming the guess about *oromardi*. *The Silmarillion* (p. 356) verifies the gloss of *mar* as "home." The first element in *Valimar* appears in the name the *Valar; val-* means "power" (*Sil,* p. 365), in the sense of Pseudo-Dionysius's classification of the angels into the ninefold ranks of seraphim, cherubim, thrones, powers, dominations, etc. Tolkien's *valar,* or "powers," are creatures best described as angels in the traditional sense; not the chubby cherubs of the Italian Renaissance, but the more intimidating angels of Scripture, who always tell the humans to whom they appear not to be afraid. (C. S. Lewis's *Perelandra* [1944] depicts similar angels.) Therefore, *Valimar* can be translated as "angel-home," or, to add a cultural translation as well, "heaven."

Apart from prepositions, articles, and the like, which may or may not be translatable from one language to another, two pairs of words occur in the text and translation of lines 3–7 and 9–10: *elen* in *eleni* and *Elentári,* and *tári* in *Elentári* and *airetári;* the common elements in the gloss are "stars," "queenly," and "Queen of the Stars." *Elentári* we translate, therefore, as "star-queen"; *eleni* as "stars"; *airetári* is clearly a compound the second element of which means "queenly," but the first half of which awaits further examination. These guesses again find confirmation at other places in the various works of the series: *The Silmarillion* lists *Elentári* as "star queen" (p. 327), and gives "lofty" as the meaning of *tara* (p. 364); *Tar-* also shows up as the title of the kings and queens of Númenor (*LR,* 3: Appendix A).

The next item is easier: Tolkien tells us (*LR,* 3 : 323) that the Elendilmir is the "single white gem, . . . bound on [the brows of the rulers of Arnor] with a silver fillet." Line 14 contains *míri,* and its context allows only the gloss "jewels." Topography helps again when we compare *Ered Luin* "the Blue Mountains" to *luini* in line 6, and gloss the word as "blue." For the sake of brevity, I will list the words translatable by reference to some other part of the work, together with the words identified by means of some grammatical element already isolated.

1 *laurië* "golden"; an adjective modifying a plural noun (cf. *laurë* "gold in color," *Sil,* p. 361).

1 *lantar* "fall"; plural, third person, present tense verb.

1 *lassi* "leaves"; plural noun of the i-class (those that form the plural by adding *-i.* Cf. *lasse-lanta,* in which the first element has the adjective end-

ing, meaning "the season of Autumn," literally, "leaf-fall," in *LR,* 3 : 386).

2–3 *yéni* "years"; pl. n., i-class.

2 *aldaran* "of trees"; pl. n. of r-class plus genitive suffix (*Sil,* p. 355, gives *alda* "tree"; cf. *Aldúya,* the day named after the two trees, *LR,* 3 : 388).

2 *únótimë* "numberless"; glossed in *LR,* 3 : 393; note adjective ending -ë.

2 *rámar* "wings"; pl. n., r-class.

3 *lintë* "swift"; identified by the adjective ending.

3 *yuldar* "drafts"; identified as a plural noun by the r-class suffix.

3 *avánier* "pass away"; *aván-* plus the present perfect plural ending -*ier.*

4 *lisse-miruvóreva* "sweet" (adj. ending -e) plus the genitive form of *miruvor* "mead" (cf. *miruvor, LR,* 1 : 304, "the cordial of Imladris"). Note that nouns of the *miruvor* class, the plural of which I do not know, have a different genitive suffix from that of the r-class nouns.

5 *Andúnë* "beyond the West" (cf. *dûn* "West," *LR,* 3 : 408).

5 *pella* "beneath."

5 *tellumar* "vaults"; pl. n., r-class (note *mar* again. Literally "deep-places"?)

6 *yassen* "in which"; relative pronoun (cf. the endings of *súrinen* "in the wind" and *lírinen* "in the song").

6 *tintilar* "twinkle, sparkle"; plural, third person, present tense verb (cf. *Tintallë* "the Kindler," l. 9).

6 *i* "the"; definite article. Quenya appears to lack an indefinite article.

7 *ómaryo* "her voice"; the ending is probably a suffixed genitive pronoun, i.e., *ómar-* "voice" -*yo* "her."

7 *airetári* "holy-queenly."

8 *man* "who"; indefinite pronoun.

8 *yulma* "cup"; singular noun, r-class.

8 *nin* "for me"; first person singular pronoun, probably a dative.

9 *Oiolossëo* "from Mount Everwhite"; this word appears to be composed of five morphemes: *Oi-* "ever" (cf. *Oialë* "forever," l.14), -*o-* a compounding element? (cf. -*o-* in *or-o-mardi*), -*loss-* "snow" (*Sil,* p. 361; cf. *Lossarnach* "the mountain-borders," lit. "the snow-borders," *LR,* 3 : 22); -*e-* adjective ending, and -*o-* "from."

10 *fanyar* "clouds"; cf. *fana* "veil." Pl. n., r-class.

10 *máryat* "her hands"; possibly *már-* "hand" (a homophone of *mar* "place," unless the accent indicates a different vowel), *-ya-* "her" (cf. *-yo* in *ómaryo*), *-t* "two" (cf. *met*, l. 13, as *me-* "us" *-t* "two").

11 *ilyë* "all."

11 *tier* "roads"; pl. n., perhaps r-class.

11 *unduláve* "are drowned"; this is the only passive verb form I have noticed.

11 *lumbulë* "shadowy"; adjective.

12 *sindanóriello* "out of the grey country"; lit. *sinda-* "grey" (cf. *Sindarin* "the Grey Elves"), *-nóri-* "country" (cf. place-name *Anórien*), *-ello* "out of" (cf. *Rómello* "out of the East").

12 *caita* "covers"; singular, third person, present tense verb.

12 *mornië* "darkness" (cf. place-name *Mordor*).

13 *falmalinnar* "foaming-waves"; a compound, but which part is which?

13 *imbe* "both."

13 *hísië* "mist."

14 *untúpa* "covers over"; again, probably a compound with *un-*, *unde-* "down"? Some parts of this analysis are questionable, and some parts of the text are still obscure: what is the meaning, for instance, of *nu* in line 6? But it is possible to make a fairly accurate word-for-word translation, preserving the original word order and displaying the syntax of Quenya:

1   Ah! golden fall leaves in the wind!
2   Years numberless as wings of trees,
3   years like swift drafts have passed-away
4   in high halls of sweet mead
5   beyond West beneath Varda's vaults
6   [of?] blue in which twinkle the stars
7   by-voice-her holy-queenly in song.
8   Now who the cup for-me refill-shall?
9   For now Kindler, Varda, Ever-snowy-from
10   like clouds hands-her-two Star-Queen has uplifted,
11   and all paths are down-drowned shadowy;
12   and grey-country-out-of spreads-over darkness
13   the foaming-waves between us-two, and mist
14   covers Calacirya's jewels forever.
15   Now lost is, to-the-East lost, heaven!

16 Farewell! May-it-be-that find-shalt-thou heaven.
17 May-it-be-that thou [emphatic] find-shalt. Farewell!

We find that just as in many highly inflected languages (Latin, for example) the word order of Quenya poetry is not inflexible, since the suffixes on the words will show their relationships. The language seems to be largely Indo-European in structure; verbs, for instance, consist of a prefix (if any), a root, and an ending that indicates (a) tense, (b) aspect, and (c) number. The paradigm below, using the root *hir* "find," shows how well Quenya verbs fit into the familiar system of Latin or Greek. A question mark means that the form is unknown (to me), and an asterisk means that the form does not occur in *LR* but has been reconstructed from uses of the suffix with other roots. All forms are indicative mood.

Present

I	*hiran	"I find"	?	"we find"
II	?	"thou findest"	?	"you find"
III	hira	"he, she, it finds"	hirar	"they find"

(forms for all persons are probably the same in the plural)

Past

I	?	"I found"	?	"we found"
II	?	"thou found"	?	"you found"
III	hire	"he, she, it found"	*hiren	"they found"

Future

I	hiruvan	"I will find"	?	"we will find"
II	hiruvalyë	"thou shalt find"	?	"you will find"
III	hiruva	"he, she, it will find"	*hiruvar	"they will find"

(second person singular is *hiruva* when the pronoun is not suffixed)

Present Perfect

I	*hirien	"I have found"	?	"we have found"
II	?	"thou hast found"	?	"you have found"
III	*hirië	"he, she, it has found"	hirier	"they have found"

Present Participle *hirielvo "our finding"

Past Participle *hirwa "found"

Tolkien's great trilogy, together with *The Hobbit* and *The Silmarillion*, is a full embodiment of historical linguistics' highest aims. If *The Lord of the Rings* is not generally considered science fiction, it is partly because it is filled with the trappings of fantasy—wizards, elves, dwarves, etc. But it is also partly because the real science that informs it, historical linguistics, is not well known publicly and is not on the surface of the story. But readers of science fiction enjoy it: Lin Carter credits them with forming its first appreciative audience.[10] And science-fiction writers continue to honor Tolkien in the sincerest way—by reference to his creations in their stories. Hal Clement's *Mission of Gravity* (1953) has as its central character a creature named Barlennan who sails a ship named the *Bree*, a reference to Tolkien's Barliman Butterbur, the owner of the inn "The Prancing Pony" in the town of Bree. In James Tiptree, Jr.'s "Your Haploid Heart" (1969; rpt. D. A. Wollheim and T. Carr, eds., *World's Best SF 1970*) a character is trying to get an egg-cell of the race he is studying, and asks himself, "How in Mordor am I going to get an ovum?" (p. 134) Here Tolkien's dark realm has become a common oath, like "Hell." Harlan Ellison's *Again, Dangerous Visions* (1972) is practically a Tolkien memorial collection: no less than three stories in the book allude to *LR:* Gene Wolfe titles three short stories "Mathoms from the Time Closet," using the Hobbit term for useless keepsakes; in "Stoned Counsel," H. H. Hollis says of a stream that "the water was certainly not crystal clear, but neither did it smoke and steam like Saruman's sewer" (p. 302), referring to Tolkien's corrupted wizard; and a character in Chad Oliver's "King of the Hill" "sometimes thought of himself as a vampire in one of the still-popular epics. ('Ah, my dear, velcome to Castle Mordor. A moment vhile I adjust my dentures.')" (p. 190) We can hope that Tolkien's greatest creation will one day be honored in fact as it is in the fictional future setting of A. Bertram Chandler's *To Keep the Ship* (1978), in which a constellation is named "The Hobbit" (p. 21).

A few words on the languages in *LR* given here merely suggest the depth of the material in the trilogy. A work the size of this book could easily be written on synchronic and diachronic features of the languages of the saga. Those interested in exploring the subject further should consult the various publications of the Mythopoeic Society of Los Angeles, California, especially *Parma Eldalamberon: The Book of Elven Tongues*. *Parma Eldalamberon*, as its masthead states, is "the journal of the Mythopoeic Linguistic Fellowship, a special interest group of The Mythopoeic Society, interested in imaginary fantasy languages and all matters linguistic and philological, especially the divers tongues of Middle-Earth and the Low Worlds." An early venture into Tolkien's work was James D. Allan's *A Glossary of the Eldarin Tongues* (Orillia, Ontario: privately printed by the author, 1972), a

work now superseded by the same author's *An Introduction to Elvish*
(Somerset, U.K.: Bran's Head, 1978). Some appreciation for the scope of
Tolkien's invention may be gained from noting that although many journals
specialize in the work of a single author (*Blake Studies, Dickens Studies
Newsletter,* etc.) this is the only instance I know of in which a journal is
devoted to the study of an invented language appearing in a literary work.

II Although J. R. R. Tolkien was a well-respected historical linguist and
academic critic, he will certainly be remembered for his fiction long
after his scholarly credentials are forgotten. In the case of Benjamin Lee
Whorf, we have nearly the reverse—a man who wrote an unsuccessful
science fiction novel, yet whose memory endures as a brilliant and innovative linguist. The story of the compilation of the Oxford English Dictionary,
from its beginning down to the young Tolkien's working as an assistant
editor, is essentially a British story; Whorf's story is an American one.

At the same time that Murray and Bradley were spending the last years of
the nineteenth century among their citation slips, Franz Boas was investigating the languages of the American Indian. Boas, born the same year as
the Philological Society resolution, 1858, was a self-taught linguist. Coming to the subject without preconceptions, he learned from his experience
with the aboriginal languages of North America that the classical method
of analyzing Western European languages, a method largely unchanged
since the time of the ancient Greeks, would not work with material so
radically different. Instead, he worked out his own methodology designed
to confront each language as it actually existed. He explained and justified
his methods in his introduction to the *Handbook of American Indian Languages* (1911):

> It is important at this point to emphasize the fact that the group of ideas ex-
> pressed by specific phonetic groups show material differences in different
> languages, and do not conform by any means to the same principles of
> classification. To take again the example of English, we find that the idea of
> *water* is expressed in a great variety of forms: one term serves to express water
> as a *liquid*; another one, water in the form of a large expanse (*lake*); others,
> water as running in a large body or a small body (*river* and *brook*); still others
> express water in the form of *rain, dew, wave,* and *foam*. It is perfectly con-
> ceivable that this variety of ideas, each of which is expressed by a single term

in English, might be expressed in other languages by derivations from the same form. . . . In Dakota, the terms *naxta'ka* (to kick), *vaxta'ka* (to bite), *ic'a'xtaka* (to be near to), *boxta'ka* (to pound) are all derived from the common element *xtaka* (to grip) which holds them together, while we use distinct words to express the various ideas.[11]

Francis P. Dinneen attributes to Boas's field experiences his realization that "the cultural tradition of peoples and not their environmental situation . . . is most influential in forming a society. He also appreciated that any description of a culture made in ignorance of the language and literature of the people would likely be misleading and superficial."[12]

In 1904 Boas met Edward Sapir, who was Benjamin Lee Whorf's mentor, as W. A. Craigie was to be Tolkien's. Sapir, trained in the classical methods of linguistic analysis, found his meeting with Boas a revelation; he abandoned his Germanic studies and began the analysis of American Indian languages after the manner of his new teacher. Sapir, one of the greatest figures in American linguistics, in turn found in Whorf his most original pupil.

Some parts of Whorf's later ideas are implied in the work of Sapir, and for this reason the principle of linguistic relativity, which we will explore later, is sometimes called the Sapir-Whorf hypothesis. Whorf would later stress the arbitrary relation between language and reality, but as early as 1912, Sapir was demonstrating that different languages segment reality differently. He points out, for example, that several American Indian languages use the same word for both sun and moon, depending on the context to make it clear which heavenly body is meant. He continues, "If we complain that so vague a term fails to do justice to an essential natural difference, the Indian might well retaliate by pointing to the *omnium gatherum* character of our term 'weed' as contrasted with his own more precise plant vocabulary."[13] He concludes, "everything naturally depends on the point of view as determined by interest." It is well known (at least among linguists) that Whorf rejected the notion that mere "interest" determined the character of a language; but the role that science fiction played in that development is not so well known. Indeed, had things turned out differently, Whorf might have gone on to become one of the pioneers of science fiction, rather than a linguist of note.

At twenty-eight, before Whorf began the linguistic work that would insure his reputation, he became troubled by what he perceived as a conflict between science and religion. In 1924, under the impact of the Scopes trial, he wrote a science fiction novel, *The Ruler of the Universe*,[14] which was never published. It pictures the destruction of Earth by a chain reaction caused by research on atomic fission for military purposes, and may be the earliest use of that theme. According to Peter C. Rollins, it was during the writing of the novel that Whorf began to consider the relation between language and thought, a consideration that culminated in his statement of the principle of linguistic relativity.

The central question of linguistic relativity is this: does our perception of reality constrain our language, or does our language constrain our perception of reality? A character in Roger Zelazny's "The Moment of the Storm" (1966; rpt. *The Doors of His Face, the Lamps of His Mouth*) ponders the question:

> It's funny how the mind personifies, engenders. Ships are always women: You say, "She's a good old tub," or "She's a fast, tough number, this one," slapping a bulwark and feeling the aura of femininity that clings to the vessel's curves; or, conversely, "He's a bastard to start, that little Sam!" as you kick the auxiliary engine in an island transport-vehicle; and hurricanes are always women, and moons, and seas. Cities, though are different. Generally, they're neuter. Nobody calls New York or San Francisco "he" or "she." Usually, cities are just "it." (P. 173)

To this point, we have a clear statement of what Whorf calls the false "common sense" notion that we find certain features or attributes in the object ("the vessel's curves") that imply a particular sex, and we assign the corresponding gender category from our language. But the character continues, coming close to the principle of linguistic relativity: "Sometimes, however, [cities] do come to take on the attributes of sex. Usually, this is in the case of small cities near to the Mediterranean, back on Earth. Perhaps this is because of the sex-ridden nouns of the languages which prevail in that vicinity" (p. 173). As the story suggests, perhaps it is the language that makes us find those features in the first place. In Spanish, for example, every noun, proper ones included, is either masculine or feminine—no neuter category exists. Thus *Toledo* is masculine and is referred to by *él*, "he," while *Salamanca* or *Madera* is feminine and referred to by *ella*, "she." Spanish, therefore, does not just allow the assignment of gender to the names of cities, it absolutely requires it. Now, to say that the Spaniard therefore thinks of one city as masculine and another as feminine is a different assertion, and an unjustified one, but the strict linguistic relativist insists that the language makes us see masculine and feminine attributes where none exist in reality. Whorf demonstrates this observation in several essays, and in one uses English gender as an example:

> One's first and "common-sense" impression of covert categories like English gender and Navaho shape-class is that they are simply distinctions between different kinds of experience or knowledge; that we say *Jane went to her house* because we know that Jane is a female. . . . But such experience is linguistic; it is learning English by observation. Moreover it is easy to show that the pronoun agrees with the name only, not with the experience. I can bestow the name *Jane* on an automobile, a skeleton, or a cannon, and it will still require *she* in pronominal references. I have two goldfish; I name one *Jane* and one *Dick*. I can still say *Each goldfish likes its food*, but not *Jane likes its food better than Dick*. I must say *Jane likes her food*.[15]

Gender assignment is an example of the Whorf hypothesis, or the principle of linguistic relativity. Whorf stated the principle most succinctly in "Science and Linguistics" in these words: "All observers are not led by the same physical evidence to the same picture of the universe, unless their linguistic backgrounds are similar, or can in some way be calibrated."[16]

Whorf drew his most effective arguments for linguistic relativity from a contrast between American Indian languages and the modern languages derived from Indo-European, principally English. One contrast he was fond of was that between Hopi verb assertions and English verb tenses. He noted that the Hopi reportive, expective, and nomic assertions translated roughly into English past, future, and present tenses but warned that "they do not refer to time or duration . . . [but] to one of three distinct realms of validity."[17] The reportive is used to state an experience witnessed by the speaker in the past or present, the expective is used for an anticipated situation, either in the future or one just beginning, and the nomic is used for statements of general truth.[18] From these and similar observations, Whorf concludes,

> Hopi may be called a timeless language. It recognizes psychological time, which is much like Bergson's "duration," but this "time" is quite unlike the mathematical time, T, used by our physicists. Among the peculiar properties of Hopi time are that it varies with each observer, does not permit of simul-

taneity, and has zero dimensions; i.e., it cannot be given a number greater than one. The Hopi do not say, "I stayed five days," but "I left on the fifth day." A word referring to this kind of time, like the word day, can have no plural.[19]

We must remember that for Whorf this difference in language meant that the Hopis viewed reality differently; he therefore goes on to speculate about how that Hopi view of reality would be described:

> Hopi grammar, by means of its forms called aspects and modes, also makes it easy to distinguish among momentary, continued, and repeated occurrences, and to indicate the actual sequence of reported events. Thus the universe can be described without recourse to dimensional time. How would a physics constructed along these lines work, with no *T* (time) in its equations? Perfectly, as far as I can see, though of course it would require different ideology and perhaps different mathematics. (P. 217)

He sees no barrier to a Hopi science that would lack such concepts as time, velocity, and acceleration.

Cyril M. Kornbluth saw the beginning of a story in these ideas. In his "Two Dooms" (1958; rpt. *A Mile Beyond the Moon*), a physicist named Royland works at a government atomic research project in the Southwest. His hobby is anthropology, and in its pursuit he has met a Hopi who leads him to Whorfian reflections:

> It was one of Nahataspe's biggest jokes that Hopi children understood Einstein's relativity as soon as they could talk—and there was some truth to it. The Hopi language—and thought—had no tenses and therefore no concept of time-as-an-entity; it had nothing like the Indo-European speech's subjects and predicates [Kornbluth errs here], and therefore no built-in metaphysics of cause and effect. In the Hopi language and mind all things were frozen together forever into one great relationship, a crystalline structure of space-time events that simply were because they were. So much for Nahataspe's people "seeing clearly." But Royland gave himself and any other physicist credit for seeing as clearly when they were working a four-dimensional problem in the X Y Z space variables and the T time variable. (P. 201)

Kornbluth seems at the end to reject a central tenet of Whorf's ideas, the notion that systems of thought produced by other languages are valuable for the different insights into reality they provide.

The main impact of Whorf's thought on science fiction comes not in such rarified matters as physics, but in areas more accessible to the layman, such as the gender example given earlier. His influence is seen in Philip

José Farmer's "Prometheus" (1961; rpt. *Down in the Black Gang*), in which an explorer on an alien planet meets a race of intelligent, birdlike beings. He teaches them a form of English since they have no language of their own, and realizing that language will have an enormous impact on their culture, realizes also that the birds present an opportunity to test the Whorf hypothesis. "Why not teach each group a different language?" he asks, "Just as an experiment? This group would be our Indo-European school; another Sinitic; another, our Amerindian; still another, Bantu. It would be interesting to see how the various groups developed socially, technologically, and philosophically. Would each group follow the general lines of social evolution that their prototypes did on Earth? Would the particular type of language a group used place it on a particular path during its climb uphill to civilization?" (p. 146). Although neither the Whorf hypothesis nor its alternate title, linguistic relativity, is mentioned by name, the experiment is as clear a test as one could wish of its accuracy. But the character is too humane to subject the creatures to an experiment without their consent, and the plan remains only an interesting speculation.

The Whorf hypothesis has a corollary: if it is true that our language determines our perception of reality, then whoever controls language controls the perception of reality as well. If language can be controlled, then would-be despots have available a subtle and efficient means of restricting thought. The frightening potential of linguistic relativity is the largest cloud on the already-gray horizon of George Orwell's *Nineteen Eighty-Four* (1949). Big Brother in that novel maintains the tyranny of Ingsoc by the time-tested methods of spying, denunciation, torture, and terror; but his hope for future years lies in the creation of a severely limited version of English called Newspeak. The intention of the creators of Newspeak is to make subversive thought impossible for want of the words to conceive it. Syme, one of the compilers of the "Eleventh Edition of the Newspeak dictionary," explains:

> Don't you see that the whole aim of Newspeak is to narrow the range of thought? In the end we shall make thoughtcrime literally impossible, because there will be no words in which to express it. Every concept that can ever be needed will be expressed by exactly *one* word, with its meaning rigidly defined and all its subsidiary meanings rubbed out and forgotten. . . . Every year fewer and fewer words, and the range of consciousness always a little smaller. . . . The Revolution will be complete when the language is perfect. Newspeak is Ingsoc and Ingsoc is Newspeak. (P. 24)

Orwell underlined his belief in the threat which Newspeak symbolized by adding an appendix on the language to his novel. Newspeak, we learn, differs "from all other languages in that its vocabulary grew smaller instead of larger every year" (p. 136). Its creators hope that each dangerous word cut from the lexicon is a dangerous thought forestalled. Of course, limiting only the number of words will not suffice; their meanings must be reduced as well. The few words remaining from the older form of English would necessarily have "their meanings extended until they contained within themselves whole batteries of words which, as they were sufficiently covered by a single comprehensive term, could now be scrapped and forgotten." As the appendix states, "the greatest difficulty facing the compilers of the Newspeak dictionary was not to invent new words, but, having invented them, to make sure what they meant: to make sure, that is to say, what ranges of words they canceled by their existence" (p. 134). Newspeak retains words such as *free*, but only in the sense of the absence of a thing, e.g., "This dog is free from lice," while the meanings "politically free" or "intellectually free" are suppressed.

But Newspeak contains the weaknesses that will lead to its eventual collapse, as Anthony Burgess has pointed out: Orwell assumes that nature is "inert and malleable," a false assumption. And "the processes of linguistic change are an aspect of nature, taking place unconsciously and, it appears, autonomously. There is no guarantee that the State's creation of Newspeak could flourish impervious to gradual semantic distortion, vowel mutation, the influence of the richer Oldspeak of the proles" (*1985*, p. 47). After all, Newspeak's use, it appears, will be limited to Party members; the proles, eighty-five percent of the population, will be excluded from indoctrination in Newspeak and therefore free of its chains. Even the Party members, or at least some of them, will have to become bilingual, since they must retain the old form of the language to communicate with the masses, and those members will also remain liberated. Finally, hubris hangs over the whole project; we have no evidence for, and much against, the belief that all the schools, newspapers, and dictionaries in existence can change the meaning of a word or prevent a change in meaning that the mass of speakers have set in motion. In 1755, Samuel Johnson, reflecting on the dictionary he had just completed, wrote:

> Those who have been persuaded to think well of my design, require that it
> should fix our language, and put a stop to those alterations which time and

chance have hitherto been suffered to make in it without opposition. With this consequence I will confess that I flattered myself for a while; but now begin to fear that I have indulged expectation which neither reason nor experience can justify. When we see men grow old and die at a certain time one after another, from century to century, we laugh at the elixir that promises to prolong life to a thousand years; and with equal justice may the lexicographer be derided, who being able to produce no example of a nation that has preserved their words and phrases from mutability, shall imagine that his dictionary can em-balm his language, and secure it from corruption and decay, that it is in his power to change sublunary nature, or clear the world at once from folly, van-ity, and affectation.

   With this hope, however, academies have been instituted, to guard the avenues of their languages, to retain fugitives, and repulse intruders; but their vigilance and activity have hitherto been vain; sounds are too volatile and subtle for legal restraints; to enchain syllables, and to lash the wind, are equally the undertakings of pride, unwilling to measure its desires by its strength.[20]

There is no reason to fear that the British lexicographers of *Nineteen Eighty-Four* will succeed at a task thought hopeless by their great ances-tor.[21]

   In one very short science-fiction story, the Whorf hypothesis works to the advantage of human beings, rather than being an instrument of their op-pression. Larry Niven, in "Three Vignettes: Grammar Lesson" (1977), presents a picture of the Earth of the future. Humanity has met several alien races, including the Chirpsithtra, beings from a society far more technolog-ically advanced than our own. In conversation with a few of them, the human narrator has occasion to remark, "The leg of your chair has pinned my pants." The aliens begin to laugh (the human has spoken in their lan-guage), but later one of them explains the reason for their mirth: "Your pardon for my rudeness. You used intrinsic 'your' and 'my,' instead of ex-trinsic. As if your pants are part of you and my chair a part of me. I was taken by surprise" (p. 22). The alien explains that they have several forms of possessive pronouns, but they have noticed no such usage in human lan-guages: "'And all your languages seem to use one possessive for all pur-poses. My arm, my husband, my mother,' she said, using the intrinsic 'my' for her arm, the 'my' of property for her husband, and the 'my' of relation-ship for her mother" (p. 22).

   It turns out that the Chirpsithtra had decided not to conquer Earth despite their considerable advantage in power because humans use the "intrinsic" possessive and would, they conclude, die defending their possessions, so closely do their languages link things that can be removed, "my hat," with things that cannot be removed, "my arm." The people of Earth are lucky that the aliens did not learn one of the human languages (Latin, for instance) that does distinguish between the grammatical categories of alienable and inalienable possession. And we are fortunate that they did not study English closely, since the usage of some verbs, *have*, *wear*, and *carry*, for instance, depends in part on just this distinction.

The fullest exposition of the Whorf hypothesis, however, occurs in Jack Vance's *The Languages of Pao* (1958), in which the principle of linguistic relativity is not central to the plot; it *is* the plot. Vance intended to explore the concept in fiction: he says that he meant the book to be "the development of an interesting concept, which may or may not be valid."[22] The people of Pao, the planet of the title, speak a language which encourages passivity by describing all subjects of discussion in terms of states, not actions. The sentence translated "There are two matters I wish to discuss with you," if rendered word for word from Paonese to English is "Statement-of-importance *in a state of readiness*–two; ear–[of speaker]–*in a state of readiness*; mouth–of this person here–*in a state of volition*" (p. 10). The italicized words are suffixes indicating condition. As a result of the language, it is stated, the Paonese are unable to resist an invasion from another planet that overthrows their emperor and sets a pretender on the throne in place of the heir, the emperor's son.

But the puppet-emperor chafes under the tribute demanded by the invaders and engages the services of a scientist from the planet Breakness to free him from it. Breakness is a planet-wide research center, whose rulers, the Dominies (or wizards, as they are sometimes called), put their talents at the disposal of anyone who will pay their fees. This particular scientist, Palafox, is a Dominie of Linguistics, and he proposes to free Pao by using the principle of linguistic relativity. As one of his sons explains, "Think of a language as the contour of a watershed, stopping flow in certain directions, channeling it into others. Language controls the mechanism of your mind. When people speak different languages, their minds work differently and they act differently" (p. 46). He continues with an example that explores the relationship between an extremely irregular language and the anarchic society which uses it:

You know of the planet Vale? . . . They are complete anarchists. Now if we examine the speech of Vale we find, if not a reason for the behavior, at least a parallelism. Language on Vale is personal improvisation, with the fewest possible conventions. Each individual selects a speech as you or I might choose the color of our garments. . . . They live to complete spontaneity—in clothes, in conduct, in language. The question arises: does the language provoke or merely reflect the eccentricity? (P. 46)

The question is answered in favor of the dominance of the language when the wizard sets forth his plan for ending the foreign dominance of Pao.

Realizing that the Paonese will never revolt while they speak their present tongue, the wizard proposes that three new languages be designed, and groups of children be trained up speaking the languages in kibbutzim isolated from the influences of the rest of the culture. The first language, called Valiant, "will be based on the contrast and comparison of strength, with a grammar simple and direct. . . . The syllabary will be rich in effort-producing gutturals and hard vowels. A number of key ideas will be synonymous; such as *pleasure* and *overcoming a resistance—relaxation* and *shame—outworlder* and *rival*" (pp. 56–57). From this group will come the soldiers, and, as the wizard predicts, "Even the clans of Batmarsh will seem mild compared to the future Paonese military" (p. 57).

A second language, Technicant, is designed to stimulate industry. Its grammar "will be extravagantly complicated but altogether consistent and logical. The vocables would be discrete but joined and fitted by elaborate rules of accordance. What is the result? When a group of people, impregnated with these stimuli, are presented with supplies and facilities, industrial development is inevitable" (p. 57).

A third language, Cogitant, is designed as a language for traders and salesmen, "a symmetrical language with emphatic number-parsing, elaborate honorifics to teach hypocrisy, a vocabulary rich in homophones to facilitate ambiguity, a syntax of reflection, reinforcement and alternation to emphasize the analogous interchange of human affairs" (p. 57). Palafox does not expect the languages to control each speaker like a robot, only to urge the speaker in the desired direction. "All these languages will make use of semantic assistance. To the military segment, a 'successful man' will be synonymous with 'winner of a fierce contest.' To the industrialists, it will mean 'efficient fabricator.' To the traders, it equates with 'a person irresistibly persuasive.' Such influences will pervade each of the languages. Naturally they will not act with equal force upon each individual, but the mass action must be decisive" (p. 57).

The third language, Cogitant, is actually the language of Breakness, which the wizard intends to use to achieve his own purposes on Pao. Eventually, the young Paonese to be trained in Cogitant are not left on Pao like the other two groups, but are transported to Breakness, to the Institute of Comparative Cultures, where they receive indoctrination in Whorfian principles:

> Language determines the pattern of thought, the sequence in which various types of reactions follow acts.
> No language is neutral. All languages contribute impulse to the mass mind, some more vigorously than others. I repeat, we know of no "neutral" language—and there is no "best" or "optimum" language, although Language A may be more suitable for Context X than Language B.
> In an even wider frame of reference, we note that every language imposes a certain world-view upon the mind. What is the "true" world-picture? First, there is no reason to believe that a "true" world-picture, if it existed, would be a valuable or advantageous tool. Second, there is no standard to define the "true" world-picture. "Truth" is contained in the preconceptions of him who seeks to define it. Any organization of ideas whatever presupposes a judgment on the world. (P. 81)

Many of these phrases would not be out of place in the writings of Whorf himself. Perhaps the denial of any true perception of reality goes against what Whorf believed; he seemed committed to the view that an accurate perception was at least possible, even though existing languages might obscure it. But it must be remembered that in the novel, the Dominies of Breakness are absolute, self-serving egotists (a philosophy which *their* language encourages).

To further his schemes, Palafox has rescued and tutored the old emperor's son, Beran; after the young man is educated, he returns to Pao and rather easily ousts the usurper. Shortly thereafter, Palafox's languages prove their value when the Paonese throw off their foreign subjugation, and the wizard now believes he has the capable tools of a vigorous people and a pliant emperor. But now the Whorf hypothesis is turned against Palafox himself; his flaw has been to allow Beran to be trained as one of the interpreter class, the young Paonese for whom Cogitant was designed.

On their own initiative, these interpreters have created still another language, more in a spirit of play than anything else. This tongue, a pidgin they name Pastiche, combines elements from Breakness, Valiant, Technicant, and several other languages. Pastiche becomes "the language of service," and its speakers, Beran among them, remain free agents because they can compare and contrast the world-views provided by all the languages at their command. Beran liberates Pao from the threat of dominance by Palafox, and by the end of the novel Beran succeeds in the final aim: although the military believe they have seized power, they agree to reunite the Paonese in a single language community, and this time the language will be Pastiche.

As M. J. E. Barnes has observed about this remarkable book, the scope of *The Languages of Pao* "is larger than single words or single sentences, the theme is linguistics."[23] If "hard" science fiction means the rigorous working out in fiction of a scientific theory, if it is an extrapolation from what is known that in no way violates our understanding of what we know, then Vance's novel is science fiction as hard as anything written by Heinlein or Clement. Yet the novel's central theory concerns language, the most human of skills, so the characters never disappear behind the gadgetry. Nor does Vance propagandize in the book, but its message is clear: the characters who suffer are those whose world-view is limited. Even this underlying warning reflects the ideas of Whorf, whose theory, according to Peter C. Rollins, was an "aggressive critique of the unacknowledged (and therefore dangerous) limitations of the world picture generated by Western science and technology."[24] The only notes characteristic of Whorf not to be found in Vance's novel are Whorf's somewhat mystical feelings about ultimate reality, shown most clearly by the linguist's later interest in Theosophy, and Whorf's Rousseau-like admiration for nontechnological cultures.

Benjamin Lee Whorf finally resists classification. One could well argue that he was better received by artists than by other linguists, who, while agreeing that language influences perception and thought, saw overstatement and inaccuracies in Whorf's arguments. Whorf was out of step as well with the behaviorist bias of American linguistics of the thirties and forties. One cannot imagine an "anti-mentalist" like Leonard Bloomfield at a Theosophy gathering. But the spirit of Whorf's work, if not the letter, was in keeping with the art of the era. Rollins clearly shows that Whorf, concerned with the systems of perception underlying non-Western tongues, sought a reality behind the veil of language: Whorf saw an enormous difference between the isolating and alienating prayer of modern Western man and the "transcendental unification of the private spirit with forces of the universe" of the religious Hopi.[25] And this attitude places Whorf in a category well-peopled by modern writers of both mainstream works (D. H. Lawrence's fascination with the Hopi comes to mind) and science fiction (compare Aldous Huxley, or the writer of a work to be discussed later, Ian Watson).

Tolkien and Whorf, both linguists, show the breadth of the discipline: one is British, the other American; one's evidence comes from history, the other's from anthropology; one begins with lexicography, the other with field work with informants. That both share a field of study demonstrates clearly that human language is a vast and in many ways mysterious subject. And that the ideas of both find a home in science fiction shows how the genre can accommodate that vast and mysterious topic.

11

A History of Linguistics
in Science Fiction: II

In 1933 Alfred Korzybski's *Science and Sanity: An Introduction to Non-Aristotelian Systems and General Semantics*[1] was published, a book whose impact on science fiction was widespread in the forties and fifties, and continues to a lesser extent today. Korzybski was a Polish aristocrat and army officer who emigrated to the United States some years after the First World War; as the founder of General Semantics, he had an influence which is sometimes difficult to distinguish from that of Whorf.

At first glance, General Semantics might seem somewhat out of place in a book on the impact of linguistics in science fiction. To begin with, General Semantics has no relation to the semantics that is a branch of linguistics. In fact, according to its believers, General Semantics includes linguistics; but then, in their opinion, General Semantics includes every part of human thought. Still, the principles of the system lead its adherents to comment frequently on human language, and to find linguistic answers to human problems; these two proclivities alone warrant the consideration of General Semantics here.

And there is a second justification for dealing with the subject: through an examination of how science fiction manifests the subject, we can learn something about the use of science generally in the field.

One may think of General Semantics as a system of thought, or a mental discipline. It seems undeniable that Korzbyski had good intentions, and his work certainly contains some points that anyone would be well advised to keep in mind, but the overall air of *Science and Sanity* is one of such quackery that one wonders how it could have ever been taken seriously. Here, however, we need only puzzle over the simpler problem of why it became popular in science fiction, and the reasons for that, I believe, are three: it was promoted by John W. Campbell, Jr.; it was popularized by widely read authors; and it was a subject uniquely suited to science fiction.

During the period of *Astounding's* domination of the magazine market, the first of these causes almost entailed the second: if Campbell was taken with an idea, he would find an author to fictionalize it; in many an issue of *Astounding*, the editorial and the stories move in counterpoint. And General Semantics had a considerable influence on John W. Campbell, Jr., according to Reginald Bretnor, himself one of the greatest admirers of Korzybski among present writers and editors.[2] One of the first fruits of that influence was A. E. van Vogt's *The World of Null-A*, first published as a serial in *Astounding* (1945) and much revised for book publication in 1948.[3] The mutual admiration of author and editor is shown by the novel's dedication to Campbell, and the editor's blurb, printed on the cover of the Berkley paperback, "one of those once-in-a-decade classics," complete with exclamation point.

Van Vogt has his own problems as a writer, some of which are mentioned elsewhere in this book, but in all fairness, many of the difficulties of *The World of Null-A* are directly traceable to its author's close attention to Korzybski's *Science and Sanity*.

For example, according to General Semantics, the only object of knowledge is structure—when the structure of the brain corresponds to the structure of space-time events in the world, true knowledge is attained. Van Vogt goes by the book when his amnesiac hero is asked if he had been served a meal aboard a plane he recalls having been on: "Gosseyn took his time remembering. It was an intensional world into which he strove to penetrate and as nonexistent as all such worlds. Memory never was the thing remembered, but at least with most people, when there was a memory, there normally *had* been a fact of similar structure. His mind held nothing that could be related to physical structure. He hadn't eaten, definitely and unequivocally" (p. 36). General Semantics is in part designed to dissuade people from making snap judgments on important questions, and in van Vogt's world, on trivial ones as well. If the picture of a man deep in contemplation over whether he has had lunch seems witless, it is nevertheless drawn by van Vogt in strict adherence to General Semantics.

Examples of the close association of book and novel abound: if you are trained in General Semantics, as is the hero of *The World of Null-A*, that training will give you "strong . . . muscles . . . temporarily cut off from the fatigue center of the brain" (p. 54), "full control of the resonance chambers in [one's] body and head" (p. 106), and a characteristic "firmness of . . . jaw" (p. 135). These fictional claims are no more ludicrous than those Korzybski made when he asserted that General Semantics would eliminate psychosomatic illnesses, among which he numbered varieties of sexual dysfunction, heart, respiratory, and digestive problems, arthritis, alcoholism, and tooth decay (p. vii).

In Korzybski's view, these and similar causes of human misery are produced by a conflict between the structure of our brains and the structure of the world. He believed that the language we speak produces actual physical changes in the brain; if our language segments reality in false ways, brain damage ("sub-microscopic colloidal lesions," p. 20) results. If language is restructured in such a way that its form reflects the structure of reality, then the brain will be brought into accord with reality, and all manner of good things will result. This was the central justification of the General Semantics system, and its chief instrument was to be a reworking of language.

That reworking of language was soon to be illustrated by the other thoroughbred in *Astounding*'s stable, Robert A. Heinlein. The proselytizing of Heinlein must have taken place early: in July of 1941 he was the guest of honor at the third annual World Science Fiction Convention in Denver. In his speech at the convention, he labelled *Science and Sanity* the most important book on the list of works he wished everyone could read, mentioned that he had seen Korzybski lecture, and recommended the Semantics conference to be held later that year in Denver.[4]

It was as a true believer of some standing, then, that Heinlein wrote "Gulf," a story that appeared in *Astounding* in November and December of 1949. In the story, a race of mutated supermen entirely jettison English because "one can think logically in English only by extreme effort, care, so bad is it as a mental tool. For example, the verb 'to be' in English has twenty-one distinct meanings, *every single one of which is false-to-fact*" (Part 2, p. 66; Heinlein's italics). Heinlein is improving on the master here, since Korzybski had contented himself with four meanings, only one of which he instructed his disciples to abjure, the so-called "is of identity," appearing in sentences like "Harold Robbins is a successful writer." For the supermen of "Gulf," *Science and Sanity* is a "monumental work," and their newly invented language will follow its precepts to achieve only true-to-fact statements, presumably. The invented language, "Speedtalk," is similar to Pohl and Williamson's Mechanese, described in chapter 3:

> Speedtalk was a structurally different speech from any the race had ever used. Long before, Ogden and Richards had shown that eight hundred and fifty words were sufficient vocabulary to express anything that could be expressed by "normal" human vocabularies, with the aid of a handful of special words—a hundred odd—for each special field, such as horse racing or ballistics. About the same time phoneticians had analyzed all human tongues into about a hundred-odd sounds, represented by the letters of a general phonetic alphabet.
>
> On these two propositions Speedtalk was based.
>
> To be sure, the phonetic alphabet was much less in number than the words in Basic English. But sounds represented by letters in the phonetic alphabet were each capable of variation several different ways—length, stress, pitch, rising, falling, et cetera. . . . There was no limit to variations but, without much refinement of accepted phonetic practice, it was possible to establish a one-to-one relationship with Basic English so that *one phonetic symbol* was equivalent to an entire word in a "normal" language; one Speedtalk word was equal to an entire sentence. (Part 2, pp. 65–66)

Of course, there are those technical vocabularies to contend with. Speedtalk accommodates them by reserving "sixty of the thousand-odd phonetic letters" usually employed for the digits ("New Men numbered to the base sixty"). When these "numbers" are prefixed by a special character that shows they are being used as words, "a pool of two hundred fifteen thousand nine hundred ninety-nine words—one less than the cube of sixty—was available for specialized meaning, without using more than four letters including the indicator. Most of them could be pronounced as one syllable. These had not the stark simplicity of basic Speedtalk; nevertheless words such as 'ichthyophagous' and 'constitutionality' were thus compressed to monosyllables" (Part 2, p. 68).

The omniscient narrator credits Korzybski as the spiritual father of Speedtalk: "Even before War II, Alfred Korzybski had shown that human thought was performed, when done efficiently, only in symbols; . . . Speedtalk did not merely speed up communication—by its structures it made thought more logical; by its economy it made thought processes enormously faster, since it takes almost as long to *think* a word as to speak it" (Part 2, p. 69).

There are two curious fallacies here, but both of them seem to me to originate with Heinlein, not Korzybski. First, it is obviously not true that it takes almost as long to think a word as to speak it—compare the speed of reading aloud with that of reading silently. Second, what possible advantage would there be to having a word like *constitutionality* be composed of one syllable? The assertion of improvement is pure efficiency expert—if something is done faster, it's done better. But the seven syllables of the word do more than take up time: the last two show the grammatical relation of the word to others like *reality, plurality, tonality,* in short, all those nouns formed from adjectives. The next syllable from the end, *-al-*, is the suffix that forms adjectives from nouns, for instance, *personal, elemental, regimental,* and so on. The next syllable forms nouns from verbs, the *-tion* of *hesitation, creation, persecution,* etc. In English, if one knows the word *constitute,* one also knows that the addition of common suffixes will produce *constitution, constitutional,* and *constitutionality.* The relationship between all of these related words (and a host of similar sets of words) would be lost in Speedtalk if, say, "constitute" is *pwn* but "constitutional" is *bbs.*

Of course, you may ask, why derive nouns from verbs and vice versa? Speedtalk does not have nouns and verbs, and for this Korzybski is clearly the inspiration: "The world—the continuum known to science and including all human activity—does not contain 'noun things' and 'verb things'; it contains space-time events and relationships between them" (Part 2, p. 66). If Speedtalk draws no distinction between nouns and verbs, it presumably draws none between adjectives—words that modify nouns— and adverbs—words that modify verbs. He bears a considerable burden of proof who claims that a language of several hundred thousand words divided into only two groups, heads and modifiers, is an improvement on any natural language.

Many writers bought General Semantics without qualification in the forties, and Korzybski's name frequently turned up in august company. A character in the future world of Henry Kuttner's *Fury* (1947 as Lawrence O'Donnell) traces the progress of logic through "Plato and Aristotle and Bacon and Korzybski and the truth machines" (p. 20). And Korzybski's influence continued, though diminished: Poul Anderson's *Brain Wave* (1954) has a psychiatrist recommend General Semantics to a neurotic patient (p. 114). By now some of Korzybski's terms are part of the common store of science-fictional ideas, yet his influence can be seen in Alexei Panshin's 1968 critical study that uses a time-index of Korzybski's devising in referring to "Heinlein $_{1939}$," [5] or in John Varley's borrowing of Korzybski's characterization of man as "a time-binding species" ("Overdrawn at the Memory Bank," 1976; rpt. D. A. Wollheim and A. W. Saha, eds., *1977 Annual World's Best SF*, p. 41).

Science fiction is a small field, but within a field it is unlikely that any system of thought ever had promoters of such dominance as Campbell, van Vogt, and Heinlein were in science fiction in the forties.

There is a third reason, too, for the success of General Semantics in science fiction—its special suitability for the field. My guide here is Norman Spinrad's essay "Rubber Sciences," in Reginald Bretnor's *The Craft of Science Fiction* (Harper & Row, 1976). Spinrad argues that the subject matter best suited for science fiction is not real science, but what he calls "rubber science"—something that sounds plausible and follows certain rules. He illustrates the idea with L. Ron Hubbard's Dianetics, but an equally good example is furnished by General Semantics. To qualify as a rubber science a subject must have suitable rewards for its acquisition, but it must not demand a lifetime's work, or even a decade of mature study: heroes of adventure novels are seldom middle-aged, let alone old folks. General Semantics qualifies here: Korzybski says of his subject that "when all is said and done, and the important semantic factors discovered, the whole issue becomes extremely simple, and easily applied, even by persons without much education" (p. 29). And the reward is great: "The full acquisition of the new s[emantic] r[eactions] requires special training; but when acquired, it solves for a given individual, without any outside interference, all important human problems I know of. It imparts to him some of the s[emantic] r[eactions] of so-called 'genius,' and thus enlarges his so-called 'intelligence'" (p. 30).

Rule six of Spinrad's rubber sciences focuses on the vocabulary of the field. Jargon is necessary, since "fiction, after all, is word magic, and a well-crafted system of magic words in itself has a certain intrinsic reality" (p. 61). The terminology of General Semantics is specialized, thereby providing the in-group recognition signals that all jargon supplies, and it springs from a very few rules. For example, the phrase "false to fact" serves as one such identifying term: Korzybski writes, "As we discover that 'identity' is invariably false to facts, this A[ristotelian] postulate must be rejected from any future non-A[ristotelian] system" (p. 146). Hence we find "false-to-fact" in the quotation above from Heinlein's "Gulf," or Bretnor's "the

languages we use in daily intercourse . . . perpetuate false-to-fact concepts"[6] and "mathematics . . . describe natural processes and relationships far more accurately than those often false-to-fact accretions that
constitute everyday speech."[7]

A sample rule from General Semantics is "a map *is not* the territory,"
which is often used metaphorically to mean "words are not the things they
represent."[8] When the hero of *The World of Null-A* believes himself to be
suffering from amnesia, he regains his composure by reciting these man-
tras: "Behind that conscious integration were thousands of hours of personal training. Behind the training was the non-Aristotelian technique of
automatic extensional thinking, the unique development of the twentieth
century which, after four hundred years, had become the dynamic philosophy of the human race. 'The map is not the territory. . . . The word is not
the thing itself'" (p. 20). A character in Philip K. Dick's *The Three Stigmata
of Palmer Eldritch* (1965) achieves an insight when he connects the map
idea with the rejection of the "is of identity": "If the map is not the territory,
the pot is not the potter. So don't talk ontology, Barney; don't say *is*" (p.
262).

Norman Spinrad's "Rubber Sciences" notes that "'New Science' is so
identified in people's minds with 'inventions' that you almost can't have
one without the other." Hence, his seventh rule is "solidify your pseudo-
science with believable hardware" (p. 62). In *Science and Sanity*, the invention is the Semantic Differential, which looks like an assembly of Ritz
and Saltine crackers, connected by wet spaghetti. Its function is to symbolize that words are not things. And its use gives you the benefits of learning a foreign language without any of the work: "a learned polyglot, or a
scholar, utilizes many nerve centres in co-ordination. In the older days,
unless one became a scholar of some sort, it was extremely difficult to train
these nerve centres in co-ordination. With the Differential we can train
simply, and comparatively quickly, all necessary nerve centres, and so im-
part to children and to practically illiterate persons the cultural results of
prolonged and difficult university training without any complicated technique" (*Science and Sanity*, p. 475). These results were to be achieved by
gazing at and fondling the Semantic Differential while contemplating difficult problems.

For some people, General Semantics turned out not to replace a college
education, but to form a part of it, thereby becoming the Transcendental

Meditation of the forties and early fifties. Van Vogt was not shy about taking responsibility for its intrusion into the halls of ivy; looking back to the publication of *The World of Null-A* from the vantage point of 1969, he says, "Today, General Semantics, then a faltering science, is taught in hundreds of universities" (p. 5). Perhaps "hundreds of universities" is an exaggeration—the fad crested in the fifties—but what academic success the subject had is due not to Korzybski or van Vogt but to S. I. Hayakawa, whose text, *Language in Thought and Action*, moved General Semantics from an unusable dogma to the more modest level of good advice. Probably a score of science-fiction writers have read *Language in Thought and Action* for every one who has struggled through *Science and Sanity*. Hayakawa's work leaves rubber science behind and forms a bridge to the most linguistically ambitious current writer, Samuel R. Delany, and his most linguistically interesting work, *Babel-17*.[9]

At first glance, it might seem that Delany borrowed at least some examples from *Science and Sanity*: Korzybski cites a paradox by Frege on page xxxiv, a paradox which turns up in *Babel-17* on page 151. But more probably Hayakawa has been an intermediary: on page 23 of *Language in Thought and Action* he speculates about the reaction of chimpanzees to symbols, and Delany's *Babel-17* incorporates the same material on page 154.

But General Semantics, despite these influences, is not the central theme of *Babel-17*—Whorfian ideas are far more important: as Robert Scholes writes in his introduction to the Gregg Press edition, the novel "begins with an epigraph from the semanticist Mario Pei: 'Nowhere is civilization so perfectly mirrored as in speech. If our knowledge of speech, or the speech itself, is not yet perfect, neither is civilization.' But it might just as well have begun with Ludwig Wittgenstein's notion that our language is the limit of our world, or the Whorfian linguistic hypothesis that language shapes perception itself, so that people from different cultures actually 'see' different worlds around them" (p. vi).[10]

Babel-17 was instantly successful; it received the Nebula Award for 1966, and the reviewers praised it highly. P. Schuyler Miller, writing in the December 1967 issue of *Analog*, said that Delany, "by making the strangely powerful language of the title the key that unlocks the doors leading into the heart of the cosmos, made painfully clear how trivial and superficial a use of semantics A. E. van Vogt really made in his classic of *Astounding*'s great years, 'World of Null-A'" (p. 164).

Babel-17 is a novel to test the strength of a critic's principles. The book is richly inventive, well written, and demonstrates the author's grasp of important generalities about language. Unfortunately, it is also wrong in many details. The novel concerns the adventures of Rydra Wong, foremost poet of her age, who has been asked by the military to decode some transmissions they have been intercepting. The task is urgent, since the transmissions coincide with a series of sabotages. In an interview with a general, she attempts to explain the difference between significant and nonsignificant variations in sound, the phoneme-allophone distinction that Chad Oliver dealt with in *The Winds of Time*, discussed in chapter 6. Delany has his heroine say:

> "You know the way some Orientals confuse the sounds of R and L when they speak a Western language? That's because R and L in many Eastern languages are allophones, that is, considered the same sound, written and even heard the same—just like the *th* at the beginning of *they* and at the beginning of *theater*."
>
> "What's different about the sound of *theater* and *they*?" [asks the general.]
>
> "Say them again and listen. One's voiced and the other's unvoiced, they're as distinct as V and F; only they're allophones in English and you're used to hearing them as if they were the same phoneme." (P. 15)

Not a bad discussion, except that the sounds at the beginning of *theater* and *they* are indeed separate phonemes, not allophones, in English. And this point is elementary and uncontroversial: Delany is just wrong here.

Technical terms are used throughout the novel without reflection on their meaning: for example, a character has had the structure of his mouth altered and the change affects his speech. We are told his "mouth, distended through cosmetisurgically implanted fangs, could not deal with a plosive labial unless it was voiced" (p. 33). He cannot make the sound *p*, and his speech is consequently distorted: instead of "They were a real close triple, Captain," Delany's character says "They were a real close tri'le, Ca'tain." The plosive labials are *b* and *p*; the position of the lips is exactly the same for each, yet the character can make the sound *b* but not *p*. The explanation of this difference makes no sense: *voiced* means that the vocal cords are vibrating in the articulation of the sound. What kind of fangs would affect the vocal cords? But assume that they do interfere in some way: the interference should hinder some muscular action (such as the vibration of the vocal cords), not hinder the *absence* of the action. Conceivably, some damage to the vocal cords could keep someone from producing voiced sounds, but a change in the lips that requires one sound and only one sound to be voiced is unheard of in experience, and what is worse, doubtful in logic.

Some of the problems of the novel were apparently caught and corrected in the changes made for the 1969 edition: in the Ace paperback of 1966 a passage reads: "'Jebel!' The word took forever to slide back and forth from postdental through labial stop and back to palatal fricative, beside the sounds that danced through her brain now" (p. 129). Perhaps because *j* is not a postdental stop nor *l* a palatal fricative, Delany revised the passage to read: "'Tarik!' The word took forever to slide from postdental, to palital [*sic*] stop, beside the sounds that danced through her brain now" (p. 94).

The uninformed reader of *Babel-17* receives misinformation about American Indian languages, English vowels, the effect of first-language speech patterns on second languages, the distinction between specific and general, and computer languages. Robert Scholes, in the introduction cited above, says that ideas like the Whorf hypothesis "function powerfully in *Babel-17*, as they did in a cruder way in Jack Vance's pioneering *The Languages of Pao*" (p. vi). To be sure, *Babel-17* is more ambitious than *The Languages of Pao*, but Delany's work is inaccurate at almost every turn, while Vance's novel carefully avoids promoting misconceptions.

Babel-17 is like a building of magnificent design, marred throughout by substandard materials. Most passers-by will be impressed by the architecture and never realize that the lights don't work and the plumbing leaks. But let us step back from our examination of the details and attend to the design ourselves.

The design of the novel dates from the 1930s: the ground plan is Whorfian. In the last chapter we saw a character of Robert Zelazny's confuse the gender of nouns with sex; Rydra Wong, Delany's heroine, falls into the same mistake in her musings: "Imagine, in Spanish having to assign a sex to every object: dog, table, tree, can-opener. Imagine, in Hungarian, not being able to assign sex to anything: *he, she, it* all the same word" (p. 81).

But the important observation to be made here concerns Delany's use of words like "having to" and "not being able to," suggesting that languages compel their speakers to think in certain ways, a suggestion that derives straight from the Whorf-Sapir hypothesis. And Delany hammers the point through the words of his character: "If you don't know the words, you can't know the ideas" (p. 110).

Delany finds some brilliant ways to illustrate this questionable idea. The Invaders, the villains of the story, have invented Babel-17 as a means of compelling their agent to carry out the sabotages referred to at the beginning. The agent, a man named Butcher, is a high-ranking captive who has had his memory destroyed, and has been retrained to think in Babel-17. The language lacks a first person singular pronoun, and this omission, as Rydra Wong points out, blinds him "to the fact that while [the language is] a highly useful way to look at things, it isn't the only way" (p. 215). She explains, "Babel-17 as a language contains a pre-set program for the Butcher to become a criminal and saboteur. If you turn somebody with no memory loose in a foreign country with only the words for tools and machine parts, don't be surprised if he ends up a mechanic. By manipulating his vocabulary properly you could just as easily make him a sailor, or an artist" (p. 215). Vance's *The Languages of Pao* is far superior on this point. Vance realized (as the wizards in his novel state) that any Whorfian linguistic influence would work on the mass of people, not on individuals. But in *Babel-17* this point is disregarded. Despite this flaw, the passage wherein Rydra Wong teaches the Butcher the use of personal pronouns is one of the cleverest pieces of writing in science fiction. She begins to instruct him in the importance of the individual by asking him to recall that a special form of the verb *to be* is used with *I*:

> After a while he asked, "What is *I*?"
> She grinned. "First of all it's very important. A good deal more important than anything else. The brain will let any number of things go to pot as long as 'I' stays alive. That's because the brain is part of I. A book is, a ship is, Tarik is, the universe is, but, as you must have noticed, I am." (P. 112)

The Butcher volunteers that *you* must be important, too, because English uses *you are*. She says, "Sometimes you frighten me," and he notices the relation between *I* and *me*. But when he speaks again, he uses the pronouns as if they were proper names:

"I and me," the Butcher said. "Only a morphological distinction, yes? The
brain figure that out before. Why does you [i.e., Butcher] frighten me [i.e.,
Wong] sometimes?" (P. 113)

The conversation continues in this way for a page, as the developing love
between the two characters becomes clear. Finally, the Butcher says,

"You will kill anyone that tries to hurt me, kill them a lot worse than you
ever killed anyone before."
"But you don't have to—"
"You will kill all of Jebel if it tries to take you and I apart and keep us alone."
"Oh, Butcher—" She turned from him and put her fist against her mouth.
"One hell of a teacher I am! You don't understand a thing—I—*I* am talking
about."
The voice, astonished and slow: "I don't understand you, you think."
. . . .
"Then listen. Right now we've met each other halfway. I haven't really
taught you about *I* and *you*. We've made up our own language, and that's
what we're talking now."
"But—"
"Look, every time you've said *you* in the last ten minutes, you should have
said *I*. Every time you've said *I*, you meant *you*." (Pp. 115–16)

After a little more, he catches on, and from a mechanical instrument of the
Invaders he becomes an independent human being again.

This description fails to do justice to either the multiplicity of Delany's
errors or the range and depth of his interest in linguistics. The book is not as
good a novel as *The Languages of Pao*, but it could have been much, much
better. The errors, after all, lie mostly in matters peripheral to the subject,
and could be removed in a revision; and the interests of the author touch
on semantics, poetics, body language, in short, the whole spectrum of
communications, a fact Robert Scholes points out in his introduction.

Considering all his work, Delany is the most adventurous and thoughtful
writer now concerning himself with human communication. From the syntactic innovation of the dialect in *Nova* through the codes of "Time Considered as a Helix of Semi-Precious Stones" and *Babel-17* he has paid
attention to problems that often do not even occur to other writers. In *The
Ballad of Beta-2* (1965) and *The Einstein Intersection* (1967) he explores,
among other things, the transmission of information through time, its

change and distortion, and its occasional reconstruction. In his more recent novels, however, although he continues his interest in language, he
has left the confines of the Whorf hypothesis behind. Foremost among
these more experimental works is *Triton* (1976).

Triton is a storehouse of linguistic themes, but not one packed with the
detail of description and observation over which Delany stumbled so badly
in *Babel-17*. His interest in *Triton* is semantics, not the Korzybskian kind,
but that which is included in the philosophy of language. A quotation
heads each of the seven chapters in the novel, and among the authors cited
are the linguistic philosophers Ludwig Wittgenstein and W. V. O. Quine.
The most useful quotation critically, though, is an epigraph that heads Appendix B; Delany quotes from Michel Foucault's *The Order of Things*:

> *Utopias* afford consolation: although they have no real locality there is never-
> theless a fantastic, untroubled region in which they are able to unfold; they
> open up cities with vast avenues, superbly planted gardens, countries where
> life is easy, even though the road to them is chimerical. *Heterotopias* are
> disturbing, probably because they . . . make it impossible to name this *and*
> that, because they shatter or tangle common names, because they destroy
> "syntax" in advance, and not only the syntax with which we construct sen-
> tences but also that less apparent syntax which causes words and things (next
> to and also opposite one another) to "hold together." This is why utopias
> permit fables and discourse: they run with the very grain of language and are
> part of the fundamental *fabula*; heterotopias . . . desiccate speech, stop words
> in their tracks, contest the very possibility of grammar at its source; they dis-
> solve our myths and sterilize the lyricism of our sentences.[11]

Whether Foucault's influence was good for Delany's art is doubtful:
George Steiner says *The Order of Things* produces, on first reading, "an
almost intolerable sense of verbosity, arrogance, and obscure platitude,"[12]
and his was one of the kinder reviews. Similarly, *Triton*'s reviewers in the
science-fiction magazines found little to praise in the novel.[13] But the influence is there: *Triton* qualifies under Foucault's definition of a heterotopia.

Particularly interesting are Foucault's remarks on speech when *Triton* is
read as a concrete embodiment of them. Some incidental characters in the
novel use language in a way that strips words of their meanings: a religious
group, "The Poor Children of the Avestal Light and Changing Secret
Name," requires its members to recite a mantra of syllables without sense
that nonetheless must be mumbled in a precise order—"Mimimomomi-

zolalilamialomuelamironoriminos."[14] These spear-carriers make a religion of the chief problem of the central character, Bron Helstrom, who had formerly been one of their number; in the words of Foucault, Helstrom's mind is sick: it "continues to infinity, creating groups then dispersing them again, heaping up diverse similarities, destroying those that seem clearest, splitting up things that are identical, superimposing different criteria, frenziedly beginning all over again, becoming more and more disturbed, and teetering finally on the brink of anxiety" (*The Order of Things*, p. xviii).

The syntax of "things" is disturbed in *Triton*: characters can change their size or sex without much difficulty; hence first names have become no more reliable an index of gender than last names are of family descent. To be sure, sexist and racist terms have disappeared from the speech of the characters in the novel, but only because of massive losses in the general use of language. People in that future age think of language, not as rising out of the nature of things, nor as a transparent medium through which reality can be seen and by which it can be classified, but as a realm of its own, a realm whose relation to reality is often tenuous, accidental, or altogether absent. Not only the common names that Foucault mentions, but proper names as well, are "shattered or tangled" in a novel in which The Spike is a woman and Flossie is a man.

The "syntax with which we construct sentences" can never be completely destroyed, of course, or nothing remains of the work as prose fiction, but Delany, in what are perhaps unhappy choices, frequently interrupts and distorts the grammar of his narrative. The reader must often reread the words, parsing as he goes; for example: "No, only the (he stumbled on lengths of plastistrut, broken styroplate, and crumbling foam) wall of the building beside him had fallen" (pp. 232–33).

Delany impresses one with the breadth of his interests and the courage of his attempts. If his recent work has not satisfied everyone, he nevertheless has ventured into fields new to science fiction. If he continues to explore the work of linguistic philosophers as an aid to his fiction, one can hope he will turn for theoretical support from the "verbosity and platitudes" of Foucault to the lucidity of Quine or Austin.

Yet it is Foucault who provides the thread that leads us to the next name in our history of linguistics in science fiction. That name is Noam Chomsky. Foucault sees the seventeenth century as the starting-point for dramatic changes in biology, economics, and linguistics. He notes specifically the

Port Royal grammarians, thinkers such as Arnauld and Cordemoy, the same theorists in whose work Chomsky saw the beginnings of transformational grammar.[15]

About ten years intervened between the statements of the principles of descriptive linguistics in the works of men like Leonard Bloomfield and the first appearance of those principles in science fiction. It has taken somewhat longer than that for transformational approaches to grammar to show up. The reasons for this lag are not clear—perhaps it has something to do with the formidable jargon of the newer theories—but whatever the cause, the first hint American readers saw of Chomsky's influence in science fiction came in John Brunner's novel *Total Eclipse* (1974), when a character says, "It's been shown that all human languages have a fundamentally identical structure—" and is immediately interrupted by his companion, who says "*What?*" (p. 86). But Chomsky's influence really burst forth in Ian Watson's *The Embedding*,[16] in which the reader can sink without a trace unless he has some understanding of terms like Universal Grammar, self-embedding, and recursion.

Beginning in 1955, the lectures and publications of Noam Chomsky, a professor of linguistics at MIT, have generated a new and radically different way of looking at language, a way that has revolutionized the study of grammar. And this claim is not inflated, even today when the word "revolution" is intemperately applied to the most trivial of changes. Chomsky began by considering two facts about language so commonplace that they frequently escape notice: first, that the acquisition of language is universal —unless there is some pathological condition or physical damage, every human being learns a language under the most chancy of circumstances; and second, that language use is creative—every day we both produce and understand sentences that are entirely new to us, and hence not explicable in terms of memory. To account for these facts and others like them, Chomsky and a growing number of linguists developed a subject popularly termed transformational grammar. That subject encompasses a number of approaches that differ from one another to a greater or lesser extent, but we need not worry about the details of the various theories here; rather, we will examine the impact on science fiction of transformational explanations of the two facts about language stated above, that everyone learns a language and that language use is creative.

The transformationalist posits that humans have a genetically transmitted ability to formulate a grammar from the data available to them in their infancy and childhood. Humans devise that grammar in such a way that their speech will conform to their analysis of the language of the community in which they find themselves. The variety of transformational grammar that Chomsky and some others espouse assumes that the grammar the child devises will have a form predetermined by the limits of our species, and that the discovery of that form can be made empirically. Thus the first fact is explained: humans learn languages because their minds are "programmed" to do so. Stated as such, the explanation has no evidence to support it, nor is it clear how direct evidence would be obtained—we just do not know enough about how the brain processes and stores information, whether that information be acquired or received as part of the genetic inheritance. Nor does the bare statement tell us anything about the form of what is inherited. At present, that form must be judged by highly inferential means: the grammarian looks at what is acceptable or unacceptable in given human languages and erects hypotheses about what is possible or impossible in all human languages from those observations.

The grammarian frequently proceeds by making the strongest possible claim and attempting to disprove it. At present that claim might go something like this: human beings are genetically equipped to intuitively perceive certain grammatical categories and to order them in specific ways by means of a small number of highly restricted rules. Those rules produce sequences of the grammatical categories (something like "proto-sentences"). These sequences are then fed through a second set of rules that adds, removes, or rearranges their components (these rules, the transformations, give the grammar its name). The result is a sentence in a specific language. The strongest claim would also maintain that the first set of rules is part of the programming, that it would be the same for any human language.

Obviously, that first set of rules must be highly abstract, but Watson's *The Embedding* outlines a procedure to gather information about it that is superior to any in use at present: at a secret research center in the novel, scientists are raising three groups of children from infancy. Each group is being taught an artificial language. As one of the scientists explains,

> Ever since Chomsky's pioneer work, we all assume that the plan for language is programmed into the brain at birth. The basic plan of language reflects our

biological awareness of the world that has evolved us, you see. So we're teaching three artificial languages as probes at the frontiers of mind. We want to find out what the raw, fresh mind of a child will accept as natural—or "real." . . . One language [tests] whether our idea of logic is "realistic"—
Or whether reality is logical. (P. 45)

The second language is taught to children raised in an environment filled with perceptual illusions, testing "what sort of tensions a language programmed to reflect them might set up in the raw human mind" (p. 46). The third language tests certain parts of the creative use of language, and will be discussed later. The most impressive thing about the experiment is its inhumanity: it subjects helpless children to the most severe kinds of stresses with no guarantee of their recovery if injured, or even their survival. The experiment is, however, of a piece with the novel's characterization of Westerners in general and Americans in particular. They are portrayed as one-dimensional villains throughout.

If the politics of *The Embedding* is nineteenth-century mythology, its linguistics is very current indeed. One of the characters gives a good summary of what I earlier called the strongest claim:

> You've got one level of information—that's the actual words we use, on the surface of the mind. The other permanent level, deep down, contains highly abstract concepts—idea associations linked together network-style. In between these two levels comes the mind's plan for making sentences out of ideas. This plan contains the rules of what we call Universal Grammar—we say it's universal, as this plan is part of the basic structure of mind and the same rules can translate ideas into any human language whatever— (P. 59)

Assuming this hypothesis to be true in outline if not in detail, would it have an effect on science fiction? George Steiner implies that it would have a profound effect:

> Despite their manifest diversity and mutual unintelligibility, all past, extant, and *conceivable* languages satisfy the same fixed set of deep, invariant, highly restrictive principles. The "wolf-child" imagined by natural philosophy or the hermit cut off by amnesia from all remembrance of former speech, will develop an idiom related to all other human tongues through a recognizable system of constraints and transformational rules. The human brain is so constructed that it cannot but do so. All grammars belong to a definable sub-class of the class of all transformational grammars, being the product of specific and

structured elements of innateness in man. A creature speaking a "language" not in this sub-class would, by definition, be non-human and we could not learn its "Martian" speech.[17]

Is human-alien communication, then, impossible? Not necessarily. For instance, some forms of muscular action are probably genetically acquired: we all learn how to walk. On the other hand, our genes do not carry the knowledge of how to play golf, yet some of us manage to play the game well. In the worst case, learning an alien language would be harder than learning a human language, and maybe only a relative few could master an alien tongue. Still, there is, in the transformational theory, no a priori reason to believe it would be impossible.

The second fact of human language that Chomsky noted, that language is creative, requires more explanation. "Creative" has a special meaning here: it means that we do not learn to speak a language by memorizing a finite set of sentences; speakers must be able to form sentences in response to an unpredictable, infinite set of real-world situations, and hearers must be able to understand these absolutely novel productions. These requirements demand that whatever grammar humans use, it must be one capable of producing an infinite number of sentences. To understand how this capacity is provided for, and to understand *The Embedding* as well, we must be aware of a few facts about transformational grammars.

A transformational grammar contains, among other things, a set of rules that "generate" or produce what may be thought of informally as preliminary sentence structures. A property called "recursiveness" is built into the rules, allowing them to operate again and again. Thus, the grammar can generate an uncomplicated sentence like this:

This is the dog.

But through the property of recursiveness, the rules provide for the generation of a sentence with the last noun modified by a relative clause:

This is the dog that worried the cat.

Or, still longer sentences:

This is the dog that worried the cat that killed the rat that ate, etc.

When the structure of the sentence above is displayed diagrammatically, the reason for the name of its type, "right-branching," is evident:

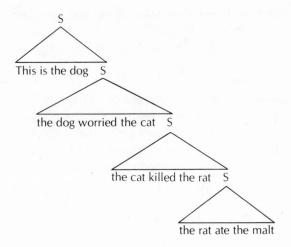

The symbol *S* in the diagram stands for "sentence"; it is the triggering element, allowing the rules to begin again, generating a new sentence beneath it. This same children's verse, by the way, is used in *The Embedding* to illustrate the process of recursion.

But right-branching structures are not the only kind of complex sentence English allows. In the sentence from "The House that Jack Built," the symbol *S* follows a noun that is last in its clause; if the symbol had followed a noun that was not final in its clause, a second kind of branching called "self-embedding" would have occurred:

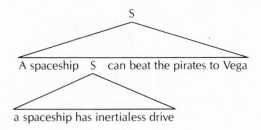

In this second diagram, the rules generated the symbol *S* following "space-ship," allowing a second sentence to be formed inside the first, or "embedded" within the first. Watson's novel takes its title from the capacity of a transformational grammar to produce embedded sentences. In the example sentence itself, the later operation of transformational rules would change its form to "A spaceship that has inertialess drive can beat the pirates to Vega."

Now we may return to *The Embedding*, and to the third experimental language taught to children in that novel. In order to be embedded as a relative clause, a sentence must have a noun phrase identical to one in the larger sentence: in the example, both embedded and outer sentences originally contained the noun phrase "a spaceship." The noun phrase in the embedded sentence is not restricted to the position of subject; it may, for example, be a direct object:

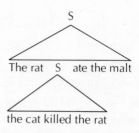

A transformation will move the identical noun phrase in the embedded sentence to the front, if it is not there already:

> The rat [the rat the cat killed] ate the malt.

In cases like this, the second identical noun phrase may be replaced by a relative pronoun:

> The rat which the cat killed ate the malt.

or removed altogether:

> The rat the cat killed ate the malt.

No one has much trouble with sentences with a single level of embedding, but if we have two levels, the result will make most people pause:

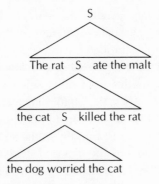

Using brackets again to show the embeddings, this sentence would appear as:

> The rat [the cat [the dog worried the cat] killed the rat] ate the malt.

The operation of the usual transformations gives us this puzzling result:

> The rat that the cat that the dog worried killed ate the malt.

The language prepared for the third group of children in the novel uses multiple levels of embedding; the sentence above would be perfectly ordinary in their speech. In fact, we are told, *three* levels of self-embedding are sometimes used.

Watson's novel is detailed to an extent seldom found in science fiction, yet succeeds in avoiding the pitfalls we have noticed in some other works. It is richly inventive in other ways, as well. It is not perfect, of course, even in linguistic terms: the author has no ear for American English, and at one point attributes to Americans a totally nonexistent dialect. But for a clear exposition, worked out in a story, of some important principles of transformational grammar, *The Embedding* has no equal.

Novels like *The Lord of the Rings*, *Nineteen Eighty-Four*, *The Languages of Pao*, *The Winds of Time*, *The World of Null-A*, *Babel-17*, *Triton*, and *The Embedding* seem so diverse that it is hard to believe there could be some common endeavor that unites them all. They range from fantasies to dystopias to unassuming entertainments to political tracts. Yet all of them share the common goal of taking some facet of language study and making it an informing principle of the literary work. Their authors seek a linguistic way of giving us important insights into man and his world, and in their search they become the spiritual descendants of the novelists of the nineteenth century whose trails through the forest of experience were those of naturalism and realism rather than fantasy or science fiction. Those writers may have taken their insights from other sciences, from economics or genetics rather than linguistics; their informing metaphors may have been a deterministic heredity or an inescapable environment rather than the determinism of Whorf or Sapir; but their aims and procedures were the same: they were captivated by theories and shared their fascination with the wider audience of their art, just like those writers of the last two chapters, who, in their works, enabled us to scan the history of linguistics in the last hundred years.

12

The Children of Sir Thomas More

Far down on the list of things destroyed by the twentieth century (but still worthy of note) comes the literary utopia. I am using the term *utopia* here in the sense certainly primary a hundred years ago: as a depiction of a model society seriously advanced as one superior to our own. Utopias in that sense are rarely written today; according to Richard Gerber, their decline began in 1905:

> [H. G. Wells's] *A Modern Utopia* is the first modern utopia; but at the same time the last modern utopia, for on the one hand it does away with the idea of a classless society, but on the other hand it is the last to present the society of functional classes in an attractive light. Others have continued to describe functional hierarchies, but their attitude has changed to one of pessimism. These pessimistic forecasts of strictly regimented societies must be considered the most important type of modern utopian fiction. . . . Their effect is all the more depressing because they do not seem very far removed from contemporary reality.[1]

Yesterday's bright horizon has clouded over, and the figure against the skyline turned out to be Jeremiah. Pessimism grips the literary form so completely that a special term, *dystopia*, was coined to describe those visions of future societies that repel rather than invite.

But there is a problem with naming a particular work a utopia or dystopia: one man's meat is another man's poison. This is a problem we traditionally solve by allowing the author's intention to rule our classification of the work. Labels are therefore not much help: B. F. Skinner, for example, intends *Walden Two* as a utopia in the most attractive and attracting sense of the word, yet many readers have disagreed with his estimation of the society he created. I believe it would be sounder to rely on features of the work rather than the intention of the author, and to distribute the terms *utopia* and *dystopia* on the basis of what is there rather than how a work's author (or even its readers) regards it.

One of those features that most merits examination is the matter of restriction. As Judson Allen points out, utopias since Plato's time have very frequently shown groups within a society restricting the activities of other members:

> The areas of society most strictly regulated involve sex, children, and war, because it is in these areas that human individuality tends most to assert itself, and to rebel against the perfect organization which philosophy, in the name of Justice, would impose.[2]

But there is another area of individual action, one in which people grow and create without the need of official philosophies or organizations—the area of language. Before reading a given work of science fiction one cannot predict whether it will raise an interesting linguistic question—perhaps 30 to 50 percent will touch on language in some way—but utopias are another matter: a high percentage will have language as a pervasive, even central, concern. Yet unless the reader considers certain key issues to be discussed in this chapter, the importance of language in a work can often be missed entirely. We move in a world of language; unless we become aware of it, it can escape our attention and we notice it no more than a fish notices the water it swims in.

One such oversight was Judson Allen's description of one of the few recent examples of the true utopia, James Cooke Brown's *The Troika Incident* (1970):

> The latest utopia of this technological sort, *The Troika Incident*, simply presumes that our inventions will make us all relatively wealthy and leisured, and then projects into a century hence the interesting trends of the present. Life seems to consist of suburban semi-communes where couples raise children, universities where swingles of all ages cultivate their *humanitas*, occasional interesting work undertaken through a placement service that resembles Merril, Lynch, Pierce, Fenner, and Smith, and a great deal of gallivanting in private vehicles which fly around as liberatingly as cars, but without traffic jams. Perfected birth control devices separate sex from the liability of children, and permit physical love to be used as one of the dimensions of conversation, rather than the ultimate act of long term commitment. Government is by consensus and seems largely to have withered.[3]

The paragraph, if condescending, is not inaccurate; but the changes Allen lists are the results, not the cause, of Brown's ideal society. The cause, as is discovered by a time-tripping spaceship crew from our own day, is a language, Panlan.

The crew members return to our time to discuss Panlan with the narrator; we find that its first form was invented in the twentieth century. Subsequently, "after the UN adopted it, . . . it was systematically taught to children" (p. 222). Its basic words "were discovered by a scientific search for the ideas that are semantically primitive in all languages. And the words themselves were built by a mathematical process that maximized their phonetic familiarity for speakers of the eight or nine most widely spoken tongues," English, Chinese, Hindi, Spanish, Russian, French, German, Japanese, and Arabic (p. 222). Children learn to speak and read Panlan starting at the age of two (p. 97); as an international tongue it has consequently become "the language of politics, . . . of travel, of science, of trade" (p. 105). Not only is it "easier to think in Panlan than in any natural language" (p. 199), but "one of the properties that was built into the international language from the beginning was . . . [that] Panlan can be understood by machines" (p. 109). There are six million words in the advanced form spoken in the future society, making it "about ten times as big as English. It has ten times as much work to do" (p. 221). As a supremely logical language, Panlan promotes and clarifies thought, and some of those clear ideas are used to refine the language further. Each new improvement facilitates even better revisions in an upward spiral as the language improves its speakers and the speakers improve the language. Citizens of the society, "children, fools, plain people," perform "logical gymnastics in speech . . . that our logicians can't even commit to paper yet" (p. 224). And Panlan "is not its name" (p. 7).

Its name is Loglan, for "logical language." *The Troika Incident* turns out, surprisingly, to spring from the same motive as *The Lord of the Rings*; it is a novel written to provide a fictional setting for a fabricated language, a language whose genesis Brown recounts:

> At the beginning of the Christmas holidays, 1955, I sat down before a bright fire to commence what I hoped would be a short paper on the possibility of testing the social psychological implications of the Sapir-Whorf hypothesis. I meant to proceed by showing that the construction of a tiny model language, with a grammar borrowed from the rules of modern logic, taught to subjects of different nationalities, in a laboratory setting, under conditions of control, would permit a decisive test.[4]

Brown's comments remind one of Philip José Farmer's "Prometheus" (discussed in chapter 10) in the intention of testing Whorf's ideas, or of Ian

Watson's *The Embedding* in the desire to test language under laboratory conditions.

The language he planned was to be "a functionally extreme one in some known or presumable way: an extremely poetic one, say, or an extremely efficient one, or extremely logical."[5] Brown's choice, for several reasons, was to emphasize logic; the logical clarity of the language would become its raison d'être, since the effect of this single quality on its speakers is the means by which the Whorf hypothesis will be judged. The language is therefore to be "uncompromisingly logical," to the extent that its speakers are affected whether they will or no; "in Loglan, one is forced to be clear."[6]

For twenty years after that decision Brown worked on Loglan, always with the hope of moving toward introducing "a culture-free language with known formal properties into a laboratory-like setting in which its effects on the behavior we call thinking could be precisely gauged."[7] But how do you get language into the lab? Brown's approach was to reduce its size, make his language "a manageable spark" in comparison with a light-ninglike natural language. If the reduced artifact can be taught to people who could then use it just as they use a natural language, he speculated, then it is possible that "*its manipulation under conditions of control* would permit us to make certain limited inferences about the natural phenomenon itself."[8] I have italicized some words above because those words are crucial to the analysis of utopias that I want to suggest. The idea of control implies a controller, manipulation implies a manipulator.

In the society of *The Troika Incident*, someone must have the power to control the use of language, and that power must be absolute. Consider an example as simple as the meaning of a word. Loglan depends on a very small number of basic words, "primitives," as they are called. Any increase in the total number of words comes from combining these primitives in regular ways. For instance, in Loglan, *morto* "dead" and *madzo* "to make" combine in a predictable manner to form *morma* "to kill," literally, "to make (someone or something) dead." Aside from the primitives and a few function words, every word in Loglan is "transparent," that is, its meaning is predictable from the meanings of its parts. And this connection between primitives and "complex" words must be maintained, or the simplicity of Loglan is impaired and its value for logical thinking is diminished. Now consider an example from English: a certain kind of shoe is called a *clog*.

Performers of a certain kind of dance, perhaps from their original footwear, come to be called *cloggers*, and the dance they perform a *clog*. These changed meanings continue, even if the dancers no longer wear the shoes called clogs.

What will prevent the same sort of thing from happening in Loglan? Suppose a musical group chooses to call themselves "The Killers," and their name is transferred to a dance they originate. The name of the dance would necessarily have some similarity to *morma*, and would appear to be a derived word. But that appearance would be false; what look like parts of the word will point the learner in the wrong direction, since nothing about those parts will state that the word means a kind of dance. Clearly, if the logic of Loglan cannot be preserved, it fails both as an instrument to test the Whorf hypothesis and as a device to make logical thinking easier. Therefore transference of meaning must be somehow prevented or rolled back (if it does occur) in the Loglan society. But effective methods of either preserving or changing the meaning of a word according to a conscious plan are unknown.

Had *The Troika Incident* shown what measures its society was willing to take to regulate word meanings, we would have had an indication within the work of how repressive the society was willing to be. As Judson Allen says, "All utopian speculation . . . [defines] a society which will foster some ideal deemed most important,"[9] and logic in language is the most important ideal in *The Troika Incident*. Would the society be willing, say, to punish individuals rather than see its ideal made more difficult of attainment? The answer to questions like these would give us a means of labelling the novel a utopia or dystopia without depending on the author's opinion of his own work or taking a poll of its readers.

And there is a further benefit to be gained: what we learn about evaluating fictional societies can equally well be used to judge existing ones; if the regimentation of the modern dystopia does not seem "very far removed from contemporary reality," we need all the help we can get.

What final judgment can we make on *The Troika Incident*? Brown shows no instances of repression of language; everything runs smoothly in the future world pictured there. Apparently we are to believe that linguistic innovation and change have ceased there, without being offered any reason why that curious cessation should have occurred. We might decide simply that there is insufficient evidence to make a judgment on the novel, but there are strong hints that its society would necessarily be a dystopia: Myra Barnes observed, from her study of language in science fiction, that "all dystopian languages technically belong to Whorf," because "all dystopian languages involve a measure of thought control." [10] I would like to argue that the relationship between dystopias and thought control is a reciprocal one—dystopian languages do indeed involve thought control; in fact, if a society promotes the control of thought or language, we judge the society, on those grounds, to be a dystopia.

The clearest exposition to date of this relationship appears in Robert M. Philmus's incisive study of the languages in Swift's *A Voyage to the Country of the Houyhnhnms* and Orwell's *Nineteen Eighty-Four*. He argues that

> The more nearly absolute a social order claims to be, the more absolutist and compulsive its demand for unanimous assent becomes. Such a degree of unanimity is not attainable in a society open to the influence of heterodox ideas. Hence, utopia insofar as it pretends to be "ultimate" aspires toward closure, whereby alternative ideas of order would be, if not unthinkable, at least inexpressible. The "closed society," in other words, can afford to tolerate only a language of assent. [11]

Philmus observes that the land of the Houyhnhnms and Oceania use different methods in their attempts to achieve closure: the rational horses would eliminate dissent by destroying the ability of language to express fictions, theories, falsehoods, indeed, anything other than a statement of fact about their self-contained society. They would chain language to their limited vision of reality. Big Brother, on the other hand, would use the instrument of Newspeak to entirely divorce language from any possible reality, making its meaning subject to continual change, even contradiction.

> Unanimity in the utopia of the Houyhnhnms depends upon the natural correspondence of word and thought. Their language, as Gulliver's use of it demonstrates, is capable of expressing what their reason tells them is not; but to speak in this way is contrary to their nature and to the dictates of their reason. The limits of customary linguistic usage among them reflect the cognitive limitations inherent in their nature and thereby insure their rationality from corruption and preserve their utopian social order.
>
> Oceania reverses the logical priorities. In *Nineteen Eighty-Four*, the program of the Party is to close off existing possibilities of cognition, to make what

has been thought in the past unthinkable, by constricting the universe of discourse. The intent of Newspeak is to perpetuate Ingsoc by impoverishing the lexicon to the point where heretical notions first become inexpressible and eventually inconceivable.[12]

Language can liberate, and Orwell's nightmare society employed an easily detected means of preventing that liberation. But as Swift showed us some centuries ago, it is not the only means. Big Brother uses the method of the bureaucrat, but the Houyhnhnms use the method of the pedant and the purist.

And there is at least a third method: that of the campaigning politician. This method separates language from the will; although words are used and sentences are spoken, the speaker makes no commitment at all. Wither, one of the chief villains in C. S. Lewis's *That Hideous Strength* (1945), uses this method throughout the novel. He is, through long habit, incapable of a straightforward statement:

> My dear young friend, the golden rule is very simple. There are only two errors which would be fatal to one placed in the peculiar situation which certain parts of your previous conduct have unfortunately created for you. On the one hand, anything like a lack of initiative or enterprise would be disastrous. On the other, the slightest approach to unauthorised action—anything which suggested that you were assuming a liberty of decision which, in all the circumstances, is not really yours—might have consequences from which even I could not protect you. But as long as you keep quite clear of these two extremes, there is no reason (speaking unofficially) why you should not be perfectly safe. (P. 253)

As Lewis's narrator observes of Wither, "the indicative mood now corresponded to no thought that his mind could entertain. He had willed with his whole heart that there should be no reality and no truth" (p. 353). The result of the method is clear: at the end of the novel, a banquet for the villains dissolves into chaos as their speech becomes meaningless babble.

These examples demonstrate that a dystopian society can attempt to manipulate language in a variety of ways. The field is so vast that an adequate study would demand a work the length of this one, and a full exploration is obviously beyond the scope of this chapter. But we can investigate one part of it. Let us look at the implications of the method of Oceania, assuming, as Rydra Wong says in *Babel-17*, that "if you don't know the words, you can't know the ideas." We can then judge that any work depicting a society which attempts to control the words assumes the rightness of Whorf's theories, and is therefore a dystopia.

Gorman Beauchamp notes that in order to constrict "the range of permissible ideas to an orthodox few, [dystopian] societies would deliberately delimit and debase the medium of ideas, words." [13] But the dystopian government has a second task: it must not only enslave words, but also prevent the natural forces of language from freeing them. New words for dissent may come from any of three sources: first, they may be borrowed from another language. Second, they may arise by attaching the proscribed meanings to already-existing words, that is, by extending or transferring the meanings of current words to include the dangerous concepts, much as, in an innocuous way, the meaning of *clog* was changed and expanded. Third, and this would be the least predictable source, the words may be coined anew.

How, then, would the opponents of freedom of thought, if the powers of the government were at their disposal, prevent these three methods? The first is probably the simplest: to prevent the borrowing of terms from another language, the tyrant forbids contact with foreign speakers and restricts the learning of other languages. The second is more difficult: to prevent the extension of meaning of words already in the language, the government must work hard at strictly regulating the meanings of words. Its most effective tools would be the available scholarly resources: only official dictionaries, grammars, commentaries on language, and the like, would be allowed. In addition, the government would have to indoctrinate the populace with its official lexicography by maintaining exclusive control of education, even from the earliest levels. Since the child's first teachers are its parents, in language as in everything else, the tyrant must prevent the parent-child relationship from becoming a teacher-student relationship. Tactics would therefore include making it difficult to keep the family group together, and making it attractive to deposit infants in state-run nurseries. The third method, coining new words, would be almost impossible to forestall; the government's shrewdest approach would be to forget about trying to prevent creation, since every speaker is a possible innovator, but rather to interrupt the spreading of the new word. It would therefore control the means of communication—tightly restrict publication, monitor and regulate radio, telephone, and correspondence. It would make travel difficult and rare in order to make word-of-mouth communication harder. Finally, on the principle that what one has done, one may do again, it would jail the inventors of new words, if it could find them.

With these methods in mind, let us examine two works that are not easily classified as utopias or dystopias, B. F. Skinner's *Walden Two* (1948) and Ursula K. Le Guin's *The Dispossessed* (1974).

Orwell's opinion of Oceania or Huxley's opinion of the dominant society in *Brave New World* is the same as that of the majority of their readers. But we cannot say that of *Walden Two*. As Philmus points out, "the difference between utopia and dystopia finally comes down to a matter of point of view. . . . In *Walden Two*, for example, B. F. Skinner depicts as utopian a technocratic social order whose totalitarian methods of 'behavioral engineering' most readers would regard as anti-utopian."[14] But Walden Two does have attractions: its citizens enjoy leisure time, meaningful work, security, and the amenities of life. On what grounds would we decide whether the work should be regarded as utopian or dystopian? An examination of uses of language in *Walden Two* provides the answer.

Before one is admitted as a member of the commune, he must accept in its entirety a body of regulations known as the Code. Thinking of the Code as similar to the *regula* of a monastic order would be a mistake: Skinner nowhere gives the complete Code, but he does quote it or refer to it in a number of places. No article specifies hours of work or play; no article discusses money or personal possessions; no article compels or forbids any deed. Every single instance of the Code given to us in the novel deals with the use of language.

Consider how our theoretical tyranny of a few paragraphs back controls the use of words: it makes communication difficult. Note in this connection that the largest meeting room at Walden Two accommodates about two hundred people; as Skinner's mouthpiece, Frazier, says: "the simple fact is, there's no good reason for bringing people together in large numbers" (pp. 43–44). The government of a dystopia would monitor and regulate radio, telephone, and correspondence; it seems no one in Walden Two has a private radio receiver, since Frazier says that "all the good radio programs are broadcast over the system of loudspeakers that we call the Walden Network, and they are monitored to remove the advertising" (p. 90). Do the individuals in the society have the option of turning off a "system of loudspeakers" as easily as they could turn off their own sets? Apparently not. I noted earlier that a tyrant would forbid contact with outsiders;

in Walden Two, the Code forbids members to talk to outsiders about the affairs of the community (p. 163), and another section forbids them to argue within the community about the Code itself (p. 164). They have no access to outside newspapers, apparently, since Frazier tells his visitors, "We have a Political Manager, who informs himself of the qualifications of the candidates in local and state elections. With the help of the Planners he draws up what we call the 'Walden Ticket,' and we all go to the polls and vote it straight" (pp. 196–97).

The notion of "outside" applies in time as well as in space: the potential dissident may find an expression of his discontent in the writings of earlier times as easily as in the speech of contemporaries. Hence, as Frazier says, "We don't teach history" (p. 237). Perhaps aware of how this appears to his visitors, he adds: "We don't keep our young people ignorant of it, any more than we keep them ignorant of mycology, or any other subject. They may read all the history they like. But we don't regard it as essential to their education. We don't turn them in that direction and not many take it" (pp. 237–38). He comes close to losing control of himself in his distaste for history: "Nothing confuses our evalution of the present more than a sense of history" (p. 239). In fact, Walden Two does keep its young people ignorant of history, and not just by neglect; they may *not* read all the history they like, since one cannot study history without documents and commentaries, and in the light of Frazier's comments, we may in justice suspect that few history books have found a place on Walden's shelves.

What they do have, he says, is "the heart of a great library—not much to please the scholar or specialist, perhaps, but enough to interest the intelligent reader for life. Two or three thousand volumes will do it" (p. 121). This is restriction with a vengeance, but Frazier is satisfied: "The secret is this. . . . We subtract from our shelves as often as we add to them. The result is a collection that never misses fire. We all get something vital every time we take a book from the shelves. If anyone wants to follow a special interest we arrange for loans" (p. 121). But special interest can obviously only be discovered within the range of subjects that the Walden library permits. How can a reader who doesn't know of the existence of a given subject follow it up? How does the librarian decide which books to remove from the shelves? If a virgin check-out slip means removal from the shelves, then Walden's library becomes a rotating best-seller list, filled with the works of Victoria Holt and Harold Robbins. If some enduring value rather than popularity is the criterion, then Walden's library must have access to competence and critical judgment in every field of thought. One cannot have best-sellers *and* monuments of scholarship in two or three thousand books. Serendipity cannot occur in the Walden library; the size of it does not permit surprises. Skinner is aware of this defect, and he has Frazier make an absurd remark rather than allow the community to suffer a damaging comparison. First, we need to examine the virulence of Frazier's dislike for the "large college library": "What trash the librarian has saved up in order to report a million volumes in the college catalogue! Bound pamphlets, old journals, ancient junk that even the shoddiest secondhand bookstore would clear from its shelves" (p. 121). But what about walking through stacks and stacks of books, letting one's eye wander until something interesting and unexpected catches it? "If anyone wants to browse, we have half a barnful of discarded volumes" (p. 121). Keeping these rejects does not make sense, in the light of what he has said. Either the barn is properly maintained as a library or it is not. (Remember, we are talking about "trash . . . ancient junk.") If the roof leaks and rats gnaw the books, then the chance to browse is an illusion, not a real alternative. On the other hand, if the building is maintained, the books catalogued and shelved, then how does the Walden library differ from the excoriated university library? It seems to me that the "half a barnful of discarded volumes" is a smokescreen: given Frazier's beliefs, those books are worthless, and their preservation is a wasteful drain on the resources of the community. Even if the books are moldering in a heap, they are still taking up space in a structure that could be put to other use. Frazier's reasoning demands that the books be destroyed, but his author is aware what his community would look like if he wrote about the Walden Two Planners' burning a pile of books every month or so. In short, the library policy at Walden Two does not differ from that of Nazi Germany.

Walden Two assumes the omnipotence of its Planners;[15] even if they do make a mistake and change an item or two in the Code, members cannot argue about it. Cut off from the outside world, the community tends toward closure in every sphere of human activity, language included. If the hermetic sealing off we see here marks a dystopia, as Philmus argues, then *Walden Two* is a dystopia on internal evidence.

Ursula Le Guin's *The Dispossessed* presents different problems. To begin with, Le Guin's attitude toward her hypothetical society is not nearly as unmixed as is Skinner's toward Walden; she subtitles her work *An Ambiguous Utopia*.

The novel takes place on a planet and its large moon, both light-years away from Earth. The planet, Urras, resembles Earth in many ways; it has a variety of nations, capitalist and communist systems, industrialized and undeveloped states. Centuries before the opening of the novel, a world-wide anarchist movement causes turmoil across the planet. To buy them off, the nations give the anarchists possession of the moon, which is almost as large as its primary and capable of supporting life.

The anarchists, Odonians as they are called after their philosopher-founder Odo, migrate to the moon, which they name Anarres. To symbolize their separation from the old world, and to cope with the practical difficulties of assimilating peoples speaking diverse tongues, they adopt a new language, Pravic. The language intentionally embodies the principles of the new society.

As I pointed out, Le Guin does not consider Anarres unambiguously good, but critics have rushed in where the author feared to tread. *The Dispossessed* drew much attention in the special Le Guin issue of *Science Fiction Studies*: Donald F. Theall saw serious flaws in the Odonian society,[16] but few others agreed with him. Judah Bierman, for example, says that "though power corrupts even in an anarchist society, though the same crippling conflicts arise in its incipient bureaucracy, still the acts themselves are part of the utopian truth of community."[17] It is hard to know how to evaluate an article that claims that power-corrupted acts are part of a utopian truth. Still stranger is Darko Suvin's article in which he asserts that the vices of Anarres demonstrate its virtues: "the very real shortcomings and backslidings of Anarres do not ultimately detract from but instead reaffirm the exemplarity of its original, Odonian impulse."[18] In the face of paradoxes like these, the only thing likely to help is a close examination of the Odonian society itself.

From the time of the settling of the moon, the language policy of the Odonians officially embraced the Whorf hypothesis. Pravic was designed to foster and protect their ideology. For example, in theory the Odonians reject all compulsion—no one is forced to work—yet Pravic exerts both positive and negative social pressure on nonconformists: the same word means both "work" and "play" (p. 81), and a special term of opprobrium exists for those few people who drift from place to place, refusing to accept "voluntary" work postings. Added to their linguistic pressure is their habit of constantly reasoning from analogy; so often have the words *healthy* and *sick* been used over the years to exalt the Odonian economic system over those of their old-world rivals that the young are often ashamed to admit physical illness (p. 104). In passing we might note that the Odonians have a place called the Asylum, located on an island, where those who commit what in other societies would be capital crimes can find refuge from retribution. Note that it is an asylum, not a penitentiary; the inmates are not punished, they receive "therapy" (p. 149). Judson Allen's comments on another subject are appropriate here: "[Samuel] Butler's *Erewhon*, with considerable force, projects a society derived from evolutionary thought, in which it is a crime to be sick, and a sickness to commit a crime. Obviously, in Erewhon as in evolutionary society, it is the strong who survive." [19]

Suppose we assume that *The Dispossessed* pictures an outright dystopian society on Anarres; in the Whorfian manner it ought to prevent the three threats to that control that the creative use of language offers. If we find the Odonians practicing the restraints cited earlier as the marks of thought control through the control of language, then our original assumption is confirmed.

First, to prevent words from being borrowed from another language, prevent contact with foreign speakers and writers. Shevek, the central character of the novel, proceeds through the school system of Anarres and moves up to university-level instruction. Yet he is almost twenty before he knows that information passes back and forth between Urras and Anarres (pp. 95–96). In the course of his studies it becomes necessary for him to learn the language of one of the nations on Urras. It comes as quite a surprise to him that he is to allow no one else to see the book he is given, the one printed in the new language. His superior, who has given him the book, tells him "those books are explosives" (p. 93). Yet he is not reading history or politics or economics, but an introductory text in physics. The Defense Department of Anarres "insists that every word that leaves here on those freighters be passed by a PDC-approved expert" (p. 101). The PDC is the central authority of Anarres, the voluntary group that arranges for production and distribution of goods in the centralized economy of the planet.

Shevek insists that ideas demand to be communicated (p. 64), and chafes under these restrictions. Yet he finds out that he has no free access to the official channels of communication with the mother planet. His letters are stopped by the managers of the one port the Odonians use, or rejected by the Defense Department. When he decides to visit Urras, he is threatened with physical violence before he leaves, and promised the same on his return.

The second problem for the thought controller is that words may change in meaning, and to prevent this change, the authorities would have two powerful weapons. To begin with, the government on Anarres controls scholarly resources on language. Twice in the novel, characters quote the dictionary definitions of words from memory in the midst of conversation (pp. 145, 231). Yet the work they quote from, Tomar's *Definitions*, does not sound like Merriam-Webster; if a dictionary, it is one in the same sense of the word as Ambrose Bierce's *Devil's Dictionary*, a work more intent on arguing a point than on defining a term.

But to guard effectively against any unauthorized change in language, the thought controller must control education. And so it is on Anarres. We see Shevek punished for "misusing" language for the first time when he is still in diapers (pp. 24–25), and again when he is eight. On the second occasion, he has thought through an amazingly advanced concept for a child of his years, the notion that a finite length can have an infinite number of parts. Yet the teacher accuses him of egotism: "Speech is sharing—a cooperative art. You're not sharing, merely egoizing" (p. 26). He is banished from the group. Already Shevek has learned to distrust words: "Nothing said in words ever came out quite even" (p. 27).

The control of education in the nursery is only effective if the children are in fact raised in government child-care centers. The pressure on Odonians to accept work-postings does not diminish after a couple decide to have children. Both husband and wife are expected by the community to contribute to the welfare of the society. Hence children are almost universally raised by the community centers, not by their parents. And Pravic, the language, helps to disrupt any incipient family bonds: singular possessive personal pronouns exist, but only for emphasis; since all things are to be shared, their use is discouraged, even with the words for relatives or body parts: "Little children might say 'my mother' but very soon they learned to say 'the mother.' Instead of 'my hand hurts,' it was 'the hand hurts me,' and so on" (p. 51). Words for family relationships are manipulated in Pravic in a second way, by having their meanings so extended that no special kind of relationship can be expressed by them. A word in the text, *tadde*, is glossed this way:

> Papa. A small child may call any adult *mamme* or *tadde*. Gimar's *tadde* may have been her father, an uncle, or an unrelated adult who showed her parental or grandparental responsibility and affection. She may have called several people *tadde* or *mamme*, but the word has a more specific use than *ammar* (brother/sister), which may be used to anybody. (P. 42)

It is instructive how frequently dystopias strive to disrupt the linguistic marks of the special affection that family names represent. *Walden Two* also had communal child-care centers; Frazier pointed out their advantages for orphans: "There is no occasion [for the orphan] to envy companions who are not so deprived, because there is little or no practical difference. It's true he may not call anyone 'Mother' or 'Father,' but we discourage this anyway, in favor of given names" (p. 143).

Finally, the society of *The Dispossessed* attacks the family by making it difficult for the group to stay together.

> Those who undertook to form and keep a partnership, whether homosexual or heterosexual, met with problems unknown to those content with sex wherever they found it. They must face not only jealousy and possessiveness . . . but also the external pressures of social organization. A couple that undertook partnership did so knowing that they might be separated at any time by the exigencies of labor distribution.
>
> Divlab, the administration of the division of labor, tried to keep couples together, and to reunite them as soon as possible on request; but it could not always be done, especially in urgent levies, nor did anyone expect Divlab to remake whole lists and reprogram computers trying to do it. (P. 215)

The reason given here is uniquely unconvincing—"We would have to reprogram the computer to do it"—and is usually heard when one is trying to correct an error on a department store bill, or to change the registration procedure at a college. Are we to believe that joint postings of husbands and wives is all that difficult a task, or that even if the task is difficult, the convenience of the machine and its programmers comes first? Families get no special privileges here, and the result is yet another way of strengthening the government's control of child-raising, and hence their control of the child's first language.

There is a third danger to be guarded against in linguistic matters; that is the coining of new words. As I said earlier, people cannot be forestalled from using language creatively, so the government concentrates on preventing dissemination of liberating words by controlling communication. The Odonians work on this problem with immense energy: the distribution and printing of books is controlled by voluntary syndicates (p. 92); when a musician in the novel tries to have some of his music published, he is outvoted and his music rejected. "The Music syndics don't like my compositions. And nobody much else does, yet. I can't be a syndicate all by myself, can I?" (p. 153). "PDC, the principal users of radio, telephone, and mails, coordinated the means of long-distance communication, just as they did the means of long-distance travel and shipping" (p. 219). "Telephone calls thus were mostly long-distance, and were handled by the PDC" (p. 220). "Letters went unsealed, not by law, of course, but by convention. Personal communication at long distance is costly in materials and labor, and since the private and public economy was the same, there was considerable feeling against unnecessary writing or calling. It was a trivial habit; it smacked of privatism, of egoizing. This was probably why the letters went unsealed: you had no right to ask people to carry a message that they couldn't read" (p. 220).

If the society of Anarres in *The Dispossessed* is not a dystopia, it has all the machinery of one, from a language designed to influence the thinking of its people through every weapon needed to keep that language from being changed. When Shevek meets an Earthwoman, an ambassador, on Urras, she tries to compliment him by remarking that his was "the only rationally invented language that has become the tongue of a great people" (p. 296). If the Odonians have become great, and they have many admirable qualities, it is in spite of a language designed for propaganda and a government willing to employ it.

Of course, *The Dispossessed* is not the first ambiguous utopia; Thomas More equivocated between asserting that his society was "the good place" and hinting, possibly, that it was "no place": "Wherefore not Utopie, but rather rightely / My name is Eutopie,"[20] yet we remember that the name of the work does not incorporate *eu*- "good," but *u*- "no." The value of the utopian novel is its use as a conjecture, as a thought-experiment in which the relative merits of different social contracts can be explored before signing.

And the experimental nature of the utopia applies equally well to all of science fiction. Conjecture is its subject, from building a better mousetrap to visions of the apocalypse, and a widening of the imagination is its product. While much of modern literature depends on a shrinking view of humanity, contenting itself with a narrowing opinion of human interests and capacities, science fiction seeks to expand that view, to prevent closure in literature, to widen the universe of discourse.

"Universe of discourse" is an appropriate term here, I think, because the phrase has another meaning, one also applicable: we do move in a world of words. Attacks on that world are caused by, or at least accompany, attacks on language itself. One of the ways we can protect and expand our freedoms is by finding out how language works. Science fiction, as I have tried to demonstrate throughout this book, is especially suited for giving instruction about language, and is a medium especially popular with the young. The pioneers of the American pulps saw science fiction as a means of teaching science. Although science fiction seldom achieves that goal, and although we have no right to demand anything more than art from its writers, the possibility is always there. And the possibility includes the chance to say something about language, something liberating and tolerant and entertaining.

Notes

1 1. Mary Shelley, *Frankenstein: or The Modern Prometheus* (Collier, 1961), p. 95. In order to cope with the truly horrendous bibliographical problems of science fiction, I have taken some liberties with the Modern Language Association system of documentation. Because literally hundreds of works are cited, I have wherever possible incorporated two critical items of bibliographical information in the text: first, many science fiction works both new and old are available only in paperback editions or collections which go in and out of print with unseemly haste. I always include, therefore, the title of the collection and the name of its editor when I am using a reprinted version. But this method will often falsify the time of composition of the novel or story, since these works are frequently reprinted not once but several times. The second item I endeavor to supply, therefore, is the year of first publication. A typical citation will look like this: Judith Merril, "The Lonely" (1963; rpt. *Best of Judith Merril*, p. 238), and is to be interpreted in this way: the author's story, "The Lonely," was first published in 1963; I am quoting from the reprinted version in *The Best of Judith Merril*, a collection of stories by that author. Fuller publishing data on *The Best of Judith Merril* will be found in the bibliography. For the most part, then, notes refer the reader either to a substantive discussion or to the citation of a critical work, since all primary sources will be identified in the text.

2. "Communication in Science Fiction," *ETC.*, 11:1 (Autumn 1953), 16.

3. "With a Piece of Twisted Wire," *SF Horizons*, 2 (Winter 1965), 58.

4. *English Journal*, 62 (1973), 998–1003.

5. "Towards an Alien Linguistics," *Vector 71*, 2:3 (December 1975), 23.

2 1. "Language and Techniques of Communication as Theme or Tool in Science Fiction," *Linguistics*, 39 (1968), 70.

2. Of course it isn't. Mary McGrory, the syndicated columnist, wrote an article that appeared in local newspapers on 26 April 1976. She finds much to admire in the style of Abigail Adams, from her reading of the Adams correspondence, but she objects to "Abigail's atrocious spelling." She cites, among others, *publick*, *an* [rather than a] *Heroine*, and *chilld* [rather than *chilled*], totally unaware that these are perfectly normal eighteenth-century spellings.

3. *Science-Fiction Handbook* (Hermitage House, 1953), p. 253. De Camp handles matters of linguistic interest as competently and imaginatively as any current writer.

4. Sturgeon's story, first published in 1954, is reprinted in *Sturgeon Is Alive and Well*. Mullen's note, correcting my originally mistaken perception of Sturgeon's technique, appears as footnote 5 to my article "The Future History and Development of the English Language," *Science-Fiction Studies*, 3:2 (July 1976), p. 141.

5. Personal letter to M. J. E. Barnes, cited in her *Linguistics and Languages in Science Fiction-Fantasy* (Arno, 1974), pp. iii–iv.

6. It is true that the *Oxford English Dictionary* records "Old English" as "in popular use applied vaguely to all obsolete forms of the language"; nevertheless, the Richard Burton–Elizabeth Taylor movie *The Sandpiper* was scored by one reviewer for (among other things) this same usage. The standards of Hollywood should not be unsurpassable for the "World's Best Science Fiction."

7. Larry Niven, "The Words in Science Fiction," *The Craft of Science Fiction*, ed. Reginald Bretnor (Harper & Row, 1976), p. 180.

8. The error Moorcock's character makes, believing that there existed just one Earthly language, satirizes the common science fiction practice of endowing a whole planet with a single tongue—"the Martian language," for example. This particular habit has been burlesqued before. Anthony Boucher's "Barrier" (1942; rpt. Kingsley Amis, ed., *Spectrum 4* [Berkley Medallion, 1966]) contains a similar incident, and is possibly the source for Moorcock's treatment. M. J. E. Barnes discusses "Barrier" at length in *Linguistics and Languages*.

9. *Science-Fiction Handbook*, p. 253.

10. H. G. Wells, *The Wheels of Chance and The Time Machine* (Everyman, 1935), p. 235. A time machine that could visit the past would of course be invaluable to historical linguists; its utility did not escape Jack Vance in his "Rumfuddle" (*Three Trips in Time and Space* [Hawthorn, 1973]). He has the inventor of a time machine of sorts write in his memoirs, "We can chart the development of every language syllable by syllable, from earliest formulation to the present" (p. 166).

11. "Parables of De-Alienation: Le Guin's Widdershins Dance," *Science-Fiction Studies*, 2:3 (November 1975), pp. 267, 268.

12. The Norton and NAL paperback editions contain an Afterword and a Nadsat dictionary by Stanley Edgar Hyman.

13. *Visions of Tomorrow: Six Journeys from Outer to Inner Space* (Arno Press, 1975), p. 160.

14. "A Critique of Science Fiction," *Modern Science Fiction: Its Meaning and Its Future*, ed. Reginald Bretnor (Coward-McCann, 1953), pp. 83–84.

15. *Before the Golden Age*, p. 373. Asimov did not stop learning; his works are notably free from linguistic errors, and he continues to be interested in language in

science fiction. On reading an earlier version of this chapter, he recalled a similar work published almost forty years ago, L. Sprague de Camp's "Language for Time-Travelers," *Astounding* (July 1938), pp. 63–72.

16. In justifying his linguistic stasis by pointing to recordings, Clarke need not have had Manning's story in mind. This particular sleight-of-hand is found several times in the science fiction of the thirties. John W. Campbell, Jr.'s "Twilight" (1934; rpt. Robert Silverberg, ed., *The Ends of Time*) portrays a visitor from 3059 A.D. who speaks American English without even an accent; he tells a man of our own time, "I can understand your speech, and you mine, because your speech of this day is largely recorded on records of various types and has influenced our pronunciation" (p. 59).

17. Bester records the same perception, but in reverse, in "The Flowered Thundermug," in *Dark Side of the Earth* (New American Library, 1964), where the police of the twenty-fifth century, searching for a man from the twentieth, note that the fugitive talks "a little funny, like a foreigner."

18. "A Standard Corpus of Edited Present-Day American English," *College English*, 26:4 (January 1965), 267. This article describes the project and corpus.

19. Among other science-fiction word-coiners who have had their inventions adopted in wider circles are Jack Williamson and Isaac Asimov. Among Williamson's contributions over his long career have been *terraform* "to adapt a planet for habitation by humans," *android* "an artificially-created intelligent being composed of biological, rather than metallic, parts," and *psion* "a particle of mental impulse without mass." These and others of more limited circulation are listed in the "Telescope" column of *Galileo*, 7 (1978), 94, where they are quoted from Mike Ashley, *Pioneer Behind the Pen: A Look at 50 Years of Jack Williamson*. Isaac Asimov tells of his creation of the word *robotics* in the first volume of his autobiography, *In Memory Yet Green* (Doubleday, 1979): "I didn't realize this until many years later, for at the time I first used the word, I thought it was a word actually used by scientists in this connection. It was, after all, analogous to 'physics,' 'hydraulics,' 'mechanics,' 'statics,' and various other words of this form used to denote a branch of physics-related science" (p. 286 [n. 7]).

20. Preface to "Et in Arcadia Ego," in *Science Fiction: Author's Choice 4*, ed. Harry Harrison (Putnam, 1974).

21. In Samuel R. Delany's *Nova* (Doubleday, 1968), p. 182. The novel is in other respects well-written and linguistically inventive, and will be cited later in another connection.

22. Readers with some interest in transformational grammars might amuse themselves by deciding how Delany's sentences can be derived.

23. *Astounding* (July 1938), pp. 63–72. John W. Campbell, Jr., long-time editor of *Astounding*, invited readers to rate the stories and articles in each issue. Their

votes were tabulated and cash bonuses awarded to the winning authors. "Language for Time-Travelers" was the first nonfiction selection ever to be ranked first by the readers.

3 1. *Problems in the Origins and Development of the English Language*, 2nd ed. (Harcourt Brace Jovanovich, 1972), p. 14. See also Thomas Pyles, *Origins and Development of the English Language*, 2nd ed. (Harcourt Brace Jovanovich, 1971), pp. 9–10, where the author refers the interested reader to Noel Perrin, "Old Macberlitz Had a Farm," *New Yorker* (27 January 1962), pp. 28–29.

2. *More Issues at Hand* (Advent, 1970), p. 87.

3. W. D. Van Gieson, Jr., and W. D. Chapman, "Machine-Generated Speech for Use with Computers, . . ." *Computers and Automation* (November 1968), p. 31.

4. For more information on the physiology of these vocal gymnastics, see Peter B. Denes and Elliot N. Pinson, *The Speech Chain: the Physics and Biology of Spoken Language* (Doubleday Anchor, 1973).

5. Williamson is credited with the coinage by Damon Knight, *In Search of Wonder*, rev. ed. (Advent, 1967), p. 58.

4 1. *The Spectator*, ed. Donald F. Bond (Clarendon, 1965), 1:151–52; No. 36, Wednesday, 11 April 1711.

2. "Men on Other Planets," in Reginald Bretnor, ed., *The Craft of Science Fiction* (Harper & Row, 1976), p. 124.

3. Simak suggests in "Census" that the surgical changes are eventually transmitted to offspring, an odd occurrence of the Lamarckian notion that an acquired characteristic can become hereditary, which Stalin's favorite biologist, Lysenko, tried to impose on Russian science.

4. And linguists have long had an interest in this sort of thing. There is an apocryphal story that the first dissertation accepted at Harvard was entitled, "When Balaam's Ass Spoke, Did Her Speech Organs Change?"

5. "On Fairy-Stories," rpt. in *Tree and Leaf* (Houghton Mifflin, 1965), p. 66.

6. Only communication between beasts and humans is examined here, not the traditional beast fable, wherein all the characters are lower animals. Chaunticleer and Pertelote, therefore, will not be considered. The eagle in *The House of Fame* may be an early example of a machine that talks, rather than an animal, since Chaucer says it is made of gold. But in either case, the work is not just the first science-fiction story in English, but the first "hard" science-fiction story, according to Dick and Lori Allen's definition in *Looking Ahead* (Harcourt Brace Jovanovich, 1975). "'Classic' or 'traditional' science fiction . . . [is] the kind of story in which the

science is 'hard,' that is, plays a major role in the story, is discussed in such a way that it appears accurate in the light of current scientific knowledge and extrapolation" (p. 5). *The House of Fame* qualifies: note the eagle's explanation of sound waves, which plays a major role in the story and appears accurate in light of the best fourteenth-century scientific knowledge.

7. See Philip Leiberman, "Primate Vocalizations and Human Linguistic Ability," *Journal of the Acoustical Society*, 44 (1968), 1574–84.

8. *College Composition and Communication*, 23 (May 1972), 142–54. Those who wish to decide the question for themselves can consult the reports of the original researchers, especially those publications by B. T. Gardner and R. A. Gardner: "Teaching Sign Language to a Chimpanzee," *Science*, 165 (1969), 664–72; "Two-way Communication with an Infant Chimpanzee," in A. M. Schrier and F. Stollnitz, eds., *Behavior of Non-Human Primates*, vol. 4 (New York: Academic Press, 1971); and "Evidence for Sentence Constituents in the Early Utterances of Child and Chimpanzee," *Journal of Experimental Psychology*, 104 (1975), 244–67.

9. See, for example, his "Decoding the Language of the Bee," *Science*, 185 (1974), 663–68.

10. John C. Lilly, *Lilly on Dolphins* (Garden City, N.Y.: Doubleday Anchor, 1975), p. vii. The preface to *Man and Dolphin*, from which I quote in the text, is here reprinted. Lilly adds, for the reprint, a retrospective comment of some wistfulness: "This prediction [of interspecies communication] was made in 1960; in 1975 it has not yet transpired. I am returning to work with interspecies communication to try a new way of approach. Maybe, by 1980, we will know, one way or another" (p. vii).

11. *Lilly on Dolphins*, p. 201; reprinted from chapter 8 of *The Mind of the Dolphin*, first published in 1967.

12. "Intelligent Life in Space," *Amazing* (March 1963), p. 95.

13. Lilly's arithmetic is often faulty. The calculations in chapter 8 of *The Mind of the Dolphin* are especially treacherous.

14. *Marine Mammals and Man: The Navy's Porpoises and Sea Lions* (Washington: Robert B. Luce, 1973), p. 110. Wood's book is a useful check on Lilly's occasional excesses.

15. Melba C. Caldwell, David K. Caldwell, and Robert H. Turner, "Statistical Analysis of the Signature Whistle of an Atlantic Bottlenosed Dolphin with Correlations between Vocal Changes and Level of Arousal," National Technical Information Service AD 708–787, abstract.

16. "Alien Minds and Nonhuman Intelligences," in Bretnor, ed., *The Craft of Science Fiction*, p. 154.

17. "Notes from a Phantom Koala," in *The Bulletin of the Science Fiction Writers of America*, 11:4 (August 1976), 17. An excellent and timely discussion of the whole field of animal communication is Donald R. Griffin's *The Question of Ani-*

mal Awareness (New York: The Rockefeller University Press, 1976). A working writer of science fiction should have Griffin's book on the reference shelf.

5 1. "The Problem of Universals in Language," *Universals of Language*, ed. Joseph H. Greenberg, 2nd ed. (MIT Press, 1963), p. 8.

2. "The Creation of Imaginary Worlds," *Science Fiction, Today and Tomorrow*, ed. Reginald Bretnor (Harper & Row, 1974), p. 236.

3. *Linguistics*, 39 (1968), 77.

4. Respectively, from Harry Harrison, "Run from the Fire," Elwood and Silverberg, eds., *Epoch* (1975), p. 417; Brian Aldiss, "The Game of God" (1958 as "Segregation"), rpt. *Starswarm* (1964), p. 71; William Barton, *Hunting on Kunderer* (1973), p. 41; Andre Norton, *Operation Time Search* (1967), p. 13; Charles Shafhauser, "A Gleeb for Earth" (1953), rpt. H. L. Gold, ed., *The Second Galaxy Reader of Science Fiction* (1954), p. 68; Katherine MacLean, "Pictures Don't Lie" (1951), rpt. Edmund Crispin, ed., *Best SF: Science Fiction Stories* (1955), p. 41; Jack Vance, "Brains of Earth" (1966), rpt. *Worlds of Jack Vance* (1973), p. 202; Larry Niven, *Ringworld* (1970), p. 12; Tony Morphett, "Litterbug" (1969), rpt. E. L. Ferman, ed., *Best from Fantasy and Science Fiction, 19th Series* (1973), p. 263.

5. Hockett, "The Problem of Universals," pp. 18–19.

6. *Astounding Science Fiction* (May 1955), p. 106.

7. For a list of some that do not fail, see Krueger, "Language and Techniques of Communication as Theme or Tool in Science-Fiction," pp. 80–82.

8. Rpt. 1968, p. ix. Eiseley also demonstrates that, unlike westerns or mystery novels, science fiction is still not quite respectable. He takes care to point out that *Voyage to Arcturus* is not really science fiction ("not a common story of adventure"), thereby excusing himself for liking it.

9. The author's name is better known as that of a character in the books of Kurt Vonnegut, Jr. In this case, however, it is the pseudonym of Philip José Farmer.

10. Krueger, "Language," p. 81.

11. *Linguistics and Languages*, p. 119. Since the story concerns the efforts of two unisexual alien explorers to understand human romance, presumably the color patches can also be used to transmit impure concepts.

12. Admittedly, *anthropologist* is not a very good word, since the objects of his study are definitely not *anthropoi*; a more accurate term sometimes found in science fiction and its criticism is *xenobiologist*.

13. Hockett, "The Problem of Universals," p. 17.

14. "The Creation of Imaginary Beings," in Bretnor, ed., *Science Fiction, Today and Tomorrow*, p. 270.

15. The linguistic function of *hmmm* seems well known, especially among the contributors to this collection; compare the quotation above with the following dialogue from Robert Sheckley's "A Suppliant in Space," also in Wollheim's *1974 Annual World's Best SF*, p. 12: "'Hmmm,' said Colonel Kettelman. 'I beg your pardon?' 'Hmmm,' said the C31 Translating Computer, 'is a polite word made by Terrans to denote a short period of silent cogitation.'"

16. Like the people of the Moon in Cyrano de Bergerac's fabulous voyage. See J. O. Bailey, *Pilgrims Through Space and Time* (Greenwood Press, 1972), pp. 223–24.

17. Showing that the author is impeded by the quotidian realities of biology no more than by those of linguistics. The book, by the way, is neither satire nor pornography, both of which genres imply intent.

6

1. The drawing is reproduced on the back cover of *Science-Fiction Studies*, 2:1 (March 1975).

2. On this fascinating subject, see Harry Harrison, *Great Balls of Fire: An Illustrated History of Sex in Science Fiction* (New York: Grosset & Dunlap, 1977).

3. From his preface to his story "Et in Arcadia Ego," in *SF: Author's Choice 4*, ed. Harry Harrison (G. P. Putnam's Sons, 1974), p. 76.

4. From his afterword to his "We Purchased People," in E. L. Ferman and Barry N. Malzberg, eds., *Final Stage* (Penguin, 1975), p. 28. Oddly enough, "We Purchased People" belies its classification in this anthology; it is *not* a first contact story.

5. It is impossible to say what incident Blish had in mind here, but the most likely candidate is the Japanese reception of the Potsdam Proclamation demanding unconditional surrender under penalty of "the utter devastation of the Japanese homeland." John Toland, in *The Rising Sun: The Decline and Fall of the Japanese Empire, 1936–1945* (Random House, 1970), outlines the Japanese government's reaction to the Proclamation. Although Prime Minister Suzuki and the Emperor desired peace, or at least negotiations, the military was steadfastly against the terms of the Proclamation, and wanted the government to officially reject it. A compromise was reached; as Toland states, "The Prime Minister would read a statement belittling the Allied terms without rejecting them. At four o'clock Suzuki told reporters, 'The Potsdam Proclamation, in my opinion, is just a rehash of the Cairo Declaration, and the government therefore does not consider it of great importance. We must *mokusatsu* it.' The word means literally 'kill with silence' but as Suzuki later told his son, he intended it to stand for the English phrase 'no comment,' for which there is no Japanese equivalent. Americans, however, understandably applied the dic-

tionary meanings: 'ignore' and 'treat with silent contempt.' On July 30 the *New York Times* headline read: JAPAN OFFICIALLY TURNS DOWN ALLIED SURRENDER UL-TIMATUM. The use of the atom bomb was inevitable" (p. 774). If this account is substantially correct, it seems that there was no mistranslation, but a poor selection of words on Suzuki's part in his statement to the press. Note that the bad choice could still have been rectified by a secret official statement to the Allies.

6. For more information about the founding of Project Ozma, see chapter 14 of Walter Sullivan's *We Are Not Alone: The Search for Intelligent Life on Other Worlds*, rev. ed. (New York: McGraw-Hill, 1966). Chapter 27 of I. S. Shklovskii and Carl Sagan's *Intelligent Life in the Universe* (New York: Dell, 1966) also deals with interstellar radio communication.

7. "Alien Communication," in *The Listener and BBC Television Review* (7 January 1965), p. 13. An excellent, longer discussion of the topic is Ralph E. Lapp's "How to Talk to People, If Any, on Other Planets," *Harper's Magazine* (March 1961), pp. 58–63.

8. *In Search of Wonder: Essays on Modern Science Fiction*, rev. ed. (Chicago: Advent, 1967), p. 71.

9. Green cites a story of his own, "A Custom of the Children of Life," in *F&SF* (December 1972) that he says was written to illustrate this point.

10. David Ketterer, *New Worlds for Old: The Apocalyptic Imagination, Science Fiction, and American Literature* (Anchor, 1974), p. 185.

11. "Extraterrestrial Translation," *Galileo: Magazine of Science and Fiction* 7 (1978), p. 20.

12. *A Sign for Cain: An Exploration of Human Violence* (Warner, 1969), p. 56.

7 1. "Strange Bedfellows: Science Fiction, Linguistics, and Education," *English Journal*, 62 (1973), 998–99. Typical of editorial opinion on the subject is Leland Sapiro's comment in "Over the Transom and Far Away," *Riverside Quarterly*, 5:4 (1973), 278–86. Sapiro, the magazine's editor, specifies what kinds of stories he will reject; under the heading "Naivete" he lists among others, "'English Spoken Here.' Here a time-traveller is addressed in English by residents of Atlantis or a scientist from Old Babylon speaks this language when he arrives in our own time. Or an extra-terrestrial invader announces, in English, 'Men of Earth, we have learned your language from your radio broadcasts'" (p. 282). Sapiro would have rejected, apparently, a story recently accepted by the editor of *Galaxy*, a representative of a type I had thought to be extinct. In Tak Hallus's "Powwow" (January 1975), the aliens land on the moon. The United States and Russia broadcast radio messages; no answer. The United States and Russia send up rockets; the aliens shoot them down. Finally, for singularly unconvincing reasons, the Americans pick an Apache chief to send as an ambassador. The aliens let him land, he speaks to them in Apache, and they answer in the same tongue! To negotiate and conclude a treaty, the chief switches to English, and so do the aliens. And not a word of explanation is ever offered to account for this breathtakingly improbable sequence of events.

2. (1947; rpt. Westport, Conn.: Greenwood Press, 1972), p. 224.

3. Pp. 110–11. The novel also contains a revealing passage in its discussion of Martian writing: "The book, for the convenience of this mode of reproduction, consists of a single sheet, generally from four to eight inches in breadth and of any length required. The writing intended to be thus copied is always minute, and is read for the most part through magnifying spectacles. A roller is attached to each end of the sheet, and when not in use the latter is wound round that attached to the conclusion. When required for reading, both rollers are fixed in a stand, and slowly moved by clockwork, which spreads before the eyes of the reader a length of about four inches at once. The motion is slackened or quickened at the reader's pleasure, and can be stopped altogether, by touching a spring" (pp. 115–16). Anyone who has made much use of a microfilm reader has probably suspected that the device was not designed for human beings, but now we have confirmation.

4. "Language and Techniques of Communication as Theme or Tool in Science-Fiction," *Linguistics*, 29 (1968), 73.

5. "Plausibility in Science Fiction," in Bretnor, ed., *Science Fiction, Today and Tomorrow*, p. 309.

6. *Mechanisms of Memory* (New York: Academic Press, 1967), p. 93.

7. Edward M. Gurowitz, *The Molecular Basis of Memory* (Englewood Cliffs, N.J.: Prentice-Hall, 1969), pp. 77–78.

8. Walter B. Essman and Shinshu Nakajima, *Current Biochemical Approaches to Learning and Memory* (Spectrum, 1973), p. 10. These authors summarize the current state of affairs this way: "In 1929, Lashley wrote: 'The whole theory of learning and of intelligence is in confusion. We know at present nothing of the organic basis of these functions and little enough of either the variety or uniformities of their expression in behavior.' The situation appears to be little better at present. There have been important finds; there have been theories. They have all contributed to some of the confusion in the field, but little to the solution of problems" (p. 17).

8 1. Cited in Barnes, *Linguistics and Languages*, p. iv.

2. *New Maps of Hell* (New York: Harcourt Brace, 1960), p. 21.

3. "The Use of Language in SF," *SF Horizons*, 1 (1964), 44.

4. "Language and Techniques of Communication as Theme or Tool in Science-Fiction," *Linguistics*, 39 (1968), 70.

5. "Strange Bedfellows: Science Fiction, Linguistics, and Education," *English Journal*, 62 (1973), 998–99.

6. Barnes, *Linguistics and Languages*, p. iv.

7. Gordon R. Dickson, "Plausibility in Science Fiction," in Bretnor, ed., *Science Fiction, Today and Tomorrow*, p. 295.

8. "Towards an Aesthetic of Science Fiction," *Science-Fiction Studies*, 2:2 (1975), 112.

9. Quoted in his *The Universe Makers* (New York: Harper & Row, 1971), p. 10.

10. "On the Poetics of the Science Fiction Genre," *College English*, 34:3 (December 1972), 381.

11. In "Towards an Aesthetic of Science Fiction," Joanna Russ likens science fiction to medieval fiction, arguing that they are both didactic in purpose and religious in tone, and names Darko Suvin as the source of this insight. I agree that this is a valid and helpful observation, and add the argument that in its dependence on authority and its extrapolative conservatism, science fiction is again medieval. Also, there is another, more basic source of the likeness: science itself, especially experimental science, draws its philosophical foundation from medieval scholastic philosophy, as its basic principles such as noncontradiction, cause and effect, and Occam's razor demonstrate.

12. "Science and Science Fiction," in *Science Fiction: the Academic Awakening*, ed. Willis E. McNelly (CEA Chapbook, 1974), pp. 30–31.

13. Preface to *The Scientific Romances of H. G. Wells* (Victor Gollancz, Ltd., 1933), p. viii. Brian Aldiss deserves thanks for calling the attention of American critics to this hard-to-locate edition in his *Billion Year Spree*.

14. "Escape Routes" (an "amalgamation and summation of several talks . . . given during the past year"), *Galaxy* (December 1974), p. 41.

15. *The Dispossessed* (Harper & Row SFBC, 1974), p. 300.

16. Foreword to Robert A. Heinlein's "All You Zombies," in *The Mirror of Infinity*, ed. Robert Silverberg (Perennial, 1973), p. 205.

17. "Science Fiction as the Imaginary Experiment," in Bretnor, ed., *Science Fiction, Today and Tomorrow*, p. 138.

18. Compiled by Franz Joseph (Ballantine, 1975).

9 1. Charles Honorton, "Error Some Place," *Journal of Communication*, 25:1 (Winter 1975), p. 105. This issue of the *Journal of Communication* contains a lengthy symposium on parapsychology, which is an excellent introduction to the subject.

2. *The Universe Makers* (Harper & Row, 1971), pp. 77–78.

3. One hesitates to call the Martians "people"; they do, after all, lay eggs. But this method of reproduction which, as mammals, they share with the Earthly platypus, does not prevent issue from the union of John Carter and Dejah Thoris, Princess of Mars. And the son, Carthoris, looks just like his father.

4. *The Creation of Tomorrow: Fifty Years of Magazine Science Fiction* (Columbia University Press, 1977), pp. 156–57.

5. *New Introductory Lectures on Psychoanalysis*, trans. and ed. James Strachey (Norton, 1933), p. 55.

6. *Encyclopedia Americana*, s.v. "Psychical Research or Parapsychology."

7. Robert L. Morris, "Building Experimental Models," *Journal of Communication*, 25:1 (Winter 1975), p. 130.

8. "A Literature against the Future," *American Scholar* (Spring 1977), p. 217. Stupple's essay casts doubt generally on the competence of the *American Scholar* editors to evaluate articles on science fiction, giving the genre yet another thing in common with linguistics.

9. *Encyclopaedia Britannica*, s.v. "Parapsychological Phenomena."

10 1. *Language: Its Nature, Development, and Origin* (1921; rpt. W. W. Norton, 1964), pp. 32–33.

2. From the Historical Introduction, *The Compact Edition of the Oxford English Dictionary*, p. v.

3. Ibid., p. x.

4. *J. R. R. Tolkien: Architect of Middle Earth*, ed. by Frank Wilson (Running Press, 1976), p. 38.

5. Foreword to *The Lord of the Rings*, rev. 2nd ed. (London: Allen & Unwin, 1974), 1:5. References to all three volumes of the work, abbreviated *LR*, are from this edition. References to *The Silmarillion*, abbreviated *Sil*, are from the 1977 edition of Houghton Mifflin.

6. *Understanding Tolkien* (Warner, 1969), p. 75.

7. *J. R. R. Tolkien*, Writers for the Seventies Series (Warner, 1972), p. 29. But see Richard Purtill, *Lord of the Elves and Eldils: Fantasy and Philosophy in C. S. Lewis and J. R. R. Tolkien* (Zondervan, 1974), especially chapter 3, for a corrective to the simple-minded view that Tolkien thought some sounds were nice and some were nasty and distributed them to the languages of the heroes and the villains respectively, on that basis.

8. *Master of Middle-Earth: The Fiction of J. R. R. Tolkien* (Houghton Mifflin, 1972), p. 15.

9. "On Fairy-Stories," p. 19.

10. *Tolkien: A Look Behind the Lord of the Rings* (Ballantine, 1969), p. 1.

11. As cited in Francis P. Dinneen, S. J., *An Introduction to General Linguistics* (Holt, Rinehart and Winston, 1967), p. 215.

12. Ibid., p. 213.

13. Edward Sapir, "Language and Environment," *The American Anthropologist*, 14 (1912), 230.

14. Described in Peter C. Rollins, "Benjamin Lee Whorf: Transcendental Linguist," *Journal of Popular Culture*, 5 (1971), 673–96.

15. "Grammatical Categories," *Language*, 21:1 (January–March 1945), 4.

16. "Science and Linguistics," *Technology Review*, 42:6 (April 1940); rpt. in *Language, Thought, and Reality: Selected Writings of Benjamin Lee Whorf*, ed. by John B. Carroll (The Technology Press of MIT, 1957), p. 214.

17. "Some Verbal Categories of Hopi," *Language*, 14:4 (October–December 1938), 276.

18. Whorf implies here and elsewhere that English past, present, and future tenses closely correspond to actions in past, present, and future time in an attempt to emphasize the contrast with Hopi. In this he is less than accurate, since the relation of English tense to time is much more complex than he admits.

19. "Science and Linguistics," p. 216.

20. From the preface to *A Dictionary of the English Language*, 1755; cited in *Dictionaries and That Dictionary*, ed. James Sledd and Wilma R. Ebbitt (Scott Foresman, 1962), p. 28. Why, one wonders, would one so aware of the paper-tiger aspects of Newspeak as Anthony Burgess cut out a similar tiger of his own to menace the reader with? All the strictures of Newspeak that he points out apply with equal force to the "Workers' English" he appends to his novel *1985*. Where Orwell's book cautioned against domination by the elite, Burgess's novel warns against domination by the working class, or rather, against domination by elite *from* the working class—union leaders. Yet Burgess patterns his chimera on Orwell's. Neither would be a significant threat either to our liberties or to our language.

21. For more examples and a discussion of the Whorf hypothesis in dystopian fiction, see Barnes, *Linguistics and Languages*, chapter 9, "The Language of Thought-Control." Barnes makes the insightful comment that dystopias necessarily take a Whorfian view of language.

22. Personal letter to M. J. E. Barnes, quoted in her *Linguistics and Languages*, p. 163.

23. Barnes, *Linguistics and Languages*, p. 159.

24. Rollins, "The Whorf Hypothesis as a Critique of Western Science and Technology," *American Quarterly*, 24 (December 1972), 565.

25. Ibid., p. 580.

11

1. 2nd ed. (Lancaster, Pa.: The Science Press, 1941).

2. "Science Fiction in the Age of Space," in Bretnor, ed., *Science Fiction, Today and Tomorrow*, p. 172.

3. I quote throughout from the 1970 Berkley Medallion paperback edition, which contains an introduction by the author. *The World of Null-A* has had an interesting history: immediately after its serial appearance in 1945, it was subjected to a scorching (and justified) review by Damon Knight in a fan magazine. The review, "Cosmic Jerrybuilder: A. E. van Vogt," is reprinted in Damon Knight, *In Search of Wonder* (Advent, 1967). In the Berkley introduction (p. 7), van Vogt admits that he revised the novel to meet Knight's objections before its hardcover publication by Simon and Schuster in 1948. The Berkley paperback gives the impression that it is the result of a second revision ("This edition specially revised . . ."), but the changes seem few and minor.

4. Forrest J. Ackerman recorded and later transcribed the speech. It appears as "Heinlein on Science Fiction," *Vertex*, 1:1 (April 1973), 46–49, 96–98. Heinlein continued to admire Korzybski: in 1959 he ranked Korzybski with Socrates and T. H. Huxley among his principal influences. See Heinlein's "Science Fiction: Its Nature, Faults, and Virtues," *Turning Points: Essays on the Art of Science Fiction*, ed. Damon Knight (Harper & Row, 1977), pp. 3–28.

5. *Heinlein in Dimension* (Advent, 1968), p. 13.

6. "Science Fiction in the Age of Space," p. 173.

7. "SF: The Challenge to the Writer," *The Craft of Science Fiction* (Harper & Row, 1976), p. 11.

8. *Science and Sanity*, pp. 750–51. Korzybski's statement that "the word is not the thing" is by no means fatuous, since the assertion is not at all obvious. But it is important to the theory of General Semantics: "The present non-aristotelian [*sic*] system is based on fundamental *negative* premises; namely, the complete denial of 'identity,' which denial *cannot be denied* without imposing the burden of impossible proof on the person who denies the denial. If we start, for instance, with a statement that 'a word is *not* the object spoken about,' and some one tries to deny that, he would have to produce an actual physical object which would *be the word*,—impossible of performance, even in asylums for the 'mentally' ill" (*Science and Sanity*, pp. 10–11). Yet Korzybski's principle is false. First, it should be noted that "thing" does not mean a concrete, physical object for Korzybski. In fact, he rejects the notion of the existence of discrete objects. "Thing," therefore, in the

sentence quoted above, can only mean what Korzybski calls a "spacetime event," that is, some segment of the flux of reality. For him, a handshake is no less a "thing" than an apple. But if events are not ruled out as things (and it is difficult to see how they can be), then some words are indeed the things themselves. There is a class of statements called performatives, in which the saying of the statement is the performance of an action (or, in Korzybski's terminology, a spacetime event). For example, the words "I promise to be here on time," when spoken under the appropriate circumstances, are in fact a promise; the words "I bet you a dollar this one will convince you," with the same qualifications, are in fact a bet.

The philosopher J. L. Austin first pointed out this class of statements in *How to Do Things with Words: The Williams James Lectures Delivered at Harvard University in 1955* (Oxford University Press, 1970). He cites examples such as those above, and says that to utter such sentences (always assuming they take place in appropriate circumstances) is to perform an action. When one says "I bet you a dollar," the words do not describe a bet; they do not state that someone is betting; they are in fact a bet. He adds, "It may be that the utterance 'serves to inform you'—but that is quite different. To name the ship *is* to say (in the appropriate circumstances) the words 'I name, &c.' When I say, before the registrar or altar, &c., 'I do,' I am not reporting on a marriage: I am indulging in it" (p. 6). Later he notes, "I am told, in the American law of evidence, a report of what someone else said is admitted as evidence if what he said is an utterance of our performative kind: because this is regarded as a report not so much of something he *said*, as which it would be hearsay and not admissible as evidence, but rather as something he *did*, an action of his" (p. 13). Performatives, therefore, are words that are things: promises, bets, marriages, and various other rituals such as christenings, bequests, and the like. Some words are space-time events.

9. First published in Ace in 1966. Delany made some revisions for the Sphere paperback of 1969, which was chosen as the text for the Gregg Press reprint of 1976 from which I quote.

10. Through some curious oversight, the Gregg Press edition does not contain the Pei epigraph that Scholes mentions; it does, however, appear in the Ace paperback.

11. *Triton*, p. 345. Delany quotes from Michel Foucault, *The Order of Things*, trans. unnamed (Pantheon, 1970; orig. pub. in French as *Les Mots et le choses* [Editions Gallimard, 1966]), p. xviii. Fantasy and science fiction meet us at every turn: Foucault says he was inspired to write the book by a passage from Jorge Luis Borges.

12. "The Order of Things," *New York Times Book Review* (28 February 1971), p. 8. Longer, harsher treatments included those of D. W. Harding, "Good-By Man," *New York Review of Books* (12 August 1971), pp. 21–22; and especially G. S. Rous-

seau, "Whose Enlightenment? Not Man's: The Case of Michel Foucault," *Eighteenth Century Studies*, 6:2 (Winter 1972–73), 238–56.

13. See, for example, Barry N. Malzberg in *The Magazine of Fantasy and Science Fiction* (September 1976), pp. 30–34; and Spider Robinson in *Galaxy* (October 1976), pp. 130–31.

14. P. 2. Delany has his technical terms under better control now, calling the chant "the dim thunder of labials and vowels" (p. 3).

15. See Noam Chomsky, *Cartesian Linguistics* (New York: Harper & Row, 1966).

16. The date of publication of Watson's *The Embedding* is 1973, in London. Although it preceded the American paperback publication of Brunner's *Total Eclipse* (1974), it was not published in the United States until after Brunner's book.

17. George Steiner, *After Babel: Aspects of Language and Translation* (Oxford University Press, 1975), p. 169.

12 1. Richard Gerber, *Utopian Fantasy: A Study of English Utopian Fiction since the End of the Nineteenth Century* (McGraw-Hill, 1973), p. 67. Originally published in 1955; the 1973 reprint adds a bibliography of "English Utopian Fantasies" from 1952 to 1971.

2. Judson Allen, "Utopian Literature: The Problem of Literary Reference," *Cithara* 11 (1972), p. 41.

3. Ibid., p. 48.

4. James Cooke Brown, *Loglan 1: A Logical Language*, 3rd ed. (Gainesville, Fla., and Palm Springs, Calif.: The Loglan Institute, 1974), p. xi. A short introduction to Loglan appeared in the June 1960 issue of *Scientific American*.

5. Ibid., p. 3.

6. Ibid., p. 12.

7. Ibid., p. 2.

8. Ibid.

9. Allen, "Utopian Literature," p. 41.

10. Barnes, *Linguistics and Languages*, pp. 150–51.

11. Robert M. Philmus, "The Language of Utopia," *Studies in the Literary Imagination*, 6:2 (Fall 1973), p. 64.

12. Ibid., p. 74.

13. Gorman Beauchamp, "Future Words: Language and the Dystopian Novel," *Style*, 8:3 (Fall 1974), p. 464.

14. Philmus, "The Language of Utopia," p. 63.

15. It may in fact assume their divinity. See Peter Wolfe, "*Walden Two* Twenty-Five Years Later: A Retrospective Look," *Studies in the Literary Imagination*, 6:2 (Fall 1973) for an analysis of Skinner's portrayal of Frazier as a god.

16. "The Art of Social-Science Fiction: The Ambiguous Utopian Dialectics of Ursula K. Le Guin," *Science-Fiction Studies*, 2:3 (November 1975), esp. pp. 261–62.

17. "Ambiguity in Utopia: *The Dispossessed*," *Science-Fiction Studies*, 2:3 (November 1975), p. 254.

18. "Parables of De-Alienation: Le Guin's Widdershins Dance," *Science-Fiction Studies*, 2:3 (November 1975), p. 267.

19. Allen, "Utopian Literature," p. 41.

20. *Utopia*, trans. Ralph Robinson (1551), (London: Dent & Sons, 1910), p. 119.

Bibliography

Science fiction magazines have seen more than a few name changes during their serial runs. I have adopted the following shortened citation forms in the bibliography:

Astounding: Astounding Stories (January 1930 [its founding] to February 1938).
Astounding Science Fiction (March 1938 to January 1960).
Astounding Science Fact and Fiction (February 1960 to September 1960).
Analog: Analog Science Fact and Fiction (October 1960 to November 1961).
Analog Science Fact–Science Fiction (December 1961 to March 1965).
Analog Science Fiction–Science Fact (April 1965 to the present).

Alternate titles of the same magazine, *Galaxy Science Fiction, Galaxy Magazine,* and *Galaxy Science Fiction Magazine,* are all cited as *Galaxy.*

"Fantasy and Science Fiction" in the title *The Magazine of Fantasy and Science Fiction,* and in the titles of the collections of stories from that magazine, is sometimes abbreviated *F&SF.*

The abbreviation *pb* indicates a paperback edition.

Nonfiction

Aldiss, Brian W. *Billion-Year Spree: The True History of Science Fiction.* Garden City, N.Y.: Doubleday, 1973.

Algeo, John. *Problems in the Origins and Development of the English Language,* 2nd ed. New York: Harcourt Brace Jovanovich, 1972.

Allan, James D. *A Glossary of the Eldarin Tongues.* Orillia, Ontario: Printed by the author, 1972.

———. *An Introduction to Elvish.* Somerset, U.K.: Bran's Head, 1978. This work may be obtained in the U.S. from Jitco, 1776 E. Jefferson Street, Rockville, Md. 20852.

Allen, Judson. "Utopian Literature: The Problem of Literary Reference." *Cithara,* 11 (1972), 40–55.

Amis, Kingsley. *New Maps of Hell.* New York: Harcourt Brace, 1960.

Anderson, Poul. "The Creation of Imaginary Worlds." In Reginald Bretnor, ed., *Science Fiction, Today and Tomorrow,* pp. 235–57.

Asimov, Isaac. *In Memory Yet Green: The Autobiography of Isaac Asimov*. Vol. 1: 1920–1954. New York: Doubleday, 1979.

———. Introduction to Carol and Frederik Pohl, eds., *Jupiter*.

Atheling, William. See James Blish.

Austin, J. L. *How to Do Things with Words*. The William James Lectures Delivered at Harvard University in 1955. New York: Oxford University Press pb, 1970.

Bailey, James Osler, *Pilgrims through Space and Time*. Westport, Conn.: Greenwood Press, 1972.

Barnes, M. J. E. *Linguistics and Languages in Science Fiction-Fantasy*. New York: Arno, 1974.

Beauchamp, Gorman. "Future Words: Language and the Dystopian Novel." *Style*, 8:3 (Fall 1974), 462–76.

Bell, Judy Winn. "The Language of J. R. R. Tolkien in *The Lord of the Rings*." In Glen GoodKnight, ed., *Mythcon I Proceedings*, pp. 35–40.

Benford, Gregory. "Science and Science Fiction." In Willis E. McNelly, ed., *Science Fiction: The Academic Awakening*, pp. 30–34.

Bierman, Judah. "Ambiguity in Utopia: *The Dispossessed.*" *Science-Fiction Studies*, 2:3 (November 1975), 249–55.

Blish, James [as William Atheling, Jr.]. *The Issue at Hand*. Chicago: Advent, 1964.

———. [as William Atheling, Jr.]. *More Issues at Hand*. Chicago: Advent, 1970.

Bova, Ben. "Intelligent Life in Space." *Amazing* (March 1963), pp. 91–101.

Bretnor, Reginald. "SF: The Challenge to the Writer." In R. Bretnor, ed., *The Craft of Science Fiction*, pp. 3–20.

———. "Science Fiction in the Age of Space." In R. Bretnor, ed., *Science Fiction, Today and Tomorrow*, pp. 150–78.

———, ed. *The Craft of Science Fiction*. New York: Harper & Row, 1976.

———, ed. *Modern Science Fiction: Its Meaning and Its Future*. New York: Coward-McCann, 1953.

———, ed. *Science Fiction, Today and Tomorrow: A Discursive Symposium*. New York: Harper & Row, 1974.

Brown, James Cooke. *Loglan 1: A Logical Language*, 3rd ed. Gainesville, Fla. and Palm Springs, Calif.: The Loglan Institute: 1975.

Caldwell, Melba C., David K. Caldwell, and Robert H. Turner. "Statistical Analysis of the Signature Whistle of an Atlantic Bottlenosed Dolphin with Correlations Between Vocal Changes and Level of Arousal." National Technical Information Service, AD 708–787.

Carter, Lin. *Tolkien: A Look Behind The Lord of the Rings*. New York: Ballantine pb, 1969.

Carter, Paul A. *The Creation of Tomorrow: Fifty Years of Magazine Science Fiction*. New York: Columbia University Press, 1977.

Chalmers, John. Letter in "Brass Tacks." *Analog* (January 1975), pp. 175–76. Slight differences in wording between the letter as it appears in *Analog* and as quoted here are due to emendations Chalmers made in a personal letter to the author dated 14 July 1977.

Chomsky, Noam. *Cartesian Linguistics*. New York: Harper & Row, 1966.

Clement, Hal. "The Creation of Imaginary Beings." In R. Bretnor, ed., *Science Fiction, Today and Tomorrow*, pp. 259–75.

de Bolt, Joe, ed. *The Happening Worlds of John Brunner*. Port Washington, N.Y.: Kennikat Press, 1975.

de Camp, L. Sprague. "Language for Time-Travelers." *Astounding* (July 1938), pp. 63–72.

———. *Science-Fiction Handbook*. New York: Hermitage House, 1953.

Denes, Peter B., and Elliot N. Pinson. *The Speech Chain: The Physics and Biology of Spoken Language*. Garden City, N.Y.: Anchor pb, 1973.

Dickson, Gordon R. "Plausibility in Science Fiction." In R. Bretnor, ed., *Science Fiction, Today and Tomorrow*, pp. 295–306.

Dinneen, Francis P., S. J. *An Introduction to General Linguistics*. New York: Holt Rinehart, 1967.

Disch, Thomas M. Preface to "Et in Arcadia Ego." In Harry Harrison, ed., *SF: Authors' Choice 4*.

Dixon, Robert M. W. "How to Understand Aliens." *Worlds of Tomorrow* (January 1966), pp. 115–22.

Doherty, G. D. "The Use of Language in SF." *SF Horizons*, 1 (1964), 43–53.

Eiseley, Loren. Introduction to David Lindsay, *A Voyage to Arcturus*. New York: Ballantine pb, 1963. Pp. 7–10.

Essman, Walter B., and Shinshu Nakajima. *Current Biochemical Approaches to Learning and Memory*. New York: Spectrum, 1973.

Evans, Robley. *J. R. R. Tolkien*. Writers for the 70s Series. New York: Warner pb, 1972.

Foucault, Michel. *The Order of Things*. New York: Pantheon, 1970. In French as *Le Mots et le choses*. Paris: Editions Gallimard, 1966.

Francis, W. Nelson. "A Standard Corpus of Edited Present-Day American English." *College English*, 26:4 (January 1965), 267–73.

Freud, Sigmund. *New Introductory Lectures on Psychoanalysis*. Translated and edited by James Strachey. New York: Norton, 1933.

Friend, Beverly. "Strange Bedfellows: Science Fiction, Linguistics, and Education." *English Journal*, 62 (1973), 998–1003.

Gaddis, Vincent H. "The New Science of Space Speech." *Worlds of Tomorrow* (August 1963), pp. 115–23.

Gardner, B. T., and R. A. Gardner. "Evidence for Sentence Constituents in the Early

Utterances of Child and Chimpanzee." *Journal of Experimental Psychology*, 104 (1975), 244–67.

———. "Teaching Sign Language to a Chimpanzee." *Science*, 165 (1969), 664–72.

———. "Two-way Communication with an Infant Chimpanzee." In A. M. Schrier and F. Stollnitz, eds., *Behavior of Non-Human Primates*. Vol. 4, ch. 3. New York: Academic Press, 1971.

Gerber, Richard. *Utopian Fantasy: A Study of English Utopian Fiction since the End of the Nineteenth Century*. New York: McGraw Hill pb, 1973. First published in 1955; the reprint adds a list of "English Utopian Fantasies," 1952 to 1971.

Goldin, Stephen. "Notes from a Phantom Koala." *The Bulletin of the Science Fiction Writers of America*, 11:4 (August 1976), 16–18.

Goldman, Stephen H. "The Polymorphic Worlds of John Brunner: How Do They Happen?" *Science-Fiction Studies*, 3:2 (July 1976), 103–12.

GoodKnight, Glen, ed. *Mythcon I Proceedings*. Los Angeles: Mythopoeic Society, 1973.

Green, Joseph. Afterword to "Encounter with a Carnivore." In Roger Elwood and Robert Silverberg, eds., *Epoch*, pp. 196–97.

Griffin, Donald R. *The Question of Animal Awareness*. New York: Rockefeller University Press, 1976.

Grotta-Kurska, Daniel. *J. R. R. Tolkien: Architect of Middle Earth*. Philadelphia: Running Press, 1976.

Gurowitz, Edward M. *The Molecular Basis of Memory*. Englewood Cliffs, N.J.: Prentice-Hall, 1969.

Harding, D. W. "Good-by Man," a Review of Michel Foucault, *The Order of Things*. *New York Review of Books* (12 August 1971), pp. 21–22.

Harrison, Harry. *Great Balls of Fire: An Illustrated History of Sex in Science Fiction*. New York: Grosset & Dunlap, 1977.

———. "With a Piece of Twisted Wire." *SF Horizons*, 2 (Winter 1965), 55–60.

Hayakawa, S. I. *Language in Thought and Action*, 2nd ed. New York: Harcourt, 1964.

Heinlein, Robert A. "Heinlein on Science Fiction." *Vertex*, 1:1 (April 1973), 46–49, 96–98. From a recording by Forrest J. Ackerman of Heinlein's Guest-of-Honor Speech at the Third World Science Fiction Convention, Denver, 4 July 1941.

———. "Science Fiction: Its Nature, Faults, and Virtues." In Damon Knight, ed., *Turning Points: Essays on the Art of Science Fiction*, pp. 3–28.

Herbert, Frank. "Men on Other Planets." In R. Bretnor, ed., *The Craft of Science Fiction*, pp. 121–35.

Hockett, Charles F. "How to Learn Martian." *Astounding* (May 1955), pp. 97–106.

———. "The Problem of Universals in Language." In Joseph H. Greenberg, ed., *Universals of Language*, 2nd ed. Cambridge, Mass.: MIT Press, 1963. Pp. 1–29.

Honorton, Charles. "Error Some Place." *Journal of Communication*, 25:1 (Winter 1975), 103–16.

Jespersen, Otto. *Language: Its Nature, Development, and Origin*. New York: Norton pb, 1964. First published 1921.

John, E. Roy. *Mechanisms of Memory*. New York: Academic Press, 1967.

Ketterer, David. *New Worlds for Old: The Apocalyptic Imagination, Science Fiction, and American Literature*. New York: Anchor pb, 1974.

Knight, Damon. *In Search of Wonder: Essays on Modern Science Fiction*. Rev. and enlarged ed. with Introduction by Anthony Boucher. Chicago: Advent, 1967.

————, ed. *Turning Points: Essays on the Art of Science Fiction*. New York: Harper & Row, 1977.

Kocher, Paul H. *Master of Middle-Earth: The Fiction of J. R. R. Tolkien*. Boston: Houghton Mifflin, 1972.

Korzybski, Alfred. *Science and Sanity: An Introduction to Non-Aristotelian Systems and General Semantics*, 2nd ed. Lancaster, Pa.: The Science Press, 1941.

Krueger, John R. "Language and Techniques of Communication as Theme or Tool in Science-Fiction." *Linguistics*, 39 (1968), 68–86.

————. "Names and Nomenclatures in Science-Fiction." *Names*, 14 (1966), 203–14.

Kučera, Henry, and W. Nelson Francis. *Computational Analysis of Present-Day American English*. Providence: Brown University Press, 1967.

Laird, Charlton. "A Nonhuman Being Can Learn Language." *College Composition and Communication*, 23 (May 1972), 142–54.

Lapp, Ralph E. "How to Talk to People, If Any, on Other Planets." *Harper's Magazine* (March 1961), pp. 58–63.

Le Guin, Ursula K. "Escape Routes." *Galaxy* (December 1974), pp. 40–44.

Leiber, Justin. "Extraterrestrial Translation." *Galileo*, 7 (1978), 18–20, 22.

Ley, Willy. "One Planet, One Language." *Galaxy* (February 1960), pp. 102–7.

Lieberman, Philip. "Primate Vocalizations and Human Linguistic Ability." *Journal of the Acoustical Society*, 44 (1968), 1574–84.

Lilly, John C. *Lilly on Dolphins*. Garden City, N.Y.: Anchor pb, 1975. Contains *Man and Dolphin* (first published 1961) in revised form; "The Dolphin in History," a lecture (no date given); *The Mind of the Dolphin* (first published 1967) in revised form; and several technical articles published in 1966 and 1968.

————. *Man and Dolphin*. Garden City, N.Y.: Doubleday, 1961.

————. *The Mind of the Dolphin*, rpt. in *Lilly on Dolphins*.

Lundwall, Sam J. *Science Fiction: What It's All About*. New York: Ace, 1971. A translation by the author of his work published in Sweden in 1969.

MacLean, Katherine. "Alien Minds and Nonhuman Intelligences." In R. Bretnor, ed., *The Craft of Science Fiction*, pp. 136–58.

McNelly, Willis E., ed. *Science Fiction: The Academic Awakening*. Supplement to

The CEA Critic, 37:1 (November 1974). Shreveport, La.: College English Association, 1974.

Malzberg, Barry N. Review of Samuel R. Delany, *Triton*. *The Magazine of Fantasy and Science Fiction* (September 1976), pp. 30–34.

Mercer, Derwent. "Alien Communication." *The Listener and BBC Television Review* (7 January 1965), pp. 13–15.

Meyers, Walter E. "The Future History and Development of the English Language." *Science-Fiction Studies*, 3:2 (July 1976), 130–42.

Miller, P. Schuyler. Review of Samuel R. Delany, *Babel-17*. *Analog* (December 1967), p. 164.

Morris, Robert L. "Building Experimental Models." *Journal of Communication*, 25:1 (Winter 1975), 117–32.

Niven, Larry. "The Words in Science Fiction." In R. Bretnor, ed., *The Craft of Science Fiction*, pp. 178–94.

Panshin, Alexei. Foreword to Robert A. Heinlein's "All You Zombies." In Robert Silverberg, ed., *The Mirror of Infinity*, pp. 204–6.

————. *Heinlein in Dimension*. Chicago: Advent, 1968.

Parma Eldalamberon: The Book of Elven Tongues. The Journal of Mythopoeic Linguistic Fellowship, Box 24150, Los Angeles, Calif., 90024.

Perkins, Lawrence A. "Target: Language." *Analog* (May 1967), pp. 81–95.

Perrin, Noel. "Old Macberlitz Had a Farm." *New Yorker* (27 January 1962), pp. 28–29.

Philmus, Robert M. "The Language of Utopia." *Studies in the Literary Imagination*, 6:2 (Fall 1973), 62–78.

Plank, Robert. "Communication in Science Fiction." *ETC.*, 11:1 (Autumn 1953), 16–20.

Pohl, Frederik. Afterword to "We Purchased People." In E. L. Ferman and B. N. Malzberg, eds., *Final Stage*, pp. 27–28.

Pournelle, Jerry. "The Construction of Believable Societies." In R. Bretnor, ed., *The Craft of Science Fiction*, pp. 104–19.

Pratt, Fletcher. "A Critique of Science Fiction." In R. Bretnor, ed., *Modern Science Fiction*, pp. 73–90.

Purtill, Richard. *Lord of the Elves and Eldils: Fantasy and Philosophy in C. S. Lewis and J. R. R. Tolkien*. Grand Rapids, Mich.: Zondervan, 1974.

Pyles, Thomas. *The Origins and Development of the English Language*, 2nd ed. New York: Harcourt Brace Jovanovich, 1971.

Ready, William. *Understanding Tolkien and The Lord of the Rings*. New York: Warner pb, 1969.

Robinson, Spider. Review of Samuel R. Delany's *Triton*. *Galaxy* (October 1976), pp. 130–31.

Rollins, Peter C. "Benjamin Lee Whorf, Transcendental Linguist." *Journal of Popular Culture*, 5 (1971), 673–96.

———. "The Whorf Hypothesis as a Critique of Western Science and Technology." *American Quarterly*, 24:5 (December 1972), 563–83.

Rousseau, G. S. "Whose Enlightenment? Not Man's: The Case of Michel Foucault." *Eighteenth Century Studies*, 6:2 (Winter 1972–73), 238–56.

Russ, Joanna. "Towards an Aesthetic of Science Fiction." *Science-Fiction Studies*, 2:2 (1975), 112–19.

Samuelson, David. *Visions of Tomorrow: Six Journeys from Outer to Inner Space.* New York: Arno, 1975.

Sapir, Edward. "Language and Environment." *American Anthropologist*, 14 (1912), 226–42.

Sapiro, Leland. "Over the Transom and Far Away." *Riverside Quarterly*, 5:4 (1973), 278–86.

Scholes, Robert. Introduction to Samuel R. Delany's *Babel-17*. Boston: Gregg Press, 1976. Pp. iii–x. A reprint of the Sphere Books pb, London, 1969.

———. *Structural Fabulation*. Notre Dame, Ind.: University of Notre Dame Press, 1975.

Scortia, Thomas N. "Science Fiction as the Imaginary Experiment." In R. Bretnor, ed., *Science Fiction, Today and Tomorrow*, pp. 135–47.

Shipman, G. R. "How to Talk to a Martian." *Astounding* (October 1953), pp. 112–20.

Shklovskii, I. S., and Carl Sagan. *Intelligent Life in the Universe.* New York: Delta pb, 1966.

Spinrad, Norman. "Rubber Sciences." In R. Bretnor, ed., *The Craft of Science Fiction*, pp. 54–70.

Steiner, George. *After Babel: Aspects of Language and Translation.* New York: Oxford University Press, 1975.

———. "The Order of Things," a review of Michel Foucault, *The Order of Things.* *New York Times Book Review* (28 February 1971), pp. 8, 28–31.

Stover, Leon E. "Social Science Fiction." In Willis E. McNelly, ed., *Science Fiction: The Academic Awakening*, pp. 21–24.

Stupple, James. "A Literature Against the Future." *American Scholar* (Spring 1977), 215–20.

Sullivan, Walter. *We Are Not Alone: The Search for Intelligent Life on Other Worlds*, rev. ed. New York: McGraw-Hill, 1966.

Suvin, Darko. "On the Poetics of the Science Fiction Genre." *College English*, 34:3 (December 1972), 372–82.

———. "Parables of De-Alienation: Le Guin's Widdershins Dance." *Science-Fiction Studies*, 2:3 (November 1975), 265–74.

Bibliography

Theall, Donald F. "The Art of Social-Science Fiction: The Ambiguous Utopian Dialectics of Ursula K. Le Guin." *Science-Fiction Studies*, 2:3 (November 1975), 256–64.

Tolkien, J. R. R. Foreword to *The Lord of the Rings*, rev. 2nd ed. London: Allen & Unwin, 1974. Vol. 1, pp. 5–8.

———. "On Fairy-Stories." *Tree and Leaf*, pp. 3–84. Originally an Andrew Lang Lecture, University of St. Andrews, 1938. First published in *Essays Presented to Charles Williams*, ed. C. S. Lewis. London: Oxford University Press, 1947.

———. *Tree and Leaf*. Boston: Houghton Mifflin, 1965.

Van Gieson, W. D., Jr., and W. D. Chapman. "Machine-Generated Speech for Use with Computers." *Computers and Automation* (November 1968), pp. 31–34.

Van Vogt, A. E. Introduction to *The World of Null-A*. New York: Berkley Medallion pb, 1974. Pp. 5–11.

Warren, David. "Language, Thought and Fantasy." *Parma Eldalamberon*, No. 5 (1977), 18–21.

Watson, Ian. "Towards an Alien Linguistics." *Vector 71* (Journal of the British Science Fiction Association), 2:3 (December 1975), 14–23.

Wells, H. G. Preface to *The Scientific Romances of H. G. Wells*. London: Victor Gollancz, 1933. Pp. vii–x.

Wertham, Frederic. *A Sign for Cain: An Exploration of Human Violence*. New York: Warner pb, 1969.

Whorf, Benjamin Lee. "Grammatical Categories." *Language*, 21:1 (January–March 1945), 1–11.

———. "Science and Linguistics." In *Language, Thought, and Reality: Selected Writings of Benjamin Lee Whorf*, edited by John B. Carroll. Cambridge, Mass.: The Technology Press of MIT, 1957. Pp. 207–19.

———. "Some Verbal Categories of Hopi." *Language*, 14:4 (October–December 1938), 275–86.

Wollheim, Donald A. *The Universe Makers*. New York: Harper & Row, 1971.

Wood, Forrest G. *Marine Mammals and Man: The Navy's Porpoises and Sea Lions*. Washington: Robert B. Luce, 1973.

Fiction

In order to keep this list to a reasonable length, I have supplied bibliographical information only for the copy I used. If that citation does not describe the first publication of the work, the date of first publication is given in parentheses immediately following the title. Readers interested in complete data on the works should consult the following very useful references:

William Contento, *Index to Science Fiction Anthologies and Collections* (Boston: G. K. Hall, 1978);

Donald B. Day, *Index to the Science-Fiction Magazines 1926–1950* (Cambridge, Mass.: MIT Science Fiction Society, 1961);

New England Science Fiction Association, *Index to the Science Fiction Magazines 1966–1970* (Cambridge, Mass.: NESFA, 1971), and supplements;

Erwin S. Strauss, *The MIT Science Fiction Society's Index to the S-F Magazines 1951–1965* (Cambridge, Mass.: MIT Science Fiction Society, 1966);

Donald H. Tuck, *The Encyclopedia of Science Fiction and Fantasy*, 2 vols. (Chicago: Advent, 1974, 1978).

The abbreviation *SFBC* in the citations below stands for the Science Fiction Book Club edition of the work.

Akers, Alan Burt. *Transit to Scorpio*. New York: DAW pb, 1972.

Aldiss, Brian W. "The Game of God." (1958 as "Segregation.") In *Starswarm*.

———. *Starswarm*. New York: New American Library pb, 1964.

———. "The Worm That Flies." (1968) In *World's Best SF 1969*, ed. D. A. Wollheim and T. Carr.

———, and Harry Harrison, eds. *Nebula Award Stories: Two*. Garden City, N.Y.: Doubleday, 1967.

Allen, Dick, and Lori Allen, eds. *Looking Ahead: The Vision of Science Fiction*. New York: Harcourt, 1975.

Amis, Kingsley, ed. *Spectrum 4*. (1965) New York: Berkley pb, 1966.

Anderson, Poul. *Beyond the Beyond*. New York: New American Library pb, 1969.

———. *Brain Wave*. New York: Ballantine pb, 1954.

———. *The Dancer from Atlantis*. Garden City, N.Y.: Doubleday SFBC, 1971.

———. "Epilogue." (1962) In *The Ends of Time*, ed. R. Silverberg.

———. "Eutopia." In *Dangerous Visions*, ed. H. Ellison.

———. "Inside Earth." (1951) In *Galaxy Reader of SF*, ed. H. Gold.

———. "Kyrie." (1968) In *World's Best SF 1969*, ed. D. A. Wollheim and T. Carr.

———. "A Little Knowledge." (1971) In *Best Science Fiction Stories of the Year*, ed. L. del Rey.

———. "Lodestar." In *Astounding: John W. Campbell Memorial Anthology*, ed. H. Harrison.

———. "Memory." (1957 as "A World Called Maanerek.") In *Beyond the Beyond*.

———. "The Queen of Air and Darkness." (1971) In *Nebula Award Stories: Seven*, ed. L. Biggle.

———. "The Serpent in Eden." In *Omega*, ed. R. Elwood.

———. "The Sharing of Flesh." (1968) In *The Hugo Winners*, ed. I. Asimov.

————. "Starfog." (1967) In *Beyond the Beyond*.

————. "Supernova." *Analog* (January 1967).

————. *Tau Zero*. (1967 as "To Outlive Eternity.") New York: Lancer pb, 1970.

———— [as Winston P. Sanders]. "The Word to Space." (1960) In *Other Worlds, Other Gods*, ed. M. Mohs.

Anthony, Piers. *Orn*. (1970) New York: Avon pb, 1971.

Asimov, Isaac. "Blind Alley." (1945) In *The Early Asimov*, 2.

————. *The Caves of Steel*. (1953) In *The Rest of the Robots*.

————. *The Early Asimov*, 2. Greenwich, Conn.: Fawcett pb, 1972.

————. *The End of Eternity*. Garden City, N.Y.: Doubleday, 1955.

————. "Hostess." (1951) In *Galaxy Reader of SF*, ed. H. Gold.

————. "In a Good Cause." (1951) In *Nightfall and Other Stories*.

————. "It's Such a Beautiful Day." (1954) In *Nightfall and Other Stories*.

————. *Nightfall and Other Stories*. Greenwich, Conn.: Fawcett pb, 1969.

————. "Not Final." (1941) In *Toward Infinity*, ed. D. Knight.

————. *The Rest of the Robots*. Garden City, N.Y.: Doubleday, 1964.

————. "What Is This Thing Called Love?" (1961 as "Playboy and the Slime God.") In *Nightfall and Other Stories*.

————, ed. *Before the Golden Age: A Science Fiction Anthology of the 1930s*. Garden City, N.Y.: Doubleday SFBC, 1974.

————, ed. *The Hugo Winners*, 1–2. Garden City, N.Y.: Doubleday, 1962–1971.

————, ed. *The Hugo Winners*, 3. Garden City, N.Y.: Doubleday, 1977.

Attanasio, A. A. "Interface." In *Epoch*, ed. R. Elwood and R. Silverberg.

Ballard, J. G. *Chronopolis and Other Stories*. New York: Putnam's, 1971.

————. "The Voices of Time." (1960) In *Chronopolis and Other Stories*.

Barton, William. *Hunting on Kunderer*. New York: Ace pb, 1973.

Bauer, Gerard M. "From All of Us." In *Frontiers 2*, ed. R. Elwood.

Bayley, Barrington J. "The Bees of Knowledge." (1975) In *The 1976 Annual World's Best SF*, ed. D. A. Wollheim and A. W. Saha.

Bester, Alfred. *The Dark Side of the Earth*. New York: New American Library, 1964.

————. "The Flowered Thundermug." In *The Dark Side of the Earth*.

————. "The Four-Hour Fugue." (1974) In *The 1975 Annual World's Best SF*, ed. D. A. Wollheim and A. W. Saha.

————. "Of Time and Third Avenue." (1951) In *A Century of SF*, ed. D. Knight.

Biggle, Lloyd, Jr., ed. *Nebula Award Stories: Seven*. New York: Harper & Row SFBC, 1973.

Bishop, Michael. "Death and Designation Among the Asadi." (1973) In *The 1974 Annual World's Best SF*, ed. D. A. Wollheim.

Blish, James. "And Some Were Savages." (1960) In *Anywhen*.

————. *Anywhen*. Garden City, N.Y.: Doubleday, 1970.

———. *Best Science Fiction Stories of James Blish*, rev. ed. London: Faber and Faber, 1973.

———. "A Dusk of Idols." (1961) In *Anywhen*.

———. *Galactic Cluster*. New York: Signet pb, 1959.

———. "No Jokes on Mars." (1965) In *Anywhen*.

———. *The Quincunx of Time*. (1954 [shorter version] as "Beep.") New York: Dell pb, 1973.

———. "Surface Tension." (1952) In *Best SF Stories of James Blish*.

———. "This Earth of Hours." (1959) In *Galactic Cluster*.

———. *VOR*. (1949 [shorter version] as "The Weakness of RVOG.") New York: Avon pb, 1958.

———. "A Work of Art." (1956) In *Best SF Stories of James Blish*.

Boucher, Anthony. "Barrier." (1942) In *Spectrum 4*, ed. K. Amis.   •

———. "Expedition." (1945) In *The Best of Science Fiction*, ed. G. Conklin.

———. "The Quest for Saint Aquin." (1951) In *Other Worlds, Other Gods*, ed. M. Mohs.

———, ed. *The Best from Fantasy and Science Fiction*. Sixth Series. Garden City, N.Y.: Doubleday, 1957.

———, ed. *The Best from Fantasy and Science Fiction*. Seventh Series. Garden City, N.Y.: Doubleday, 1958.

———, ed. *The Best from Fantasy and Science Fiction*. Eighth Series. Garden City, N.Y.: Doubleday, 1959.

———, ed. *A Treasury of Great Science Fiction*. 2 vols. Garden City, N.Y.: Doubleday, 1959.

Boult, S. Kye. "The Safety Engineer." In *The Alien Condition*, ed. S. Goldin.

Bova, Ben, ed. *The Science Fiction Hall of Fame*. Vols. 2A and 2B. Garden City, N.Y.: Doubleday SFBC, 1973.

Brackett, Leigh. *The Sword of Rhiannon*. (1949 as "Sea-King of Mars.") New York: Ace pb, 1953.

Bradbury, Ray. "Forever and the Earth." (1950) In *Big Book of Science Fiction*, ed. G. Conklin.

———. "Pillar of Fire." (1948) In *A Treasury of Great SF*, ed. A. Boucher.

Brown, James Cooke. *The Troika Incident: A Tetralogue in Two Parts*. Garden City, N.Y.: Doubleday, 1970.

Broxon, Mildred Downey. "The Stone Have Names." In *Fellowship of the Stars*, ed. T. Carr.

Brunner, John. *The Dramaturges of Yan*. New York: Ace pb, 1972.

———. *Total Eclipse*. New York: DAW pb, 1974.

———. "You'll Take the High Road." In L. Niven, J. Brunner, and J. Vance, *Three Trips in Time and Space*.

Budrys, Algis. "For Love." (1962) In *The Seventh Galaxy Reader*, ed. F. Pohl.
Bulwer-Lytton, Edward George Earle. *The Coming Race*. New York: Routledge, 1877.
Burgess, Anthony. *A Clockwork Orange*. New York: Norton pb, 1962.
———. *1985*. Boston: Little, Brown, 1978.
Burroughs, Edgar Rice. *The Gods of Mars*. (1912) In *The Gods of Mars and The Warlord of Mars*. Garden City, N.Y.: Doubleday SFBC, 1971.
———. *Llana of Gathol*. (1941 as "The City of Mummies," "Black Pirates of Barsoom," "Yellow Men of Mars," and "Invisible Men of Mars.") In *Llana of Gathol and John Carter of Mars*. Garden City, N.Y.: Doubleday SFBC, 1977.
———. *The Master Mind of Mars*. (1927) In *The Master Mind of Mars and A Fighting Man of Mars*. Garden City, N.Y.: Doubleday SFBC, 1973.
———. *A Princess of Mars*. (1912) Garden City, N.Y.: Doubleday SFBC, 1970.
———. *Swords of Mars*. (1934–35) In *Swords of Mars and Synthetic Men of Mars*. Garden City, N.Y.: Doubleday SFBC, n.d.
Butler, Samuel. *Erewhon*. London: Trübner, 1872.
Campbell, John W., Jr. "The Brain Stealers of Mars." (1936) In *Before the Golden Age*, ed. I. Asimov.
———. "The Last Evolution." (1932) In *The Best of John W. Campbell*, ed. L. del Rey.
——— [as Don A. Stuart]. "The Machine." (1935) In *The Best of John W. Campbell*, ed. L. del Rey.
——— [as Don A. Stuart]. "Out of Night." (1937) In *The Best of John W. Campbell*, ed. L. del Rey.
——— [as Don A. Stuart]. "Twilight." (1934) In *The Ends of Time*, ed. R. Silverberg.
——— [as Don A. Stuart]. "Who Goes There?" (1938) In *The SF Hall of Fame*, 2A, ed. Ben Bova.
Carr, Terry. "The Dance of the Changer and the Three." (1968) In *World's Best SF 1969*, ed. D. A. Wollheim and T. Carr.
———, ed. *Fellowship of the Stars*. New York: Simon & Schuster SFBC, 1974.
Chandler, A. Bertram. *The Hard Way Up*. New York: Ace pb, 1972.
———. *To Keep the Ship*. New York: DAW pb, 1978.
———. *The Way Back*. New York: DAW pb, 1978.
Chayefsky, Paddy. *Altered States*. New York: Harper & Row Book Club Edition, 1978.
Cherryh, C. J. *Hunter of Worlds*. Garden City, N.Y.: Doubleday SFBC, 1977.
Clarke, Arthur C. *Childhood's End*. New York: Ballantine pb, 1953.
———. *The City and the Stars*. New York: Signet pb, 1956.
———. "People of the Sea." *Worlds of Tomorrow* (April, June 1963).
———. "The Star." (1955) In *The Hugo Winners*, 1, ed. I. Asimov.

Clement, Hal. *Mission of Gravity*. (1953) New York: Pyramid pb, 1962.

――――. "Uncommon Sense." *Astounding* (September 1945).

Conklin, Groff, ed. *The Best of Science Fiction*. New York: Crown, 1946.

――――, ed. *Big Book of Science Fiction*. New York: Crown, 1950.

Crispin, Edmund [Robert Bruce Montgomery], ed. *Best SF: Science Fiction Stories*. London: Faber, 1955.

de Camp, L. Sprague. "The Blue Giraffe." (1939) In *The SF Bestiary*, ed. R. Silverberg.

――――. *Lest Darkness Fall*. (1939) Garden City, N.Y.: Doubleday SFBC, n.d.

de Ford, Miriam Allen. "The Apotheosis of Ki." (1956) In *Special Wonder*, ed. J. McComas.

Delany, Samuel R. *Babel-17*. (1966) Boston: Gregg, 1976.

――――. *The Ballad of Beta-2*. New York: Ace pb, 1965.

――――. *Driftglass*. New York: New American Library pb, 1971.

――――. *The Einstein Intersection*. New York: Ace pb, 1967.

――――. *Nova*. Garden City, N.Y.: Doubleday SFBC, 1968.

――――. "The Star Pit." (1967) In *Driftglass*.

――――. "Time Considered as a Helix of Semi-Precious Stones." (1968) In *Driftglass*.

――――. *Triton*. New York: Bantam pb, 1976.

del Rey, Judy-Lynn, ed. *Stellar 1*. New York: Ballantine pb, 1974.

del Rey, Lester. "Natural Advantage." (1976) In *The 1977 Annual World's Best SF*, ed. D. A. Wollheim and A. W. Saha.

――――, ed. *The Best of John W. Campbell*. Garden City, N.Y.: Doubleday SFBC, 1976.

――――, ed. *Best Science Fiction Stories of the Year*. New York: Ace pb, 1973.

Dick, Philip K. "Autofac." (1955) In *Beyond Control*, ed. R. Silverberg.

――――. *Galactic Pot-Healer*. New York: Berkley pb, 1969.

――――. *The Three Stigmata of Palmer Eldritch*. Garden City, N.Y.: Doubleday, 1965.

Dickson, Gordon R. "The Christmas Present." (1958) In *The Star Road*.

――――. "Jackal's Meal." (1969) In *The Star Road*.

――――. *The Star Road*. New York: DAW pb, 1974.

――――. "Twig." In *Stellar 1*, ed. J-L. del Rey.

Doar, Graham. "The Outer Limit." (1949) In *Big Book of SF*, ed. G. Conklin.

du Maurier, George. *Trilby*. New York: Harper, 1894.

Elder, Michael. *Flight to Terror*. New York: Pinnacle pb, 1973.

Ellison, Harlan. "A Boy and His Dog." (1969) In *World's Best SF 1970*, ed. D. A. Wollheim and T. Carr.

――――, ed. *Again, Dangerous Visions*. Garden City, N.Y.: Doubleday SFBC, 1972.

――――, ed. *Dangerous Visions*. Garden City, N.Y.: Doubleday SFBC, 1967.

Elwood, Roger, ed. *And Walk Now Gently through the Fire, and Other Science Fiction Stories*. Philadelphia: Chilton, 1972.

——, ed. *Frontiers 2: The New Mind*. New York: Collier pb, 1973.

——, ed. *Omega*. Greenwich, Conn.: Fawcett pb, 1973.

——, and Robert Silverberg, eds. *Epoch*. New York: Berkley SFBC, 1975.

——, and Virginia Kidd, eds. *Saving Worlds*. Garden City, N.Y.: Doubleday, 1973.

Farmer, Philip José. *Down in the Black Gang*. Garden City, N.Y.: Doubleday, 1971.

——. *The Fabulous Riverboat*. New York: Putnam's, 1971.

——. *Flesh*. (1960) New York: New American Library pb, 1969.

——. "Prometheus." (1961) In *Down in the Black Gang*.

—— [as Kilgore Trout]. *Venus on the Half-Shell*. New York: Dell pb, 1974.

Ferman, Edward L., ed. *The Best from Fantasy and Science Fiction*. 18th Series. New York: Ace pb, 1972.

——, ed. *The Best from Fantasy and Science Fiction*. 19th Series. New York: Ace pb, 1973.

——, and Barry N. Malzberg, eds. *Final Stage*. New York: Penguin pb, 1975.

——, and Robert P. Mills, eds. *Twenty Years of Fantasy and Science Fiction*. New York: Putnam's, 1970.

Foster, Alan Dean. "Dream Done Green." In *Fellowship of the Stars*, ed. T. Carr.

——. "With Friends Like These." (1971) In *The 1972 Annual World's Best SF*, ed. D. A. Wollheim.

Fyfe, Horace B. "Ransom." (1952) In *Special Wonder*, ed. J. McComas.

Gallun, Raymond Z. "Old Faithful." (1934) In *Before the Golden Age*, ed. I. Asimov.

Gerrold, David and Larry Niven. *The Flying Sorcerors*. (1970 [shorter version]) New York: Ballantine pb, 1971.

Godwin, Francis. *The Man in the Moone*. (1638) Hereford, Eng.: Nagrom, 1959.

Gold, H. L., ed. *Galaxy Reader of Science Fiction*. New York: Crown, 1952.

——, ed. *The Second Galaxy Reader of Science Fiction*. New York: Crown, 1954.

Goldin, Stephen, ed. *The Alien Condition*. New York: Ballantine pb, 1973.

Gordon, Rex [Stanley Bennett Hough]. *First on Mars*. (1956 in Great Britain as *No Man Friday*.) New York: Avon Equinox pb, 1976.

Green, Joseph. "A Custom of the Children of Life." *Magazine of Fantasy and Science Fiction* (December 1972).

——. "Encounter with a Carnivore." In *Epoch*, ed. R. Elwood and R. Silverberg.

Greg, Percy. *Across the Zodiac*. 2 vols. London: Trübner, 1880.

Haldeman, Joe. *The Forever War*. (1974) New York: Ballantine pb, 1976.

——. *Mindbridge*. New York: St. Martin's SFBC, 1976.

Hallus, Tak. "The Linguist." *Galaxy* (February 1975).

——. "Powwow." *Galaxy* (January 1975).

Hamilton, Edmond. "The King of Shadows." (1947) In *What's It Like Out There? and Other Stories.*

————. *What's It Like Out There? and Other Stories.* New York: Ace pb, 1974.

Harris, Larry M. "Lost in Translation." *Analog* (August 1961).

Harrison, Harry. "Run from the Fire." In *Epoch*, ed. R. Elwood and R. Silverberg.

————, ed. *Astounding: John W. Campbell Memorial Anthology.* New York: Ballantine pb, 1974.

————, ed. *SF: Authors' Choice 4.* New York: Putnam's, 1974.

Harrison, M. John. *The Pastel City.* New York: Avon pb, 1971.

Heinlein, Robert A. "Gulf." *Astounding* (November, December 1949).

————. *The Moon Is a Harsh Mistress.* (1965) New York: Berkley pb, 1968.

————. *Stranger in a Strange Land.* (1961) New York: Berkley pb, 1968.

————. *Time for the Stars.* New York: Ace pb, 1956.

————. "Waldo." (1942) In *A Treasury of Great SF*, 1, ed. A. Boucher.

Herbert, Frank. *Dune Messiah.* New York: Berkley pb, 1969.

Hollis, H. H. "Stoned Counsel." In *Again, Dangerous Visions*, ed. H. Ellison.

Holly, Joan C. "The Gift of Nothing." In *And Walk Now Gently*, ed. R. Elwood.

Hough, Stanley Bennett. See Rex Gordon.

Hughes, Zach. *The Legend of Miaree.* New York: Ballantine pb, 1974.

Jacobs, Harvey. "The Egg of the Glak." (1968) in *The Best from F&SF*, 18th Series, ed. E. Ferman.

Jenkins, Will F. See Murray Leinster.

Jesby, Ed. "Ogre." (1968) In *The Best from F&SF*, 18th Series, ed. E. Ferman.

Kapp, Colin. "The Old King's Answers." *Galaxy* (September 1973).

Karp, David. *One.* New York: Vanguard, 1953.

Knight, Damon. *The Best of Damon Knight.* Garden City, N.Y.: Doubleday SFBC, 1976.

————. "Cabin Boy." (1951) In *Galaxy Reader of SF*, ed. H. Gold.

————. "Extempore." (1956 as "The Beach Where Time Began.") In *Best of Damon Knight.*

————. "Stranger Station." (1956) In *Looking Ahead*, ed. D. Allen and L. Allen.

————, ed. *A Century of Science Fiction.* New York: Simon & Schuster, 1962.

————, ed. *Science Fiction of the Thirties.* Indianapolis, Ind.: Bobbs-Merrill SFBC, 1975.

————, ed. *Toward Infinity.* New York: Simon & Schuster, 1968.

Koontz, Dean. *Demon Seed.* New York: Bantam pb, 1973.

Kornbluth, Cyril M. "Friend to Man." (1951) In *The Best of C. M. Kornbluth*, ed. F. Pohl.

————. *A Mile Beyond the Moon.* Garden City, N.Y.: Doubleday, 1958.

————. "The Slave." (1957) In *A Mile Beyond the Moon.*

———. "Time Bum." (1953) In *A Mile Beyond the Moon*.

———. "Two Dooms." (1958) In *A Mile Beyond the Moon*.

Kuttner, Henry. *The Best of Henry Kuttner*. Garden City, N.Y.: Doubleday SFBC, 1975.

———. "The Big Night." (1947) In *The Best of Henry Kuttner*.

——— [as Lawrence O'Donnell]. *Fury*. (1947) New York: Magnum pb, n.d.

———. "The Iron Standard." (1943) In *The Best of Henry Kuttner*.

Lanier, Sterling. "Such Stuff as Dreams." *Analog* (January 1968).

Le Guin, Ursula K. "The Author of the Acacia Seeds and Other Extracts from the *Journal of the Association of Therolinguistics*." In *Fellowship of the Stars*, ed. T. Carr.

———. *The Dispossessed*. New York: Harper & Row SFBC, 1974.

———. *The Left Hand of Darkness*. New York: Walker pb, 1969.

———. "Mazes." In *Epoch*, ed. R. Elwood and R. Silverberg.

———. "The New Atlantis." In *The New Atlantis*, ed. R. Silverberg.

———. "The Word for World Is Forest." In *Again, Dangerous Visions*, ed. H. Ellison.

Lehmann, W. P. "Decoding of the Martian Language." *The Graduate Journal*. A Publication of the Dean of the Graduate School of the University of Texas. 7:1 (December 1965).

Leiber, Fritz. "Deadly Moon." (1960) In *Ships to the Stars*.

———. *Ships to the Stars*. New York: Ace pb, 1964.

Leinster, Murray [Will F. Jenkins]. "Dear Charles." (1953) In *Twists in Time*.

———. "First Contact." (1945) In *The Best of SF*, ed. G. Conklin.

———. "Proxima Centauri." (1935) In *Before the Golden Age*, ed. I. Asimov.

———. "Sidewise in Time." (1934) In *Before the Golden Age*, ed. I. Asimov.

———. *Twists in Time*. New York: Avon pb, 1960.

Lem, Stanislaw. *Solaris*, trans. Joanna Kilmartin and Steve Cox. New York: Berkley pb, 1971.

Levin, Ira. *The Stepford Wives*. New York: Random House Book Club Edition, 1972.

———. *This Perfect Day*. New York: Random House, 1970.

Lewis, C. S. *Out of the Silent Planet*. (1938) New York: Macmillan pb, 1965.

———. *Perelandra*. (1943) New York: Macmillan pb, 1965.

———. *That Hideous Strength* (1945) New York: Macmillan pb, 1965.

Lindsay, David. *A Voyage to Arcturus*. (1920) New York: Ballantine pb, 1968.

McAllister, Bruce. "Benji's Pencil." (1969) In *The Best from F&SF*, 19th Series, ed. E. Ferman.

McCaffrey, Anne. "The Ship Who Sang." (1961) In *Looking Ahead*, ed. D. Allen.

McComas, J. Francis, ed. *Special Wonder: The Anthony Boucher Memorial An-*

thology of Fantasy and Science Fiction. New York: Random House, 1970.

Macfarlane, W. "Quickening." *Galaxy* (September 1973).

MacLean, Katherine. "Pictures Don't Lie." (1951) In *Best SF: Science Fiction Stories*, ed. E. Crispin.

⸻. "Small War." In *Saving Worlds*, ed. R. Elwood and V. Kidd.

⸻. "Unhuman Sacrifice." (1958) In *A Century of SF*, ed. D. Knight.

MacLennon, Phyllis. "Thus Love Betrays Us." (1972) In *The 1973 Annual World's Best SF*, ed. D. A. Wollheim and A. W. Saha.

Manning, Laurence. "The Man Who Awoke." (1933) In *Before the Golden Age*, ed. I. Asimov.

Meek, S. P. "Awlo of Ulm." (1931) In *Before the Golden Age*, ed. I. Asimov.

⸻. "Submicroscopic." (1931) In *Before the Golden Age*, ed. I. Asimov.

Meredith, Richard C. "Choice of Weapons." *Worlds of Tomorrow* (March 1966).

Merle, Robert. *The Day of the Dolphin*, trans. Helen Weaver. Greenwich, Conn.: Fawcett pb, 1970.

Merril, Judith. *The Best of Judith Merril*. New York: Warner pb, 1976.

⸻. "Daughters of Earth." (1952) In *The Best of Judith Merril*.

⸻. "The Lonely." (1963) In *The Best of Judith Merril*.

⸻. "Whoever You Are." (1952) In *The Best of Judith Merril*.

Miller, P. Schuyler. "Tetrahedra of Space." (1931) In *Before the Golden Age*, ed. I. Asimov.

Miller, Walter M., Jr. *A Canticle for Leibowitz*. (1960) New York: Bantam pb, 1961.

⸻. "Command Performance." (1952) In *The Second Galaxy Reader*, ed. H. Gold.

Mitchison, Naomi. *Memoirs of a Spacewoman*. New York: Berkley pb, 1962.

Mohs, Mayo, ed. *Other Worlds, Other Gods*. New York: Avon pb, 1971.

Montgomery, Robert Bruce. See Edmund Crispin.

Moorcock, Michael. *An Alien Heat*. New York: Harper & Row, 1972.

Moore, Ward. "No Man Pursueth." (1956) In *The Best from F&SF*, 6th Series, ed. A. Boucher.

Morphett, Tony. "Litterbug." (1969) In *The Best from F&SF*, 19th Series, ed. E. Ferman.

Morressy, John. *Stardrift*. New York: Popular Library pb, 1973.

Niven, Larry. *All the Myriad Ways*. New York: Ballantine pb, 1971.

⸻. "Becalmed in Hell." (1965) In *Twenty Years of F&SF*, ed. E. Ferman and R. Mills.

⸻. "The Ethics of Madness." (1967) In *Neutron Star*.

⸻. "The Fourth Profession." (1971) In *The 1972 Annual World's Best SF*, ed. D. A. Wollheim.

⸻. "How the Heroes Die." (1966) In *The Shape of Space*.

———. *Neutron Star*. New York: Ballantine pb, 1968.

———. "Rammer." In *Best SF Stories of the Year*, ed. L. del Rey.

———. *Ringworld*. New York: Ballantine pb, 1970.

———. *The Shape of Space*. New York: Ballantine pb, 1969.

———. "Three Vignettes. 3: Grammar Lesson." *Cosmos* (May 1977).

———, and Jerry Pournell. *The Mote in God's Eye*. New York: Simon & Schuster, 1974.

———, John Brunner, and Jack Vance. *Three Trips in Time and Space: Original Novellas of Science Fiction*. New York: Hawthorn, 1973.

Nolan, William F. *Alien Horizons*. New York: Pocket Books pb, 1974.

———. "Promises to Keep: A Science Fiction Drama." In *Alien Horizons*.

Norman, John. *Priest-Kings of Gor*. New York: Ballantine pb, 1968.

Norton, Andre [Alice Mary Norton]. *Operation Time Search*. New York: Harcourt Brace, 1967.

O'Donnell, Lawrence. See Henry Kuttner.

Oliver, Chad. "King of the Hill." In *Again, Dangerous Visions*, ed. H. Ellison.

———. *The Winds of Time*. Garden City, N.Y.: Doubleday, 1957.

Orwell, George. *Nineteen Eighty-Four* (1949), ed. Irving Howe. New York: Harcourt Brace, 1963.

Osborne, Robertson. "Contact, Incorporated." (1949 as "Action on Azura.") In *Big Book of SF*, ed. G. Conklin.

Panshin, Alexei. *Rite of Passage*. New York: Ace pb, 1968.

Piper, H. Beam. "Omnilingual." *Astounding* (February 1957).

Piserchia, Doris. *Star Rider*. New York: Bantam pb, 1974.

Pohl, Carol, and Frederik Pohl, eds. *Jupiter*. New York: Ballantine pb, 1973.

Pohl, Frederik, ed. *The Best of C. M. Kornbluth*. Garden City, N.Y.: Doubleday SFBC, 1976.

———, ed. *The Seventh Galaxy Reader*. Garden City, N.Y.: Doubleday, 1964.

———, and C. M. Kornbluth. "Mute Inglorious Tam." *Magazine of Fantasy and Science Fiction* (October 1974).

———, and Jack Williamson. "Doomship." (1973) In *The 1974 Annual World's Best SF*, ed. D. A. Wollheim.

———, and Jack Williamson. *Starchild*. New York: Ballantine pb, 1965.

Rotsler, William. *Patron of the Arts*. New York: Ballantine pb, 1973.

Runyon, Charles W. "Sweet Helen." (1969) In *Twenty Years of F&SF*, ed. E. Ferman and R. Mills.

Russell, Eric Frank, and Leslie T. Johnson. "Seeker of Tomorrow." (1937) *SF of the Thirties*, ed. D. Knight.

St. Clair, Margaret. "Prott." (1953) In *Best SF: Science Fiction Stories*, ed. E. Crispin.

Sanders, Winston P. See Poul Anderson.

Schachner, Nat. "Past, Present, and Future." (1937) In *Before the Golden Age*, ed. I. Asimov.

Schmitz, James H. *The Demon Breed*. (1968 [shorter version] as "The Tuvela.") New York: Ace pb, 1968.

Scott, Robin S. "Who Needs Insurance?" (1966) In *Nebula Awards: Two*, ed. B. Aldiss. See also Robin Scott Wilson.

Shafhauser, Charles. "A Gleeb for Earth." (1953) In *The Second Galaxy Reader of SF*, ed. H. Gold.

Sheckley, Robert. *Can You Feel Anything When I Do This?* Garden City, N.Y.: Doubleday, 1971.

———. "Game: First Schematic." In *Can You Feel Anything When I Do This?*

———. *Mindswap*. (1965 [shorter version]) New York: Delacorte, 1966.

———. "The People Trap." (1968) In *The Best from F&SF*, 18th Series, ed. E. Ferman.

———. "A Suppliant in Space." In *The 1974 Annual World's Best SF*, ed. D. A. Wollheim.

Sheldon, Walt. "I, the Unspeakable." (1951) In *Galaxy Reader of SF*, ed. H. Gold.

Shelley, Mary. *Frankenstein, or The Modern Prometheus*. (1818) New York: Collier pb, 1961.

Shirley, John. "Uneasy Chrysalids, Our Memories." In *Epoch*, ed. R. Elwood and R. Silverberg.

Silverberg, Robert. *Beyond Control*. New York: Dell pb, 1974.

———. *Downward to the Earth*. (1969) Garden City, N.Y.: Doubleday SFBC, 1970.

———. "Ishmael in Love." (1970) In *World's Best SF 1971*, ed. D. A. Wollheim and T. Carr.

———. "Schwartz Between the Galaxies." In *Stellar 1*, ed. J-L. del Rey.

———, ed. *The Ends of Time*. New York: Hawthorn, 1970.

———, ed. *The Mirror of Infinity*. New York: Perennial pb, 1973.

———, ed. *The New Atlantis*. New York: Hawthorn, 1975.

———, ed. *The Science Fiction Bestiary*. New York: Thomas Nelson, 1971.

Simak, Clifford D. *All the Traps of Earth and Other Stories*. Garden City, N.Y.: Doubleday, 1962.

———. "Census." (1944) In *City*.

———. *City*. (1952, as a collection.) Garden City, N.Y.: Doubleday SFBC, n.d.

———. "Desertion." (1944) In *City*.

———. "Installment Plan." (1959) In *All the Traps of Earth and Other Stories*.

———. *Shakespeare's Planet*. New York: Berkley SFBC, 1976.

———. "The World of the Red Sun." (1931) In *Before the Golden Age*, ed. I. Asimov.

Skinner, B. F. *Walden Two*. (1948) New York: Macmillan pb, 1962.

Smith, Cordwainer [Paul Linebarger]. "Alpha Ralpha Boulevard." (1961) In *The Ends of Time*, ed. R. Silverberg.

Snyder, Cecil. *The Hawks of Arcturus*. New York: DAW pb, 1974.

Sonnemann, W. K. "The Council of Drones." (1936) In *SF of the Thirties*, ed. D. Knight.

Spinrad, Norman. "A Child of Mind." (1965) In *The Last Hurrah of the Golden Horde*.

———. *The Last Hurrah of the Golden Horde*. Garden City, N.Y.: Doubleday, 1970.

Stuart, Don A. See John W. Campbell, Jr.

Sturgeon, Theodore. "The Hurkle Is a Happy Beast." (1949) In *The SF Bestiary*, ed. R. Silverberg.

———. "The Stars Are the Styx." (1950) In *The Galaxy Reader*, ed. H. Gold.

———. *Sturgeon Is Alive and Well*. New York: Putnam's, 1971.

———. "To Here and the Easel." (1954) In *Sturgeon Is Alive and Well*.

———. "The [Widget], the [Wadget], and Boff." (1955) In *A Treasury of Great SF*, 1, ed. A. Boucher.

Sutton, Jeff. *Alton's Unguessable*. New York: Ace pb, 1970.

Swift, Jonathan. *Gulliver's Travels*. (1726) In *Gulliver's Travels and Other Writings*, ed. Louis Landa. Cambridge, Mass.: Riverside, 1960.

Szilard, Leo. *The Voice of the Dolphins and Other Stories*. New York: Simon & Schuster, 1961.

Tall, Stephen. "The Bear with the Knot on His Tail." (1971) In *The 1972 Annual World's Best SF*, ed. D. A. Wollheim.

———. *The Ramsgate Paradox*. New York: Berkley pb, 1976.

Tiptree, James, Jr. "I'll Be Waiting for You When the Swimming Pool Is Empty." (1971) In *Best SF Stories of the Year*, ed. L. del Rey.

———. "Your Haploid Heart." (1969) In *World's Best SF 1970*, ed. D. A. Wollheim and T. Carr.

Tolkien, J. R. R. *The Lord of the Rings*. 3 vols.: *The Fellowship of the Rings, The Two Towers, The Return of the King*. Rev. 2nd ed. London: Allen & Unwin, 1974.

———. *The Silmarillion*. Boston: Houghton Mifflin, 1977.

Trout, Kilgore. See Philip José Farmer.

Tubb, E. C. "Evane." (1973) In *The 1974 Annual World's Best SF*, ed. D. A. Wollheim.

Vance, Jack. "Brains of Earth." (1966) In *The Worlds of Jack Vance*.

———. *City of the Chasch*. New York: Ace pb, 1968.

———. "The Dogtown Tourist Agency." In *Epoch*, ed. R. Elwood and R. Silverberg.

———. "The Dragon Masters." (1962) In *The Hugo Winners*, 2, ed. I. Asimov.

———. *The Eyes of the Overworld*. New York: Ace pb, 1966.

———. *The Languages of Pao*. (1958) New York: Ace pb, 1966.

———. "The Last Castle." (1966) In *Nebula Award Stories: Two*, ed. B. Aldiss.

———. "The Moon Moth." (1961) In *The Worlds of Jack Vance*.

———. "Rumfuddle." In L. Niven, J. Brunner, and J. Vance, *Three Trips in Time and Space*.

———. *The Worlds of Jack Vance*. New York: Ace pb, 1973.

Van Scyoc, Sydney J. "Deathsong." (1974) In *The 1975 Annual World's Best SF*, ed. D. A. Wollheim and A. W. Saha.

Van Vogt, A. E. "Resurrection." (1948) In *Toward Infinity*, ed. D. Knight.

———. "The Weapon Shops of Isher." (1951 [enlarged version]) In *A Treasury of Great SF*, 1, ed. A. Boucher.

———. *The World of Null-A*. (1948 [revised version]) New York: Berkley, 1974.

Varley, John. "Overdrawn at the Memory Bank." (1976) In *The 1977 Annual World's Best SF*, ed. D. A. Wollheim and A. W. Saha.

Vonnegut, Kurt, Jr. *Cat's Cradle*. (1963) New York: Dell pb, 1964.

Watson, Ian. *The Embedding*. London: Gollancz, 1973.

Weinbaum, Stanley G. *The Best of Stanley G. Weinbaum*. New York: Ballantine pb, 1974.

———. "The Lotus Eaters." (1935) In *The Best of Stanley G. Weinbaum*.

———. "A Martian Odyssey." (1934) In *The SF Bestiary*, ed. R. Silverberg.

———. "Valley of Dreams." (1934) In *The Best of Stanley G. Weinbaum*.

Wellman, Manly Wade. "Pithecanthropus Rejectus." (1938) In *SF of the Thirties*, ed. D. Knight.

Wells, Herbert George. *Men Like Gods*. New York: Macmillan, 1923.

———. *A Modern Utopia*. New York: Scribner's, 1905.

———. *The Time Machine*. (1895) In *The Wheels of Chance and The Time Machine*. London: Dent, 1935.

White, Cecil B. "The Retreat to Mars." (1927) In *The Best of SF*, ed. G. Conklin.

White, William Anthony Parker. See Anthony Boucher.

Williamson, Jack. "Jamboree." (1969) In *Those Who Can*, ed. R. Wilson.

Wilson, Richard. "A Man Spekith." (1969) In *World's Best SF 1970*, ed. D. A. Wollheim and T. Carr.

Wilson, Robin Scott, ed. *Those Who Can: A Science Fiction Reader*. New York: Mentor pb, 1973. See also Robin S. Scott.

Wolfe, Gene. "Mathoms from the Time Closet." In *Again, Dangerous Visions*, ed. H. Ellison.

Wollheim, Donald A., ed. *The 1972 Annual World's Best SF*. New York: DAW SFBC, 1972.

———, and Arthur W. Saha, eds. *The 1973 Annual World's Best SF*. New York: DAW SFBC, 1973.

———, and Arthur W. Saha, eds. *The 1974 Annual World's Best SF*. New York: DAW SFBC, 1974.

———, and Arthur W. Saha, eds. *The 1975 Annual World's Best SF*. New York: DAW SFBC, 1975.

———, and Arthur W. Saha, eds. *The 1976 Annual World's Best SF*. New York: DAW SFBC, 1976.

———, and Arthur W. Saha, eds. *The 1977 Annual World's Best SF*. New York: DAW SFBC, 1977.

———, and Terry Carr, eds. *World's Best Science Fiction 1969*. New York: Ace SFBC, 1969.

———, and Terry Carr, eds. *World's Best Science Fiction 1970*. New York: Ace SFBC, 1970.

———, and Terry Carr, eds. *World's Best Science Fiction 1971*. New York: Ace SFBC, 1971.

Wyndham, John. "Pillar to Post." (1951) In *The Second Galaxy Reader of SF*, ed. H. Gold.

Yep, Lawrence. "The Selchey Kids." (1968) In *World's Best SF 1969*, ed. D. A. Wollheim and T. Carr.

Zelazny, Roger. *The Doors of His Face, the Lamps of His Mouth*. New York: Avon pb, 1974.

———. *Doorways in the Sand*. New York: Harper & Row SFBC, 1976.

———. "The Moment of the Storm." (1966) In *The Doors of His Face, the Lamps of His Mouth*.

———. *To Die in Italbar*. Garden City, N.Y.: Doubleday, 1973.

Index